A Psalm in Your Heart

VOLUME 2
PSALMS 76–150

GEORGE O. WOOD

Gospel Publishing House
Springfield, Missouri
02-0785

Each chapter in this book first appeared in Dr. Wood's column, "A Psalm in My Heart," in the *Pentecostal Evangel*.

Library of Congress Catalog Card Number 97-71906
International Standard Book Number 0-88243-785-2

Printed in the United States of America.

The Groaning and the Glory

It is not widely known that the late Charles de Gaulle, president of France, and his wife Evonne were the parents of a Down's syndrome child.

The de Gaulles, despite their overloaded schedules, tried to spend some time every day with their daughter, who was both a treasure and a concern. Often at night, after Evonne would put the girl to bed, she would ask, "Oh, Charles, why couldn't she have been like the others?"

As predicted by the doctors, the de Gaulles' daughter died in her youth. They held a private graveside service for her, and after the benediction the small company began to leave, except for Evonne. In her grief, she could not pull away. Charles went back to her and said, "Come, Evonne. Did you not hear the blessing? She is now like the others."

¹In Judah God is known; his name is great in Israel. ²His tent is in Salem, his dwelling place in

Step into the future

The apostle Paul stirringly reminds us of that day when the glory will outweigh the groaning. (See Romans 8:18–25.) This psalm sounds the same theme by fast forwarding us into that future moment when God's victory is total and complete. No more Down's syndrome or disease, dangerous or dark night, lost wanderings in canyons deep. Fields of conflict and disappointment lie silent, all enemies vanquished.

What's surprising about this psalm is that it is written by one who lived after

3

the devastation of Jerusalem by the Babylonians. (See Psalm 74:3.) Asaph pens these words at a time when Jerusalem groaned in ruins and occupation. But the Psalmist prophetically leaps into a future hour when enemies lie plundered and the Lord reigns resplendently.

Zion. ³There he broke the flashing arrows, the shields and the swords, the weapons of war. Selah

Take a second look at the past

The sting of conquest and pillaging hurts worse in the locales of Judah, Jerusalem, and the temple mount in Zion. In those very places where the burning was greatest and the weeping most bitter, God has returned. (See vv. 1–3.)

In Babylon's successful siege of Jerusalem, God's name seemed so insignificant and powerless, neither known nor great. But where His people departed in chains, sackcloth, and tears, now He has taken up residence. The place of distress has again become Salem, the city of peace. The instruments of war that penetrated the flesh, pierced the heart, crushed the spirit: These are now all broken.

Will you look at your defeats in the same fashion? At the very spot where you suffered the most, God will return someday to transform your most grievous loss into an absolute triumph. Could this be how in part He "will wipe away all tears"? Will He take us back to the scenes where we were sickened, held powerless, victimized and betrayed, hurt and abandoned, grieved beyond all consolation, and show us that He has the last word in turning our greatest sorrows into permanent joys?

Think of that battlefield in your life. You feel defeated now. Your enemies have the upper hand, well-armed with flashing arrows, shields, and swords (offensive and defensive weapons). But, there is another day coming. Hold that day in your heart. Don't let it go. God will revisit your battlefield and exercise His might on your behalf. Your enemy will be defenseless in that day.

Once you've experienced such total victory, your admiration for the Lord knows no bounds, for He is resplendent with light, more majestic than mountains rich with game (v. 4). Only One is to be feared—the God of Jacob (vv. 5,6), the Lord of those who struggle. He is the one we should have "feared" in the beginning instead of fearing all our other fears (v. 7). For His power, unlike the powers which held us subject, remains absolute. Fear neither death, nor illness, nor desolation, nor betrayal, nor lack, nor any such thing.

Benefit now

When God acts, you, the afflicted, are saved (vv. 8–10).

What should be your response to such a victory? Recall once more that Asaph writes of triumph while Jerusalem remains yet devastated. Will you, following his example, join in praising God for the certain and wonderful conclusion to a most difficult chapter in your own life?

This psalm, by reaching into the future to catch a glimpse of the coming glory, gives us a lesson for the present: "Make vows to the Lord your God and fulfill them" (v. 11). In other words, get on with God's will for your life. Say an unequivocal yes to Him. Your surrender will take you through Golgotha and Calvary. You can't take a route around that. But after-

4You are resplendent with light, more majestic than mountains rich with game.

5Valiant men lie plundered, they sleep their last sleep; not one of the warriors can lift his hands. 6At your rebuke, O God of Jacob, both horse and chariot lie still.

7You alone are to be feared. Who can stand before you when you are angry?

8From heaven you pronounced judgment, and the land feared and was quiet—9when you, O God, rose up to judge, to save all the afflicted of the land. Selah 10Surely your wrath against men brings you praise, and the survivors of your wrath are restrained.

11Make vows to the Lord your God and fulfill them; let all the neighboring lands bring gifts to the One

ward, the garden of resurrection waits: "Let all the neighboring lands bring gifts to the one to be feared. He breaks the spirit of rulers; he is feared by the kings of the earth" (vv. 11,12).

to be feared. [12]He breaks the spirit of rulers; he is feared by the kings of the earth.

Is God feared now by His enemies or yours? Not at all. They presently withhold gifts to Him, lacking in awe for Him. But the Day is coming when Jesus is acknowledged by all as victor over all.

Cherish the Lord in your heart. Remember, as did Asaph and the de Gaulles, that a day is coming when Down's syndrome and all other syndromes that are down will be gone.

Prayer of response

Lord Jesus, sometimes I feel like I'm trapped in a maze. I lose perspective and get confused. Thank You for always knowing where I am and for giving me this psalm as a photograph of my future in You.

My thoughts on Psalm 76 . . .

For Sleepless Nights

Psalm 77

Recently, I hosted out-of-town family members for a visit to a local attraction, Marvel Cave. Prior to the tour, our guide assembled the group for a photograph—the younger children standing in the front rows.

A darling 5-year-old girl began crying because she thought she had lost her parents, who were hidden in the upper row from her view.

I thought, *How like real life. I also panic when I feel alone and don't sense my Heavenly Father near me.*

Remembering the wrong things

Asaph feels alone in this psalm, in total contrast to his mood in Psalm 76. There Asaph leaped ahead to the final day when all conflict dissolved into victory. Here, he stands within the present moment, the tide of battle very much in doubt: "I cried out to God for help; I cried out to God to hear me" (v. 1).

It's hard to have faith during such a time. "When I was in distress, I sought the Lord; at night I stretched out untiring hands and my soul refused to be comforted" (v. 2). Why? Because you have momentarily lost hope in a brighter day.

Asaph groans, muses, and grows faint as he remembers God (v. 3) and remains comfortless in the unspoken

> ¹I cried out to God for help; I cried out to God to hear me.
>
> ²When I was in distress, I sought the Lord; at night I stretched out untiring hands and my soul refused to be comforted.
>
> ³I remembered you, O God, and I groaned; I mused, and my spirit grew faint. Selah

feeling that God does not remember him.

Sleeplessness (v. 4), a frequent companion to depression, plunges you into reveries of better times (v. 5) and the happy tunes of yesterday (v. 6).

But those joy-drenched moments butt against the harshness of present reality: life is so very hard and God has disappeared (vv. 7–9). Like the frightened child at Marvel Cave, you have lost sight of Father—and feel, therefore, that He has also lost sight of you.

Reprogramming the memory

"Selah," say Asaph and you. Yes, just think of it. And you do over and over. You keep asking the endless circular question: When will this ever end?

Is the key with us or with God?

In this psalm, the solution lies within us. At verse 10, the mood changes as Asaph shifts from his own personal problems (vv. 1-9) to the record of God's activity on our behalf (vv. 10-20). The transition is signaled by the opening word "then" (v. 10).

Before then he remembered God and groaned (v. 5). After then he remembered God's past miracles of provision and redemption.

Before then he thought only about the former days with their past haunting melodies (vv. 5,6). After then he focuses on what God did in earlier times.

You will continue to grow faint (v. 3) as long as you exclude from your meditations the activity of God on your behalf. You must turn from focusing on your own life to recalling what the Lord has done for you.

4You kept my eyes from closing; I was too troubled to speak.

5I thought about the former days, the years of long ago;

6I remembered my songs in the night. My heart mused and my spirit inquired:

7"Will the Lord reject forever? Will he never show his favor again? 8Has his unfailing love vanished forever? Has his promise failed for all time? 9Has God forgotten to be merciful? Has he in anger withheld his compassion?" Selah

10Then I thought, "To this I will appeal: the years of the right hand of the Most High." 11I will remember the deeds of the Lord; yes, I will remember your miracles of long ago. 12I will meditate on all your works and consider all your mighty deeds. 13Your ways, O God, are holy. What god is so great as our God? 14You are the God who performs miracles; you display

Remembering the right things

Remember the right things. That's what Asaph does. Through an act of will, he orders his memory to reach back into the long ago of God's miracles, His wondrous deeds.

If you permit your memories to dwell exclusively on your own hurts you will never find your way out. Your past experience will tell you that you cannot trust anyone, even God.

But you open a door for faith to enter when you begin thinking of what the Lord has done.

In the depth of depression, it's hard to keep your mind on the Lord, so centered are you on your own pain. But begin the discipline of practicing the Lord's presence—even if it's only one minute out of every hour. You will learn gradually to increase the time spent reflecting on His realities, your history with Him, His dealings with people—and these thoughts will become strong and long enough to form a meditation (v. 12).

As you think about the Lord, you come face-to-face with His character. Who is He? I pick up the Bible for the answer and find that historically He hears the cries of His people. There is no one else who possesses His power to rescue and redeem (vv. 13–15).

Those ancient descendants of Jacob and Joseph (v. 15) are no more worthy of deliverance than you. You don't have any solutions for your dilemma, just as they had none for theirs. Like them, all you can do is groan. But God hears you and delivers.

Within the Old Testament context, the Exodus (vv. 16-20) was God's greatest your power among the peoples. 15 With your mighty arm you redeemed your people, the descendants of Jacob and Joseph. Selah 16 The waters saw you, O God, the waters saw you and writhed; the very depths were convulsed. 17The clouds poured down water, the skies resounded with thunder; your arrows flashed back and forth. 18Your thunder was heard in the whirlwind, your lightning lit up the world; the earth trembled and quaked. 19Your path led through the sea, your way through the mighty waters, though your footprints were not seen. 20You led your people like a flock by the hand of Moses and Aaron.

deed, the high-water mark of His work for His people. For Asaph, the divine deliverance from Egypt involved more than reciting history; it served as encouragement of what God is capable of doing in the present hour. The God of then is the Lord of now. His path can lead through your sea.

The psalm ends abruptly. Nothing more need be said, for to state You led is to declare You lead.

The Exodus of the New Testament is even greater, for Jesus led us out of bondage to the devil, death, and sin through His death on a cross for our sins and His resurrection from the dead. Life is now at work in you.

Tears turned into smiles on the face of the little girl at Marvel Cave when she spotted her mom and dad. And it will be no different with you. Your faithful Lord has never let you out of His sight. Away with despair. Turn your eyes upon Jesus.

Prayer of response

Jesus, I have many memories—some very painful and others joyful. But I ask that my meditation on things past will not be devoid of remembering what You have done for me and anticipating all You will yet do. You are my faithful Friend, my Lord and Savior.

My thoughts on Psalm 77 . . .

Quo Vadis?

Psalm 78

Tradition has it that Simon Peter faced certain martyrdom in Rome and, as he had years earlier, fled the scene. The Lord met him on the Appian Way and asked him, *Quo vadis?* (Where are you going?)

When Peter answered, the Lord replied He was going into Rome to be crucified again—in Peter's place. Shamed, Peter turned around.

Even if this story cannot be verified, we do know Jesus daily asks us, "Where are you going?"

This psalm reviews the history of God's relationship with His people Israel who repeatedly went away from Him despite God's gracious and powerful care. We read the psalm best when we apply it to ourselves, for we also are prone to wander or rebel.

⁷Then they would put their trust in God and would not forget his deeds but would keep his commands. ⁸They would not be like their forefathers—a stubborn and rebellious generation, whose hearts were not loyal to God, whose spirits were not faithful to him.

⁹The men of Ephraim, though armed with bows, turned back on the day of battle;

The wrong way in hard times

Asaph opens with the clear intention that the truths stated should be passed down to our children and our children's children (vv. 1–8). Each generation chooses to either put its trust in God and not forget His deeds (v. 7) or become stubborn and rebellious, not loyal to God, not faithful to Him (v. 8). You make that choice personally as well.

Most of this psalm fleshes out examples of those disloyal and unfaithful to God. Example one: "The men of Ephraim, though armed with bows, turned back on the day of battle" (v. 9).

We do not know from the Scriptures the historical setting for this reference. However, one can picture the scene of trauma in the camp of Israel when on the *day* of battle, one of its key armed divisions pulled out of the engagement. They would not be the last of those who would injure the work of God by departing at the moment of greatest need. Why did they leave? Because they forgot what He had done (v. 11).

Verses 12–16 detail the wonders God did for Israel in Egypt and the wilderness.

But all these mighty acts did not quiet the rebellious heart (v. 17). In His mercy, God continued providing for His people. They accused Him of not spreading a table in the desert (vv. 19,20). The Lord answered by giving them manna and meat, and then judged them severely for their mistrust (vv. 21–31).

"In spite of all this, they kept on sinning; in spite of his wonders, they did not believe" (v. 32). Thus, God again acted against them (v. 33), but only so long as they rebelled. At their first blush of repentance, God would relent (vv. 34,35).

The wrong way in good times

You draw the wrong conclusions from God's forbearance when you think you can fool Him with words (v. 36) which cloak a devious heart (v. 37). "Yet he was merciful; he atoned for their iniquities and did not destroy them. Time after time he restrained his anger and did not stir up his full wrath. He remembered that they were but flesh, a passing breeze that does not return" (vv. 38,39).

Have you contrasted your own waywardness with God's mercy? How many

¹¹They forgot what he had done, the wonders he had shown them.

¹⁷But they continued to sin against him, rebelling in the desert against the Most High.

¹⁹They spoke against God, saying, Can God spread a table in the desert? ²⁰When he struck the rock, water gushed out, and streams flowed abundantly. But can he also give us food? Can he supply meat for his people?"

³²In spite of all this, they kept on sinning; in spite of his wonders, they did not believe.

³³So he ended their days in futility and their years in terror.

³⁴Whenever God slew them, they would seek him; they eagerly turned to him again. ³⁵They remembered that God was their Rock, that God Most High was their Redeemer.

³⁶But then they would flatter him with their mouths, lying to him with their tongues; ³⁷Their hearts were not loyal to him, they

times have you put the Lord to the test and rebelled against Him in your own wilderness, grieving Him in your wasteland (vv. 40,41)? It's easy to forget the Lord's deliverance; therefore, we must engage in the discipline of remembering (vv. 42–54).

Even after arriving in the Promised Land, Israel continued to provoke the Lord (vv. 55–58). Spiritual failures do not occur only in wilderness moments when we are desolate and desolated: They happen when we enjoy life to the full. In Canaan, as well as in the desert, loyalty is tested. Are you faithful to the Lord when you have plenty?

The northern tribes weren't; therefore, God abandoned them. He rejected Israel completely (vv. 59–67) and turned to the south, to the tribe of Judah (vv. 68–72).

Asaph wrote years later, after Judah had also failed and was carried away into captivity by the Babylonians. But Asaph remains silent regarding the final fall. Why?

The right way in all times

For Asaph, the destiny of God's people remained tied to the tribe of Judah (v. 68), and more importantly one member of that family—David (vv. 70–72). At the writing of this psalm, however, David had been dead for at least 400 years. What possible hope could he provide?

Asaph dimly understood at best. Only David's son, the Good Shepherd, can pastor you with integrity of heart and with skillful hands. (See John 10:1–18.)

Perhaps like ancient Israel, you have failed God and today you are heading away from Him. You knew better than to sin. Now you have reaped the conse-

were not faithful to his covenant.

[38]Yet he was merciful; he forgave their iniquities and did not destroy them. Time after time he restrained his anger and did not stir up his full wrath. [39]He remembered that they were but flesh, a passing breeze that does not return.

[40]How often they rebelled against him in the desert and grieved him in the wasteland! [41]Again and again they put God to the test; they vexed the Holy One of Israel.

[55]He drove out nations before them and allotted their lands to them as an inheritance; he settled the tribes of Israel in their homes. [56]But they put God to the test and rebelled against the Most High; they did not keep his statutes. [57]Like their fathers they were disloyal and faithless, as unreliable as a faulty bow. [58]They angered him with their high places; they aroused his jealousy with their idols.

[68]But he chose the tribe of Judah, Mount Zion, which he loved.

quences of your own rebellious choices. What's ahead for you?

Jesus does not want to stand over you in judgment, but to lift you up in mercy. Asaph's hope was in the promises God made to David; your hope lies in God's promises fulfilled in Jesus, the Son of David. (See Matthew 1:1; Acts 2:30.) In all the moments when you doubted the Lord, tested Him, complained, or rebelled, He never stopped loving or caring for you.

Your destiny will be good only if you answer His *quo vadis?* by following Him with all your heart.

> 70He chose David his servant and took him from the sheep pens; 71from tending the sheep he brought him to be the shepherd of his people Jacob, of Israel his inheritance. 72And David shepherded them with integrity of heart; with skillful hands he led them.

Prayer of response

Lord Jesus, only one thing amazes me more than the deceitfulness of my own heart, and that's Your steadfast love for me. I am so grateful You did not send me away when I sent You away. May I, unlike ancient Israel, be content with Your provisions for me rather than pining away with grumbling and rebellion over what I seek that You choose not to give, over what I crave that is outside Your will.

My thoughts on Psalm 78 . . .

Desecration

While walking in a cemetery recently, I noticed a plastic bouquet of flowers atop a tombstone. What attracted my eye was a large handwritten note in the center of the arrangement.

Thinking someone had a written message to the deceased, I read it. The note had been laminated for protection from the elements, but its message was directed to the living: "Jack was known as a kind and honest man. We suffer from our loss of him. Jack was loved. If you steal these flowers, it's like a slap in the face."

How sad, I thought, *that dear family members suffer intensified sorrow because of the cruelty of unfeeling people who would rob a grave of flowers.*

We call such an act desecration, from the Latin, *secrate,* or sacred. To *desecrate* means to violate the sanctity of.

When the worst happens

¹O God, the nations have invaded your inheritance; they have defiled your holy temple, they have reduced Jerusalem to rubble.

²They have given the dead bodies of your servants as food to the birds of the air, the flesh of your saints to the beasts of the earth. ³They have poured out blood like water all around Jerusalem, and there

Asaph, in this psalm, expresses the desecration felt by the nation of Israel after its conquest and plunder by the Babylonians: "O God, the nations have invaded your inheritance; they have defiled your holy temple, they have reduced Jerusalem to rubble" (v. 1).

The psalm depicts the nightmare atrocities against God's people: a bloodbath all around the city, unburied bodies eaten by scavenger birds and beasts, a people whose plight engenders no sympathy from others—only scorn (vv. 2-4).

Perhaps you also feel violated. The spouse you trusted cheated on you; a business partner took advantage of you; the child you dearly love now as an adult shows disrespect or contempt; the friend in whom you confided betrayed your confidence and gossiped your deeply personal secrets. You find it difficult to believe in happy endings.

Like the unburied corpse in this psalm, you feel ravaged. Perhaps you have been raped, assaulted, a victim of another's violence. All the props have been knocked out of your self-esteem, and you too feel scorned and derided.

The prayer of the violated

Remember, this psalm is a prayer. When you find yourself desecrated, it's important to follow Asaph's example. Don't make the mistake of talking only to yourself or others about your sorrow. Bring it to the Lord.

It's not just your honor at stake; it's His. Notice how Asaph reminds the Lord that what has been ravaged is *Your* inheritance, *Your* temple, *Your* servants.

When you have been trampled on, your tendency is to feel totally worthless. But you are not. You are God's possession. (See 1 Corinthians 6:20.) If there has been a fire in your life, He's determined to repair the damage. The problem right now is that you see only the smoldering ruins of your loss and not the shining future God has planned.

You are now caught in the crack of time where you can do nothing but wait. With Asaph, you ask, "How long?" (v. 5).

There's usually no quick answer to that question. Here's what Asaph teaches us to pray while waiting.

is no one to bury the dead. **⁴We are objects of reproach to our neighbors, of scorn and derision to those around us.**

⁵How long, O Lord? Will you be angry forever? How long will your jealousy burn like fire?

That the offender will be punished (vv. 6,7). It's not politically correct today to think of God pouring out His wrath. Nevertheless, the Lord is committed to judging the whole world. (See 2 Corinthians 5:10; Hebrews 12:23.)

In His own time, He will address the wrong done against you by another. You can be confident of that.

That our own wrongs will be forgiven (vv. 8,9). Sometimes you get the treatment you deserve. Asaph recognized that Israel suffered oppression from Babylon not just because Babylon was mean, but because Israel sinned.

Part of God's recovery plan for you, if you have been desecrated, is that you conduct an inventory of your own life. Unlike ancient Israel, you may not bear any responsibility for the grief and loss you have suffered. Don't try to make yourself feel guilty when you did not do wrong. On the other hand, if your own attitudes or actions were sinful, admit that and make amends. Ask the Lord to forgive you.

That a better day will come (vv. 10-13). Asaph looks ahead to payback time, when those who dished it out will be paid back seven times worse. Oh, the relishing of such a delicious prospect.

Maturing Christians, however, don't hold on to vengeful feelings for long because we know they are not healthy, that God can be trusted to do the right thing with every person, and we won't answer to God for anyone other than ourselves.

We close the prayer where Asaph did—by focusing upon God's endearment to us. The desecration is for a short time. it will pass. But we, the sheep of His pasture, will praise Him forever.

⁶Pour out your wrath on the nations that do not acknowledge you, on the kingdoms that do not call on your name; ⁷for they have devoured Jacob and destroyed his homeland.

⁸Do not hold against us the sins of the fathers; may your mercy come quickly to meet us, for we are in desperate need. ⁹Help us, O God our Savior, for the glory of your name; deliver us and forgive our sins for your name's sake.

¹⁰Why should the nations say, "Where is their God?" Before our eyes, make known among the nations that you avenge the outpoured blood of your servants. ¹¹May the groans of the prisoners come before you; by the strength of your arm preserve those condemned to die. ¹²Pay back into the laps of our neighbors seven times the reproach they have hurled at you, O Lord. ¹³Then we your people, the sheep of your pasture, will praise you forever; from generation to generation we will recount your praise.

I went back to that grave with the laminated note and laid some fresh flowers in front of the tombstone. And that's what God does with your life, except He really knows you. When another robs something precious from you, He shows up with fresh flowers.

Prayer of response

Lord Jesus, thank You for holding me safe and secure in moments I feel so naked and unprotected. I, too, have felt as worthless as a pile of rubble, and I am humbled beyond words to think You would value me enough to regard me as Your temple.

My thoughts on Psalm 79 . . .

A Second Chance

The Georgia Tech Golden Tornado laid claim to the mythical national football championship after a strange 8–7 victory over the Golden Bears of California in the 1929 Rose Bowl Classic.

The margin of victory came from a play in the first half. Neither side had scored. Tech had the ball on its own 25-yard line and fumbled. Roy Riegels, California's center and team captain, snatched up the ball and started for the Georgia goal line. But after a few steps, he became disoriented—some say it was because he had been taking a ferocious pounding from the opposing all-American Georgia Tech center—wheeled about and headed for his own goal line.

Seventy thousand stunned fans watched as Riegels streaked 75 yards down the field. His teammate, Benny Lom, chased him and finally overtook and tackled him 1 foot short of the opposite goal. Riegels was too crestfallen for words. He dropped to the ground, jerked off his helmet, and vented dismay.

California tried to punt out of the situation, but Georgia Tech blocked the kick, scoring a 2-point safety, providing them the ultimate margin of victory.

What strikes me about the story, however, is not the long wrong way run—it's the fact that Coach Nibbs Price started Roy Riegels in the second half. It is reported that Riegels sat in a corner of the locker room with a blanket over his head, put his face in his hands, and cried like a baby. Coach Price announced to his team moments before the second half began, "The same team that played the first half will start the second."

Riegels, however, appeared not to hear him or respond; so Price came over to him, put his hands on Riegels' shoulders, and said, "Roy, get up and go on back. The game is only half over."

Coping with consequences of bad choices

Psalm 80 concerns a whole team—the northern tribes of Israel—who ran the wrong direction, away from God. Now devastated by the consequences of their actions, they come—not to a coach—but to the Shepherd of Israel, making a thrice-repeated request to get back in the game, "Restore us, O God; make your face shine upon us, that we may be saved" (vv. 3,7,19).

Have you, like Riegels or ancient Israel, ever run the wrong way? Then, this psalm is for you.

Little do you realize when you head away from the Lord that God will later allow you to reap what you have sown. You will not like that harvest of unpleasant consequences. "The pleasures of sin are but for a season." (See Hebrews 11:25.) They are wonderful pleasures or we would never engage in them. But in the end the pleasure turns to pain, and you are left in ruins.

Then the God you neglected becomes your only hope of recovery (vv. 1-3). I ask God to awake, when in reality it is myself who has been asleep.

Asaph describes the trauma for Israel after being conquered, pillaged, and ruled by a foreign power. He recognizes the price the nation paid for its rebellion against the Lord: the people now shed tears by the bowlful (vv. 4-6).

The glimmer of hope

All you can do is offer up a prayer: "Restore us, O God Almighty" (v. 7).

In the midst of agony, regret, and repentance we remember our relation-

[1]Hear us, O Shepherd of Israel, you who lead Joseph like a flock; you who sit enthroned between the cherubim, shine forth [2]before Ephraim, Benjamin and Manasseh. Awaken your might; come and save us. [3]Restore us, O God; make your face shine upon us, that we may be saved.

[4]O Lord God Almighty, how long will your anger smolder against the prayers of your people? [5]You have fed them with the bread of tears; you have made them drink tears by the bowlful. [6]You have made us a source of contention to our neighbors, and our enemies mock us.

[7]Restore us, O God Almighty; make your face shine upon us, that we may be saved.

ship with God before the season of sin. God's goodness became evident in what He did for us (vv. 8–11).

The Lord brought you as a vine out of the captivity of Egypt, where you were bound in sin and served harsh masters. Under God's careful planting, you grew and prospered. Your root flourished (vv. 9, 11), but now the vine is cut down (v. 16). The good news is that the root itself is still in the ground (vv. 14,15). God has trimmed you in judgment, but not uprooted you.

Although you have endured the amputation of many things, the Lord has not cut you off altogether.

Like Roy Riegels, you know you ran the wrong way. Will the Lord let you have a second chance? Like the Psalmist your help rests with the Man at God's right hand. Asaph had no photograph of the Man at God's right hand, but we know Him—Jesus Christ, our Lord. (Compare v. 17 with Acts 2:33; Romans 8:34; Ephesians 1:19-21.) We can reach out to Him, even in our darkest moments when the full flood of judgment rages against us for our own sins.

I wonder if Asaph did not have more confidence at the end of his prayer for God's restoration (v. 19) than he did in the beginning (v. 3) or the middle (v. 7). There is value in praying through, in asking more than once. The ask-seek-knock sequence in prayer shows the value of pressing into the Lord with our need. (See Matthew 7:7.)

Roy Riegels came back from his mistake to play a ferocious second half in that famous 1929 Rose Bowl game, even blocking a Georgia Tech punt and recovering it for California.

8You brought a vine out of Egypt; you drove out the nations and planted it. 9You cleared the ground for it, and it took root and filled the land. 10The mountains were covered with its shade, the mighty cedars with its branches. 11It sent out its boughs to the Sea, its shoots as far as the River.

14 Return to us, O God Almighty! Look down from heaven and see! Watch over this vine, 15the root your right hand has planted, the son you have raised up for yourself.

16Your vine is cut down, it is burned with fire; at your rebuke your people perish.

17Let your hand rest on the man at your right hand, the son of man you have raised up for yourself. 18Then we will not turn away from you; revive us, and we will call on your name. 19Restore us, O Lord God Almighty; make your face shine upon us, that we may be saved.

The Scottish preacher Alexander Whyte described the Christian life as falling down and getting up, falling down and getting up, falling down and getting up, all the way to heaven. It's much easier to fall down than to get back up.

Like Roy Riegels, I want to play well the rest of my life for Jesus—even if I have embarrassed myself by running the wrong way. How about you?

Prayer of response

Lord Jesus, give me a second chance to serve You. Forgive me for running the wrong direction. Thank You for saying to me, "Child of Mine, get up, go on back. The game is only half over."

My thoughts on Psalm 80 . . .

"If"

I n her book, *God is No Fool,* Lois Cheney spins the tale of a man who kept coming to God with if only's. If only I had extra money, I'd give it to God. If only I had some extra time, I'd give that to God. If only I had a talent or special skill, God would have it.

So the Lord gave the man what he asked for: money, time, and talent. God waited and waited. At long last, God took back what He had given. After a while, the man prayed again, "If only You returned some of my money, time, or talents, I'd give them to You."

Here's what the Lord has on His mind.

God said, "Oh, shut up."

I chuckle at the comeuppance given the dishonest man, whose fickle disposition bears a remarkable resemblance to God's audience in this psalm.

You would never know from reading the opening call to worship (vv. 1–5) that God was displeased with His congregation. Instead, you find a gracious invitation to enthusiastically adore God with voice (v. 1), instruments (v. 2), and at high holy-day seasons (vv. 3–5).

The worship hour takes a sharp turn when God takes the pulpit after the song service (vv. 6–16). He doesn't tell us to shut up, but He does expect us to shape up.

This psalm speaks relevantly to our believers' gatherings today where often the praise and worship are protracted and exuberant. When the drums, guitars, and electronic keyboard are still, we may be ready to head for the door, ending the psalm at verse 5. But God tells us to sit back down. He hasn't had a chance to preach yet. He has spotted gaps between our words and deeds, worship and walk.

23

Did you forget?

Asaph reminds us that God "went out against Egypt, where we heard a language we did not understand" (v. 5). How so? Israel lived in Egypt 400 years—they certainly knew Egyptian.

What did they not understand? This: That under a Pharaoh who knew not Joseph, Egypt no longer spoke in soft, seductive welcome tones but in brittleness and contempt.

As a metaphor for this present world, Egypt represents periods in your own life when you spent a season in sin—and the evil you played with masked its harsh demanding nature with a soft skin of warmth and soothing words of comfort. You felt accepted and cared for, as Israel did in Egypt, but the world is never a committed friend to the people of God. It speaks a language the Lord's people do not understand: the tongue of self-interest, ego fulfillment, murder of the innocents, hatred for what is moral and right, contempt for God himself.

So often we look at the exterior of holy things and holy events. No doubt ancient Israel focused on remembering the great deeds of God in the Exodus—the external acts: the plagues, the parting sea, the manna. But God remembers the internal effect His deliverance has upon us. The reason for the miracles: "I removed the burden from your shoulders" (v. 6).

Did you quarrel?

Exodus 17 and Numbers 20 tell the story of the two times Israel failed the test of trusting God in the desert to supply water. The location was known as Meribah, or quarreling. Today, Meribah

1Sing for joy to God our strength; shout aloud to the God of Jacob! 2Begin the music, strike the tambourine, play the melodious harp and lyre. 3Sound the ram's horn at the New Moon, and when the moon is full, on the day of our Feast; 4this is a decree for Israel, an ordinance of the God of Jacob. 5He established it as a statute for Joseph when he went out against Egypt, where we heard a language we did not understand.

6He says, "I removed the burden from their shoulders; their hands were set free from the basket.

in your own life is not a matter of geography, but attitude.

Do you have a place in your life where you feel God has let you down? Do you feel God has put you in a spot, a terribly desolate place without sufficient resources to stay alive? Having done a wonderful work in your life, do you think God is now at the point of abandoning you to die by the thirst of unmet need? Do you, like Israel, want to return to Egypt with its bondage, under the romantic but fictional notion that Egypt will change back its hard face into softness and speak your language?

Our Meribahs are places of God's testing, and God remembers what we do with them. Meribah means you are being called upon to trust God for provision of your needs, even when you don't have a clue as to how He will provide. Provide He will, if you trust Him.

Did you listen?

God's people frequently suffer from spiritual attention deficit disorder. Note the Lord's own three-peated complaint: If you would but listen to me (v. 8). My people would not listen to me (v. 11). If my people would but listen to me (v. 13).

What's the problem here? Meribah did not just occur in the wilderness—it's a perpetual test. At every juncture in life we are called upon to either trust God or go our own way. The Lord knows we face this issue over and over. That's why He calls for absolute surrender to Him (v. 8). Say no to your addiction to false anythings, and God will fully satisfy you with His provisions.

However, when you insist on your own way against God's, you write the

7In your distress you called and I rescued you, I answered you out of a thundercloud; I tested you at the waters of Meribah. Selah 8"Hear, O my people, and I will warn you—if you would but listen to me, O Israel! 9You shall have no foreign god among you; you shall not bow down to an alien god. 10I am the Lord your God, who brought you up out of Egypt. Open wide your mouth and I will fill it. 11"But my people would not listen to me; Israel would not submit to me. 12So I gave them over to their stubborn hearts to follow their own devices. 13"If my people would but listen to me, if Israel would follow my ways, 14 how quickly would I subdue their

prescription for disaster (v. 12). But if you open your life to receive whatever the Lord has in His hand to give you, you will discover a wonderful satisfaction (vv. 10,14,16).

The psalm closes (vv. 15,16) with two alternatives depending upon whether or not we listen. Which one will you choose? Will the Lord in that day have to say to you, "Oh, shut up"?

enemies and turn my hand against their foes! [15]Those who hate the Lord would cringe before him, and their punishment would last forever. [16]But you would be fed with the finest of wheat; with honey from the rock I would satisfy you."

Prayer of response

Lord Jesus, help me to be more concerned about Your "if" questions than my own. Too often I chafe over difficult circumstances and blame You for not making things easier. In my own Meribahs, help me to ask the right questions—and more importantly, help me to hear the questions You are asking me.

My thoughts on Psalm 81 . . .

One God or Many?

Psalm 82

Mormons understand this psalm as one which corroborates their belief in polytheism (many gods) despite the clear teaching of the Scripture: "The Lord is God; besides him there is no other" (Deuteronomy 4:35).

In Mormon theology, verse 1 describes an assembly of gods and verse 6 holds the promise of deity for humans. Joseph Smith, the founder of Mormonism, put it this way: "How many gods there are I do not know, but as we are now, God once was; and as God now is, we will one day become."

Such a view, however, misreads the whole of Scripture as well as this particular psalm.

Who are the "gods"?

Jesus himself tells us the psalm does not refer to gods, but to humans: The gods are those to "whom the word of God came" John 10:34,35). Who is the "whom" Jesus speaks of? The people of Israel—to whom the Old Testament was given.

¹God presides in the great assembly; he gives judgment among the "gods":

Within Israel itself, human judges acted on God's behalf to enforce His laws. They are told not to show partiality because judgment belongs to God. (See Deuteronomy 1:17.) Solomon is said to have sat on the throne of the Lord (1 Chronicles 29:23), even though he literally sat on an earthly chair. Making decisions is such a god-like function that the Hebrew word for God, *Elohim,* is even used for human judges. (See Exodus 21:6; 22:8,9.)

Great Britain has a House of Lords, and everyone understands that parliamentary body does not consist of gods. In the same way, the assembly referred to in this psalm is not one of many gods, but persons who have the God given capacity to make decisions.

Why are they assembled?

God holds us responsible for the decisions we make. To have power of choice (Deuteronomy 30:19,20) is part of what it means for us to be created in the image of God (Genesis 1:27).

Psalm 82 anticipates the day when God holds responsible those who act unjustly. (See 2 Corinthians 5:10.) Such a scene from the future is designed to compel those in the present to change their behaviors lest they too find themselves in that disgraced assembly.

The scene begins with the heavenly court in session—God himself presiding. On trial are the then "gods" of Israel—the judges or leaders and people: mortal persons who die as mere men even though they held the title "sons of the Most High" (v. 6).

Only one question is asked the defendants: "How long will you defend the unjust and show partiality to the wicked?" (v. 2).

We err, however, if we apply this question only to ancient Israel and not to ourselves. God holds all governing authorities responsible to act justly—that's why He instituted government. (See Romans 13:1–7.) But He also holds us accountable for proper self-government.

2"**How long will you defend the unjust and show partiality to the wicked? Selah**

On a personal level, how do you treat other people? Are you fair? Are you cruel or merciful, honest or deceptive? Do you use others to fulfill your selfish purposes or serve them instead? Would you want any other persons to treat you better than you have them?

What do family members honestly think of you? Do they regard you as caring or overbearing, as demanding or giving, as complaining or grateful?

The answers to all these questions have to do with self-government. How are you managing your life? What decisions are you making so your inner life and external deeds align with God's intention and purpose in giving you life?

What happens to them?

The question in verse 2 results from the indictment given: that those on trial have not "defend[ed] the cause of the weak and fatherless; maintain[ed] the rights of the poor and oppressed, rescue[d] the weak and needy; deliver[ing] them from the hand of the wicked" (vv. 3,4). In other words, the "gods" (leaders) of Israel had been interested only in feathering their own nests—not in caring for the vulnerable or acting justly. God regards such gods as know nothings, for they live without a moral compass (v. 5).

What is the Lord God going to do with them—the pompous or powerful rulers who revel in their perks and defend actions which promote evil?

First, He reminds them of their high calling: He gave them power of choice. In this sense, they were "gods" (v. 6).

But they have failed to govern their own lives as God desires; therefore, He promises to displace them (v. 7).

³Defend the cause of the weak and fatherless; maintain the rights of the poor and oppressed. ⁴Rescue the weak and needy; deliver them from the hand of the wicked.

⁵"They know nothing, they understand nothing. They walk about in darkness; all the foundations of the earth are shaken.

⁶"I said, 'You are "gods"; you are all sons of the Most High.'

⁷But you will die like mere men; you will fall like every other ruler."

Are you in the assembly?

Quite clearly, this disgraced group includes only those who have not conducted their lives in a manner pleasing to God. Thus, Asaph stands outside that assembly and offers a closing comment. He has been watching the dialogue from God to the "gods." He yearns for the moment just spoken of when those of bad conduct will be dislodged from their power to inflict harm on others—the hour when the Lord himself brings the unrighteous into His supreme court (v. 8).

Asaph's longing becomes the prayer of every believer pressed down by the selfish and harmful choices of others: "Rise up, O God, and judge the earth" (v. 8).

> [8]Rise up, O God, judge the earth, for all the nations are your inheritance.

Prayer of response

Lord Jesus, this psalm tells me about one assembly I do not want to be a part of—standing before You condemned for acting unkindly, inconsiderately, or unlovingly toward others. Let me instead be in that other assembly to whom You say, "Well done, good and faithful servant."

My thoughts on Psalm 82 . . .

Trouble on Every Side

Your circumstances may seem so overwhelming you feel like the very seasick passenger who had turned several shades of green and was leaning over the rail of the ocean liner.

The steward came along, sized up what was happening, and threw out this cheerful word: "Don't be discouraged. Just remember, no one's ever died yet of seasickness."

The nauseous man, his face ashen, looked up at the steward and replied: "Oh, don't say that. It's only the hope of dying that's keeping me alive."

Have things gone wrong in a big way for you? You face several calamities at once and no help is in sight You feel surrounded by trouble, evil, or sorrow, and you cannot see a path of escape? Only the hope of dying is keeping you alive?

Welcome to Psalm 83—a prayer for God to defend you and take action against your problems.

Is help on the way?

You realize how serious things are, but does God? You are not alone if you feel more alert to the danger than God. The Psalmist opens his prayer by asking the Lord to snap out of passivity (v. 1).

¹O God, do not keep silent; be not quiet, O God, be not still.

Unfortunately, from our perspective, God all too often is silent, quiet, or still. Like Jesus' disciples in a storm, we panic while He is asleep. (See Mark 4: 35–41.) Our Heavenly Helper seems

31

oblivious to threats we clearly perceive. In so many of life's dark passages and excruciating pressures, life seems unresponsive.

You are left on your own to deal with the terror. Like the Psalmist, You wish for God to speak (v. 1), and failing to do so—at least that He might open His eyes and take a look at what you're facing (v. 2).

But the Psalmist's tone is not accusatory. Deep down , he knows God cherishes him (v. 3) and that beyond his own personal safety, God's honor is at stake (v. 4). The enemies are referred to not as "mine," but "yours."

Some of the peoples against Israel in this psalm were close relatives—making the hurt more intense. Edom and Ishmael, respectively, were half brothers to Jacob and Isaac. Moab and Ammon were the sons of Lot. The other neighbors comprise a circle about Israel on all sides (vv. 5–8).

Even as the Psalmist clearly knew the names of his problems, so you also know the identity of what assails you. Take comfort, God does, too.

He'll do it again

As you deal with the current threat to your well-being, remember what God has done for you in the past (vv. 9–12). God's people have a battle-scarred history. If the Lord has helped before, what makes you think He will fail you this time?

The Psalmist ran through selected names of Israel's vanquished enemies, but we have a longer list because we know Jesus. We remember Christ was "delivered over to death for our sins and . . . raised to life for our justification"

²See how your enemies are astir, how your foes rear their heads.

³With cunning they conspire against your people; they plot against those you cherish.

⁴"Come," they say, "let us destroy them as a nation, that the name of Israel be remembered no more."

⁵With one mind they plot together; they form an alliance against you—⁶the tents of Edom and the Ishmaelites, of Moab and the Hagrites, ⁷Gebal, Ammon and Amalek, Philistia, with the people of Tyre. ⁸Even Assyria has joined them to lend strength to the descendants of Lot. Selah

⁹Do to them as you did to Midian, as you did to Sisera and Jabin at the river Kishon, ¹⁰who perished at Endor and became like refuse on the ground. ¹¹Make their nobles like Oreb and Zeeb, all their

(Romans 4:25), that "having disarmed the powers and authorities, he made a public spectacle of them, triumphing over them by the cross" (Colossians 2:15). Therefore, we take hope for "the God of peace will soon crush Satan under your feet" (Romans 16:20).

Rather than seeing your adversities as formidable and unstoppable—a season of prayer (vv. 1–12) puts faith in your heart to believe instead that they are as blowable as tumbleweed and combustible as chaff (vv. 13–15). Don't be deceived into thinking your problems are permanent. God, in His time, will make them go poof before the might of His wind or go up in smoke in the flame of His judgment.

Use this psalm, as all psalms, to pray. What's the first thing you focus on when you have a real big problem? Your own need. That's what happened in this psalm. Asaph is concerned that God may not do anything—so he asks God to start speaking and looking.

When Asaph gets to the end of the psalm, his external situation is no different than at the beginning. The enemies are still out there. God has not yet done anything. But in prayer, Asaph has been reminded that God has acted before to defend His people, that God's cause is at stake in his own personal danger, and that when God applies His power the terrifiers become the terrified (v. 15).

Will you perish because of the hardships you presently face? No. But your adversities will. Your problems are temporary, but God's action against them is permanent (vv. 16,17).

Asaph ends with a prayer that God will reveal himself as Lord to the foes of

princes like Zebah and Zalmunna, 12who said, "Let us take possession of the pasturelands of God."

13Make them like tumbleweed, O my God, like chaff before the wind. 14As fire consumes the forest or a flame sets the mountains ablaze, 15so pursue them with your tempest and terrify them with your storm.

16Cover their faces with shame so that men will seek your name, O Lord. 17May they ever be ashamed and dismayed; may they perish in disgrace.

Israel (v. 18). Perhaps, in your situation, you need also to pray for a revelation of God's presence in your own life.

Will you let the Holy Spirit help you, through this psalm, minimize what threatens you and maximize instead God's future for you?

18Let them know that you, whose name is the Lord—that you alone are the Most High over all the earth.

Prayer of response

Lord Jesus, the enemy wants me to feel hopeless and overwhelmed. I want You to deliver me immediately from harm, but so far You have chosen to give me day–by–day strength. This pause does not mean victory denied, only delayed. Cherish (v. 3) me in every plot against me. My heart rests in the security of Your strength.

My thoughts on Psalm 83 . . .

The View From Baca Valley

I love to walk Balboa Island in Newport Beach, California, in the evening. A sidewalk circles the island's 2.6-mile perimeter. On my left—water, boats, near and distant harbor lights. Always on my right expensive homes built next to one another, most of them with open curtains or shutters inviting passersby to look in on warmly and richly furnished interior decors.

I have often wondered what it would be like to live in houses so beautiful.

Psalm 84 finds us far removed from the charm of Balboa. But it's written by a walker—a psalmist on pilgrimage who looks through the window of memory and anticipation at life within the temple courts. His present path finds him in a valley named Baca (v. 6), a word thought to indicate a tree or shrub that grows in arid places. Geographically and psychologically, it's really the valley of hardship or weeping, and a long climb up and out to Mount Zion where stands the temple.

But Baca lies in your way. You can't go around it. You must not stay in it. Valleys, by their very nature, are depressed places. They enhance our longing to be somewhere else. Who would not prefer the serenity and security of God's courts over hardship and weeping? Why cry from deepest need if you're already in God's presence on the mountaintop, within protected walls (vv. 1,2)?

Nostalgically the psalm writer thinks of the small sparrows and their access to the temple courts and even the altar (v. 3)—a wistful contrast for one far down below.

How do you get out of Baca?

Look beyond the present

In the valley, don't get hemmed in and lose your perspective. The Psalmist refreshed his spirit by anticipating when the valley would lie far behind (vv. 1,2). You will not always be in a dry and sorrowful place. Others have made it to the top and the Psalmist thinks of them (v. 4).

Rather than being envious of those whose struggles are past, the Psalmist blesses them. *Oh, if saints and angels praise You today in the temple, I choose to join their song even while in Baca. I will lift up my hands and voice, and declare Your wonderful glory, and that Your deeds to the children of men are not at an end. Your mercy endures forever!*

Look for increased strength

Your stamina is not enough. You need His (v. 5). But strength is also developmental (v. 7). When first entering the valley of tears, the pilgrim feels overwhelmed and not ready for the test that takes place there. However, the tremendous external pressure acts to develop a counter prevailing strength of spiritual muscle and stamina. You go from strength to strength as you let trials become the pulleys, barbells, and bench presses of your soul.

Set your heart on pilgrimage. A walker keeps moving. You know it will be an arduous climb out of your valley of hurt—but you are determined to keep going upward. You will not give up, give in, or give out.

Look for the good

Insist the trial become a blessing. Note the pilgrim makes the dry barren Baca a place of springs (v. 6). You dig around in

[1]How lovely is your dwelling place, O Lord Almighty! [2]My soul yearns, even faints, for the courts of the Lord; my heart and my flesh cry out for the living God.

[3]Even the sparrow has found a home, and the swallow a nest for herself, where she may have her young—a place near your altar, O Lord Almighty, my King and my God.

[4]Blessed are those who dwell in your house; they are ever praising you. Selah

[5]Blessed are those whose strength is in you, who have set their hearts on pilgrimage.

[6]As they pass through the Valley of Baca, they make it a place of springs; the autumn rains also cover it with pools.

your desert and make it yield resources to refresh. And God adds to your efforts rain from above.

What compelling encouragement. You discover water in the place you wept. God sends rain where you shed tears. When you are done with Baca, it's no longer hard, barren, dry ground—God worked with you to make an oasis in your personal desert.

So keep toiling on the upward climb, pilgrim. One day Baca will be behind you. Good things lie ahead (vv. 10,11). Your reasoning can become hopelessly twisted in the valley of Baca. You were tempted to make it a place of bitterness, despair, and unforgiveness. You felt like giving up on life. You should not have been treated the way you were, and your emotions ranged from deep-seated anger over the injustice you suffered to dark seasons of depression.

This psalm tells us God's people transform Baca before they leave it. Baca becomes a blessing and not a curse.

Look with faith

You may be going through a period when you wish you could trade places with someone else. Times are tough and so difficult to endure. You longingly look through windows at other people's happiness and wish you could be in that idyllic setting.

God has a better place for you. You will not be on the outside looking in. That place is inside God; and if you're only the doorkeeper there, that's a better spot than anything outside of Him (v. 10). You see things clearly when He illumines your life as the sun, shades you as a shield, and gives you honor and favor (v. 11).

7They go from strength to strength, till each appears before God in Zion. 8Hear my prayer, O Lord God Almighty; listen to me, O God of Jacob. Selah 9Look upon our shield, O God; look with favor on your anointed one.

10Better is one day in your courts than a thousand elsewhere; I would rather be a doorkeeper in the house of my God than dwell in the tents of the wicked. 11For the Lord God is a sun and shield; the Lord bestows favor and honor; no good thing does he withhold from those whose walk is blameless.

We can let the valley of Baca diminish our confidence in the Lord, or we can choose to trust Him. The Psalmist did the latter—four times referring to God as "O Lord Almighty" (vv. 1,3,8,12). He knew no difficulty was beyond God's power to cure, and that nothing would ever be stronger than God's power to ultimately deliver.

> [12]O Lord Almighty, blessed is the man who trusts in you.

Prayer of response

Lord Jesus, in the valley of hardship I feel so weak. I wonder if I can make it. But I remember You are the Almighty. I trust You in this Baca. My heart is set on pilgrimage, and I know with Your help I'll make my test a testimony, my hurt a healing, and my loss a gain. I thank You that Your Word encourages me that Baca is not the end of the journey—only a stop along the way.

My thoughts on Psalm 84 . . .

Starting Over

My Aunt Ruth Plymire served a lifetime as missionary to Chinese and Tibetan people. On her tombstone is etched this two-word epitaph: "No regrets."

Few persons could say the same thing. Most of us have regrets. We wish we could have a second chance at some of the decisions we muffed. We may think it impossible to recover from the disastrous effects of our own personal choices.

Perhaps someone told you that serving God was like a fork in the road. If you made the wrong turn, you could never get back. I prefer the comparison to the will of God being a river. If you leave the river, bank your canoe, and get lost in the woods, the solution is to head back to the river. You may not be as far downstream as you would have been had you not wandered off, but you can be back in the current of God's will and blessing.

Psalm 85 is written for people who have failed God, regret doing so, and want to find a place of beginning again. How do you do that?

¹You showed favor to your land, O Lord; you restored the fortunes of Jacob.

Take time to remember

This psalm speaks to us when we experience hurtful personal consequences because of our own sin.

C.S. Lewis said God whispers to us in our pleasures and shouts at us in our pain. Indeed, without pain we would have little incentive to change, but adversity forces us to cry out for help.

The enemy wants us to think God

won't hear us; that our last rebellion or inattention went beyond the limit; that we have journeyed too far from even God's grace.

²You forgave the iniquity of your people and covered all their sins. *Selah*

Not so. Our ability to come back from devastation lies not in our goodness, but His. He is the One who shows favor, restores our fortunes, forgives our iniquity, covers our sins, and turns from anger.

³You set aside all your wrath and turned from your fierce anger.

I know people who refuse to forgive what someone did to them. Not only do they remain unforgiving but they never tire of telling others how bad that person is. How different with God who not only forgives but covers our sin. He is not interested in broadcasting our failures but in erasing the bad episodes from our life's videotape.

Unfortunately there are even so-called believers who don't understand this principle in God. They are always looking for dirt in others and are quite willing to spread their information far and wide.

Recovering from spiritual failure begins as you remember God wants you well, that He has helped others in the past, and He will help you.

Ask God for favor

Remembering God's past mercy gives the Psalmist confidence to seek restoration, reviving, joy, and salvation.

⁴Restore us again, O God our Savior, and put away your displeasure toward us.

As the American Civil War neared its end, it is reported that Abraham Lincoln was asked how he intended to treat the vanquished South. He responded: "As if they had never rebelled."

So with the Lord. We may freely ask Him to put away His displeasure with us. Indeed, when we are under God's disciplinary judgment, it feels like "forever" and "through all generations" (v. 5).

⁵Will you be angry with us forever? Will you prolong your anger through all generations?

But the Lord will grant our request for renewal when we ask with the same sincere spirit as this Psalmist.

Why does He do this? Because He possesses unfailing love (v. 7). The opposite of unfailing love is failing love. Few of us have remained immune from persons who professed love for us one day, only to withdraw it later. The Lord is no fair-weather friend—He loves us even when we're at our worst.

Listen to what God says

Prayer involves both speaking and listening. When you're hurting, you may find it easier to ask God for help than to be quiet and listen for His response.

What is He saying to you in the stillness of your spirit?

The Psalmist hears Him speak peace. The Hebrew word for peace, *shalom,* means far more than a cessation of conflict or trouble. It represents fulfillment, wellness and contentment, the absence of lack.

When you suffer emotional, relational, or spiritual pain, it's because you lack something you feel you dearly need. God wants to move His peace into that great void in your life. He'll do so, plus help you "not to return to folly" (v. 8)—the senseless or self-destructive patterns of behavior which brought you despair in the first place.

The blessed life

The psalm closes with an emphasis on being a person of love and faithfulness, righteousness and peace.

These two sets of virtues are often divorced in our culture. Thus, we hear a

6Will you not revive us again, that your people may rejoice in you?
7Show us your unfailing love, O Lord, and grant us your salvation.

8I will listen to what God the Lord will say; he promises peace to his people, his saints—but let them not return to folly. 9Surely his salvation is near those who fear him, that his glory may dwell in our land.
10Love and faithfulness meet together; righteousness and peace kiss each other. 11Faithfulness springs forth from the earth, and righteousness looks down from heaven.

lot about love and peace, little about faithfulness and righteousness. But true love never exists without faithfulness, and true peace never comes without inward integrity. You cannot say you love someone whom you have abandoned, and your peace is plastic if you violated God's will to get it.

God knows that when we receive the gift of His goodness, our living environment prospers (v. 12) and we make good choices (v. 13).

> ¹²The Lord will indeed give what is good, and our land will yield its harvest.
>
> ¹³Righteousness goes before him and prepares the way for his steps.

Prayer of response

Lord, I began this psalm by asking You to restore my fortunes, and I conclude it by recognizing You do something even better. I wanted You to change my circumstances, and You changed me instead.

My thoughts on Psalm 85 . . .

Poor and Needy

How refreshing. Finding a psalm of David again—the only one in Book III of the Psalms (73–89)—like rediscovering a long lost friend.

I want to say, "How are you, David?" As if I need to ask. He's in trouble, pouring out his soul to God for help, not sure he is going to make it, yet continuing to trust. So what else is new?

How I love David's honesty. I understand now why Jonathan felt so close to him. Here is a man with a sensitive and transparent heart in the midst of a troubled and talented life: fabulous musician and poet, mighty warrior, respected leader.

¹Hear, O Lord, and answer me, for I am poor and needy.

²Guard my life, for I am devoted to you. You are my God; save your servant who trusts in you.

³Have mercy on me, O Lord, for I call to you all day long.

⁴Bring joy to your servant, for to you, O Lord, I lift up my soul.

Help!

But it's the tenderness within David that endears him to us, the open vulnerability from which his plea spills out like toothpaste squeezed from the fingerprints of pressure: "Hear, O Lord, and answer me, for I am poor and needy" (v. 1).

If you had it all together, you would not need to cry for God's help all day long (v. 3). Like David, are you in need of God's protection (v. 2), His mercy (v. 3), and relief from depression (v. 4)?

Look up!

Such desperate seasons trigger a gush of inner hurt, a giving vent to griefs or

43

fears buried deep within. But David permits his faith to invade his feelings. He switches from a catharsis of personal pain to a celebration of the goodness of the Lord upon whom he calls (vv. 5–10).

A friend of mine is a leader of many churches in a country where four of his pastors have been martyred in the past 4 years. He recounted to me that they have learned a new lesson in thanksgiving; that in the times you hurt so badly you can't find anything to thank God for in your circumstances, the Holy Spirit gives you reasons to thank Him for who He is; that despite your adversities, He is in control. That's the spirit of David. Through prayer, he is transported out of his personal anguish into remembering the nature of the Lord he serves. The first thing coming to his consciousness is awareness of God's forgiveness and love toward those who call (v. 5).

Is your valley longer, darker, and deeper because you have not done this? In your time of trouble, have you spent yourself trying your own solutions? Has your "day" of trouble lasted a whole lot longer because you didn't throw yourself upon God right at the beginning? It's not too late. Have the confidence, as did David, that the Lord will indeed answer you (vv. 6,7)—that He will not leave you struggling alone, a victim to defeat and despair.

Have you reached the place where your hope is in God and no other (vv. 8–10)?

God's way of saving you out of trial may not be to perform an external deed of deliverance on your behalf. Perhaps the work He wants to do is inward. Maybe the way out of your trial is not the remaking of your circumstances, but the

5You are forgiving and good, O Lord, abounding in love to all who call to you.

6Hear my prayer, O Lord; listen to my cry for mercy. 7In the day of my trouble I will call to you, for you will answer me.

8Among the gods there is none like you, O Lord; no deeds can compare with yours. 9All the nations you have made will come and worship before you, O Lord; they will bring glory to your name. 10For you are great and do marvelous deeds; you alone are God.

way you think and talk. Prayer changes you from being negative to becoming a person of faith.

Look inside

David explores this prospect in making himself available to God for instruction. He asks for the split ends of his life to be made whole: that the one end which sought his own way, and the other end which sought God would both be united into one undivided self. Your request for teaching must be backed up by commitment to live the truth taught (v. 11).

David gains spiritual altitude as this psalm progresses. Early in the psalm (v. 5) he acknowledged that God abounded in love toward "all" who call upon Him. Now he has the personal assurance that God's love is great toward "me," along with a quickening in his spirit that God's deliverance has been given (vv. 12,13).

How can David begin the psalm with a desperate call for help, only to speak of being delivered a few seconds later?

It's because the solution to his trial—and possibly yours—lies on the inside. In contemplating God's love, forgiveness, and sovereignty, David has already emerged from the abyss of despair. Emotionally he had been in the grave—worse, the deepest part of the grave (v. 13). But his words of confidence in the Lord, like an elevator, have already moved him out of the emotional basement.

I'm okay now

Thus, David can now look out on his foes, his danger, and not be overwhelmed (v. 14). God will give you strength to deal

11Teach me your way, O Lord, and I will walk in your truth; give me an undivided heart, that I may fear your name.

12I will praise you, O Lord my God, with all my heart; I will glorify your name forever. 13For great is your love toward me; you have delivered me from the depths of the grave.

14The arrogant are attacking me, O God; a band of ruthless men seeks my life—men without regard for you.

with the trial because that's His character—He is compassionate and gracious, completely faithful to you (vv. 15,16).

Notice that the last two verbs in the psalm, "helped" and "comforted," are in the past tense (v. 17). Why so? The enemies were still very much alive and their threat intensely real. What has changed in David's external circumstances? Nothing. But everything is different on the inside of David.

Prayer nourishes one's heart. Early in life, David had learned with Goliath that the battle is won on the inside before there ever is an outward manifestation of victory. So, this psalm ends with David sure that his enemies will be put to shame—not himself. What a contrast from how the psalm began.

15But you, O Lord, are a compassionate and gracious God, slow to anger, abounding in love and faithfulness. 16Turn to me and have mercy on me; grant your strength to your servant and save the son of your maidservant.

17Give me a sign of your goodness, that my enemies may see it and be put to shame, for you, O Lord, have helped me and comforted me.

Prayer of response

Lord Jesus, I don't have the strength to handle this trial. I really feel helpless, yes, poor and needy. But I lift my eyes from my need to You. You will never fail me—not because I'm good—but, because You are who You are: loving, faithful, powerful, and completely dependable. My hope is in You.

My thoughts on Psalm 86 . . .

Born in Zion

In the first week on her job as the only woman ever to serve as United States Secretary of State, Madeleine Albright, 59, learned a family secret—she was of Jewish ancestry.

She had never known that her parents were Czech Jews and that two of her grandparents, as well as an aunt, died in concentration camps during the Holocaust.

What a jolt to discover that your roots differ from what you believed your whole life.

Psalm 87 celebrates the ancestry of all those born in Zion—or Jerusalem. But it has shocking news. The birth records of Zion are not limited to a single ethnicity. Those born elsewhere have opportunity to change their point of origin.

Glorious Zion

The original singers of this psalm, the Sons of Korah, often composed music connected with worship in the temple at Jerusalem. They were the praise and worship leaders of their day. Like prophets, in this psalm they speak words beyond their own ability to fully understand. Only in looking back can we now see what the Holy Spirit had in mind when He inspired the Sons of Korah to write it.

It's clear that the earthly city of Jerusalem held special favor with God. He loved it more than all cities (v. 2). Why? On its holy mountain, He had placed

¹He has set his foundation on the holy mountain; ²the Lord loves the gates of Zion more than all the dwellings of Jacob.

47

the temple—through which a show-and-tell object lesson was given for centuries that we might know how sinful people may have fellowship with God and forgiveness of sins.

If glorious things may be said of the earthly city of Jerusalem (v. 3), how much more the New Jerusalem above coming down from heaven as a bride beautifully dressed for her husband (Revelation 21:1–4; 22:1–6)? All the hurts and dangers will be gone in the eternal city: There will be no more sea (i.e., separation from those we love), death, mourning, crying, pain, curse, or night.

Who belongs?

The stunning news of Psalm 87, however, begins at verse 4 with recitation of those whom God himself says are "born in Zion."

Who are these native-borns? Five ancient enemies.

First is Rahab—not the harlot Rahab who saved the spies at Jericho (Joshua 2), but the nickname given by Isaiah to Egypt (Isaiah 30:7). Not only will Egyptians—the oppressors of Israel in slavery be "born in Zion"—but also the Babylonians who destroyed Zion and carried its people into captivity.

The mighty foreign powers of Egypt to the south and Babylon to the northeast are followed by smaller local enemies who gave Israel fits throughout its history: Philistia and Tyre (now Lebanon). Finally, even the more remote foreign power threat, Cush (present-day Ethiopia) is included among those "born in Zion."

How could this be? The Lord himself signs their names into the birth registry of Zion (v. 6).

³**Glorious things are said of you, O city of God: Selah**

⁴**"I will record Rahab and Babylon among those who acknowledge me— Philistia too, and Tyre, along with Cush—and will say, 'This one was born in Zion.' "**

⁵**Indeed, of Zion it will be said, "This one and that one were born in her, and the Most High himself will establish her."** ⁶**The Lord will write in the register of the peoples: "This one was born in Zion." Selah**

The Sons of Korah, in the distance, have seen the gleaming international city of those born again into the family of God from every tribe, nation, and language. Their psalm celebrates the Jerusalem above (Galatians 4:26) where a true Jew is one inwardly (Romans 2:29).

In noting Egyptians, Babylonians, Philistines, Ethiopians, and citizens of Tyre as native born to Zion, this psalm breathes the spirit of Ephesians 2:11–22, in which Gentiles "are no longer foreigners and aliens, but fellow citizens with God's people and members of God's household" (Ephesians 2:19).

Birth registry

When you apply for a passport, you are required to furnish proof of who you are by presenting a certified copy of your birth certificate. The original copy is stored at the courthouse in the county where you were born. That certificate entitles you to citizenship in your country of origin.

But there is a hall of records beyond the county courthouse. It's called the Lamb's Book of Life (Revelation 21:27). Only those whose names are in that registry enter the New Jerusalem. Jesus tells us to rejoice if our names are written there (Luke 10:20).

How do you get your name into that registry? Jesus tells us it comes through being born again (John 3:5). You experience new birth when you receive Jesus into your life, believe on His name, confess with your lips He is Lord, and believe in your heart that God raised Him from the dead (John 1:12,13; Romans 10:8–10). When you do that, God says of you: "That one was born in Zion."

The New Testament urges us to live with the realization that "our citizenship is in heaven. And we eagerly await a Savior from there, the Lord Jesus Christ, who . . . will transform our lowly bodies so that they will be like his glorious body" (Philippians 3:20,21). How fitting that a glorious city (v. 3) has glorious people.

No wonder the psalm concludes with the anthem sung by us, the citizens of Zion above, "All my fountains are in you" (v. 7). All that truly sustains us comes not from ourselves or others, but from the Lord himself.

Madeleine Albright only learned late in life of her earthly ancestry. How about you? If Zion—God's heavenly city—is your choice of final destination, then your name is already there in its registry of new births.

⁷As they make music they will sing, "All my fountains are in you."

Prayer of response

Thank You, Lord, for regarding me as born in Zion. I have loved some places where I have lived better than others; may I love best the place You love most.

My thoughts on Psalm 87 . . .

The Pit

Many believe this psalm was written especially for Jesus to pray the night before His crucifixion.

The details certainly fit such a moment. So does the layout of the Church of St. Peter in Gallicantu ("rooster crow"), believed to be built over the three-level house of the high priest. This is where Jesus stayed the night before the Crucifixion (Matthew 26:57–68; Mark 14:53–65; Luke 22:54–62).

The Lord's trial evidently occurred on the upper level in view of Mark's description of Peter being in the courtyard "below" (Mark 14:66). The courtyard actually is outside the middle level of the house, and farther beneath it lie two rooms: one accessible by stairs where prisoners were bound and flogged; another, a windowless, doorless stone pit into which a prisoner was lowered by ropes through a hole in the top.

In all likelihood, Jesus had been led down the stairs from the main hall. On His descent to the room where He would be beaten and the pit in which He would be held, He passed the courtyard at the precise moment His closest friend and lead disciple disowned Him for the third time. Jesus looked "straight at Peter" (Luke 22:61). Had Jesus still been on the upper level, He would have looked "down," not "straight at."

With Peter's denial and curses ringing in His ears, the Lord continues down into the flogging room (Luke 22:63–65).

The Gospels themselves never tell us about the pit, but some place would have been needed for the detainment of Jesus before His delivery after sunrise to Pilate.

The plea in the pit

Many times I have stood in that small cell at the base of St. Peter in Gallicantu, sensing that even as Psalm 22 was written for Jesus to pray while on the cross, so this Psalm appears uniquely designed as a prayer for Jesus in the pit while waiting for His transfer unto death.

Assuming this is the case, then Psalm 88 is the next prayer Jesus prayed after saying in Gethsemane, "Father . . . not my will, but thine, be done" (Luke 22:42).

Have you ever prayed the Gethsemane prayer in a very tough circumstance in your own life? Your temptation is to think that once the Lord sees your yieldedness, your outer circumstances will improve. Psalm 88 indicates the reverse—a descent into a terrible dark hole of aloneness where there are no angels to strengthen and no friends to arouse from slumber.

The darkness of the pit closes in on you, and the only bright hope in the whole psalm lies in its opening two verses—you are still talking to God. No solution for the dilemma of the pit is found within the psalm. The entire prayer is a one-way conversation—God doesn't say a thing. But the fact you pray at all to the "God who saves [you]" attests to your belief and hope that He is listening.

After praying this desperate psalm of black night and deep abyss, you may yet face worse things. For Jesus, crucifixion followed the pit: pain piled on top of pain. But all along, keep crying out to God.

The peril of the pit

A soul (emotions and mind) full of trouble, physically drawing close to death, no strength left to draw upon—

¹O Lord, the God who saves me, day and night I cry out before you.
²May my prayer come before you; turn your ear to my cry.
³For my soul is full of trouble and my life draws near the grave.
⁴I am counted among those who go down to the pit;

Jesus acknowledges himself as one "set apart with the dead, like the slain who lie in the grave."

The end of verse 5 matches the mood of Psalm 22:1—that God himself has forsaken and forgotten. In actual fact, He has not—as the end of Psalm 22 indicates and as the Lord himself knew—but God gives us permission to vent our emotions in prayer. And sometimes our feelings suggest that God doesn't even know our address anymore.

The problem of the pit

In Gethsemane, Jesus described His soul as "overwhelmed with sorrow to the point of death" (Mark 14:34). The pit intensifies that sorrow. In His aloneness, the wrath of God lies heavily upon Him. He bears God's judgment, which we deserved, as all His friends forsake Him—including the last, Peter, who repulsed Him with shouted curses and denials. He is confined and cannot escape.

Questions come (vv. 10–12)—for which He knows all the answers are yes. But in the pit you leave them unanswered. Why? There has been no response to the cry for help, and you interpret that as God's rejection (vv. 13,14).

The panic of the pit

We all like neat endings. But some prayers don't end prettily. This one closes on a note of total and complete despair.

Earlier in the evening, Jesus told His friends: "I am not alone, for my Father is with me" (John 16:32). Here, that confession is not present.

⁵I am set apart with the dead, like the slain who lie in the grave, whom you remember no more, who are cut off from your care. ⁶You have put me in the lowest pit, in the darkest depths. ⁷Your wrath lies heavily upon me; you have overwhelmed me with all your waves. *Selah* ⁸You have taken from me my closest friends and have made me repulsive to them. I am confined and cannot escape; ⁹my eyes are dim with grief. I call to you, O Lord, every day; I spread out my hands to you. ¹⁰Do you show your wonders to the dead? Do those who are dead rise up and praise you? *Selah* ¹¹Is your love declared in the grave, your faithfulness in Destruction? ¹²Are your wonders known in the place of darkness, or your righteous deeds in the land of oblivion?

¹³But I cry to you for help, O Lord; in the morning my prayer comes before you. ¹⁴Why, O Lord, do you reject me and hide your face from me?

¹⁵From my youth I have been afflicted and close to death; I

But you must remember that what you prayed prior to the pit is still good. God refuses to allow the last verse of this psalm to be His final word for Jesus or for you.

You may forget when you are in the pit that it is not God's permanent location for you. But the problem with the pit lies in your feeling that this is the end. Only later will you look back and say as did Jesus: "He has not despised or disdained the suffering of the afflicted one . . . but has listened to his cry for help" (Psalm 22:24).

have suffered your terrors and am in despair. [16]Your wrath has swept over me; your terrors have destroyed me. [17]All day long they surround me like a flood; they have completely engulfed me. [18]You have taken my companions and loved ones from me; the darkness is my closest friend.

Prayer of response

Lord Jesus, life will never be as dark for me as it was for You in those horrible moments You suffered. I thank You for enduring the pit and the cross in order to rescue me. When I am in my own pit, I know You are with me, even when I wonder if You're there at all. You know my aloneness since You were in a far darker place. I am grateful that You, and not the darkness, are my closest friend.

My thoughts on Psalm 88 . . .

Saturday

Psalm 89

Have you noticed the four Gospels say nothing about the day between Good Friday and Easter Sunday morning?

In his award-winning book, *The Jesus I Never Knew* Philip Yancey says, "In a real sense we live on Saturday. . . . Human history grinds on, between the time of promise and fulfillment. Can we trust that God can make something holy and beautiful and good out of a world that includes Bosnia and Rwanda, and innercity ghettos and jammed prisons in the richest nation on earth? It's Saturday on planet Earth; will Sunday ever come?"

The disciples of Jesus had to wait until Sunday in order to call Friday "good."

Psalm 89, within its Old Testament context, also fits the mood of Saturday. Yesterday (vv. 1–37) God made an unconditional promise that David's kingly line would continue forever. Today (vv. 38–51), it appears God has renounced His covenant. The hope for a better tomorrow lies in one brief burst of praise (v. 52).

¹I will sing of the Lord's great love forever; with my mouth I will make your faithfulness known through all generations. ²I will declare that your love stands firm forever, that you established your faithfulness in heaven itself.

Yesterday

There's no hint in the opening anthem (vv. 1,2) that Israel lay in ruins and under occupation or that David's sons were kings no more. Faith shines best when you declare God's truth even though it contradicts how you feel. God's love stands firm forever, and His faithfulness is established in heaven itself.

How can he be so confident? Because God made a covenant without contingencies that David's throne would be established throughout all generations (vv. 3,4). If Jesus is not the fulfillment for that promise, then God broke His word because Israel has had no king these past 2,600 years.

³You said, "I have made a covenant with my chosen one, I have sworn to David my servant, ⁴"I will establish your line forever and make your throne firm through all generations.' " Selah

As the Psalmist contemplates the character of the one who made such a promise, he looks to heaven (vv. 5–8) and earth (vv. 9–18) for illustration of God's incomparability, awesomeness, power, and faithfulness.

The presence of faithfulness means God can be utterly relied upon. The laws of mathematics, physics, genetics, gravity, and space all owe their existence to the predictability and dependability of God. Indeed, faithfulness does surround Him (v. 8).

⁸O Lord God Almighty, who is like you? You are mighty, O Lord, and your faithfulness surrounds you.

It is this God who unilaterally selected David, promising to give him faithful love and a throne forever (vv. 9–29), assuring him that the covenant would hold even if David's sons forsook God's law and violated His decrees (vv. 30–33). Never, however, would God annul His own agreement or lie to David. David could rest in the reliability of God's own word that his line would endure eternally (vv. 34–36).

Today

Now, no one sat on David's throne. Its splendor was gone, cast down to the ground. The nation itself had been subdued and plundered; its conquered people ridiculed among the nations (vv. 38–51).

Hard times may lead you to believe things about God that are not true. God never renounced His covenant with

David, despite what the Psalmist thought (v. 39). The Lord doesn't strike you down when you accuse Him of things that are not true. He allows you in prayer to express what's on your heart, and waits for your distorted emotions to fall in line with the objective truth.

We know that the devastation lamented in the latter part of this psalm did not mean God had broken His promise to David; but rather that He had kept His word to punish David's sons when they forsook His law (vv. 30–32). There's a world of difference between discipline and abandonment—the Psalmist confuses the two and misreads God's discipline of Israel as an abandonment of His promises.

Have you felt like saying: "Lord, You must not love me anymore or You would not have allowed this to happen." Then you're in the same boat as the Psalmist here. Don't make his mistake. Don't interpret tough times as a sign that God no longer cares for you even if you are being disciplined for your own sin as was Israel.

It's on Saturday that we ask a question like this: "O Lord, where is Your former great love, which in your faithfulness you swore to David?" (v. 49).

Tomorrow

The Psalmist has been in a nosedive toward deep depression. But at the last moment he pulls hard on spiritual levers, lifting his faith upward split seconds before he hits dirt and ground: "Praise be to the Lord forever! Amen and Amen" (v. 52).

What happened? There doesn't appear to be any logical connection between the

30"If his sons forsake my law and do not follow my statutes, 31if they violate my decrees and fail to keep my commands, 32I will punish their sin with the rod, their iniquity with flogging.

49O Lord, where is your former great love, which in your faithfulness you swore to David? 50Remember, Lord, how your servant has been mocked, how I bear in my heart the taunts of all the nations, 51the taunts with which your enemies have mocked, O Lord, with which they have mocked every step of your anointed one. 52Praise be to the Lord forever! Amen and Amen.

despair of verses 38–51 and the conclusion of verse 52 except that faith entered his heart. He believed God for tomorrow. There would be an answer to his questions and his needs.

In the face of overwhelming problems, you must defy them by the same shout of trust. If the Psalmist had had the benefit of the New Testament's answer to his questions, he would have been beside himself with joy. Instead of a single concluding verse of praise, there would have been a whole book.

As people of Saturday, we live between Jesus' first coming and His second. I like how Yancey closes his book by relating what's carved onto a tombstone in a cemetery in rural Louisiana. Just one word: "Waiting."

Prayer of response

Lord Jesus, help me to be honest enough to admit when my suffering results directly from my own sins, rather than blaming You or other people. I want to live Saturdays strengthened by what You did for me yesterday, and encouraged by what you have planned for me tomorrow, always grateful for Your faithfulness. What You have promised will come true.

My thoughts on Psalm 89 . . .

Our Greater Address

I n his play, *Our Town,* Thorton Wilder tells of a letter received in the village of Grover's Corner, New Hampshire, by a little girl named Jane Croft from her minister. He addressed the envelope: "Jane Croft, Sutton County, New Hampshire, United States of America, Continent of North America, Western Hemisphere, the earth, the solar system, the universe, the mind of God."

Jane discovered she had a larger address than she had ever imagined.

Psalm 90 is a reminder that we also have a larger address; that moments of disillusionment, frustration, despair, and defeat are not the last word. So often at gravesides the words of this psalm have been read alongside the triumphant hope given in 1 Corinthians 15.

The four divisions of the psalm compare God's eternity (vv. 1,2) to our mortality (vv. 3–6), and set in contrast our recognition of God's wrath (vv. 7–12) with our plea for grace (vv. 13–17).

The eternity of God

This psalm sees further than the Hubble telescope, for it peers upon what lies beyond time and space: the everlasting God, the same Lord to whom we belong.

¹Lord, you have been our dwelling place throughout all generations.

Notice the Psalmist in verse 1 carefully chooses the pronoun "our." Had he said "my" he would have excluded you. Had he said "they" he would have excluded himself. When we say, "Lord,

You have been our dwelling place in all generations," we identify ourselves as members of the household of faith. We are in the same company as Abraham and Sarah, Isaac and Jacob, Deborah and Ruth, Moses and David, Peter and Paul, Mary and Martha.

The One in whom they lived and moved is the one in whom we abide. If He sustained them, will He not also you? He has no thought of retiring from being God—from everlasting to everlasting He can be counted upon.

Our mortality

As a 17-year-old I wrote these lines about death:

Icy cold fingers reached out for me,
Clutching at my soul.
I could not fight the arrogant intruder,
Whose name was death.

Now, 40 years later, I realize death is gaining ground on me through the aging process. This psalm forces me to face stark realities. If Jesus does not return soon, casket and grave are waiting.

Moses—to whom this psalm is attributed—turns from His contemplation of God's eternity (vv. 1,2) to his own mortality (vv. 3–6). His key thoughts lie compressed in these four words: "dust," "day," "watch," and "dew."

God turns us back to the dust (Genesis 3:19). Someone described our bodies as liquefied dirt. We are such complex life forms—it's hard to accept that one day our earthly bodies will again be specks of inanimate matter.

The Psalmist says your life is so short that a thousand of your years are but a day with God. That means that 70 years of your time totals 9 1/2 seconds on His

2Before the mountains were born or you brought forth the earth and the world, from everlasting to everlasting you are God.

3You turn men back to dust, saying, "Return to dust, O sons of men." 4For a thousand years in your sight are like a day that has just gone by, or like a watch in the night. 5You sweep men away in the sleep of death; they are like the new grass of the morning—6 though in the morning it springs up new, by evening it is dry and withered.

clock. It gets worse. On further reflection, you are less than a day—only a "watch," that is, a 4-hour span in the evening, or 1 1/2 seconds in God's eternal day.

Finally, you are compared to grass— fresh in the morning, withered by evening.

God's wrath

What is our emotional reaction to mortality? Horror. God's judicial sentence of death has been imposed because of our sins (vv. 7–12; Genesis 2:17). He has the tapes, the videos, the transcript of our entire life. He has seen every deceptive intention, act, and word. There's no place to hide.

This psalm offers only a partial solution for our dilemma with death's certainty. It tells us to number our days that we may gain a heart of wisdom. In other words, live well and rightly one day at a time. That's little consolation when you consider your last words will not be witty or articulate, but a "moan" (v. 9).

A plea for grace

At verse 13, the psalm moves from despair to hope. If death awaits him, then the least he can do is ask God for a joyful (vv. 14–16) and meaningful (v. 17) life. As Christians, we anticipate so much more.

We know that to be absent from the body is to be present with the Lord (2 Corinthians 5:8); that Christ will bring with Him all those who have fallen asleep and at the resurrection they will be raised first and then we who remain (1 Thessalonians 4:13–18). We look forward to having an imperishable and immortal body (1 Corinthians 15:35–58) given us

7We are consumed by your anger and terrified by your indignation. 8You have set our iniquities before you, our secret sins in the light of your presence. 9All our days pass away under your wrath; we finish our years with a moan. 10The length of our days is seventy years—or eighty, if we have the strength; yet their span is but trouble and sorrow, for they quickly pass, and we fly away. 11Who knows the power of your anger? For your wrath is as great as the fear that is due you. 12Teach us to number our days aright, that we may gain a heart of wisdom.

13Relent, O Lord! How long will it be? Have compassion on your servants. 14Satisfy us in the morning with your unfailing love, that we may sing for joy and be glad all our days. 15Make us glad for as many days as you have afflicted us, for as many years as we have seen trouble. 16May your deeds be shown to your servants, your splendor to their children.

by the One who said: "I am the resurrection and the life. He who believes in me will live, even though he dies; and whoever lives and believes in me will never die" (John 11:25,26).

Remember the story about Jane Croft's address? The last line was "the mind of God." It's more biblical to place the name of Christ last since "all things were made by him" (John 1:3) and "in him all things hold together" (Colossians 1:17). Put your name in place of Jane Croft. Where would a letter find you today? Is the last line on your greater address "Christ"? Do you live and move and have your being in Him (Acts 17:28)?

Someday all the intermediary lines between your name and Christ will be gone, it'll just be you . . . in Christ Jesus—no forwarding necessary. He is your final and greater address.

[17]May the favor of the Lord our God rest upon us; establish the work of our hands for us—yes, establish the work of our hands.

Prayer of response

Lord Jesus, I am so thankful to have a permanent home in You. I am grateful my final destination is not the grave but glory. Because my earthly life is so brief, I ask You to help me live every day wisely and in such a way that it counts for You.

My thoughts on Psalm 90 . . .

In God We Trust

At first blush, this psalm seems to fly in the face of our own Christian experience. Its promise of immunization from danger and insulation from adversity cuts cross-grain against our own encounters with accidents, illness, and misfortune.

The devil, by means of this psalm, tempted Jesus to trigger the angelic protections assured in verses 11 and 12 (Matthew 4:5–7). Three years later, at His arrest in Gethsemane, Jesus again refused to invoke the guarantee of angelic rescue (Matthew 26:53). The bright promise of this psalm became instead a taunt on the lips of His crucifiers, "He trusts in God. Let God rescue him" (v. 14; Matthew 27:43).

If the Lord's experience and ours do not square with the nothing-will-ever-harm-those-who-love-God spirit of this psalm, how do we understand and apply it?

A secure place

¹He who dwells in the shelter of the Most High will rest in the shadow of the Almighty. ²I will say of the Lord, "He is my refuge and my fortress, my God, in whom I trust."

The opening verses find their New Testament counterpart in Romans 8:31–39. When you have made God your dwelling place, you are secure on the day of trouble. In Psalm 91, the emphasis lies on physical protection in this life, while in Romans, immunity from adversity applies only to the spirit. Here the focus is on "nothing will hurt you." In Romans, the emphasis lies on "nothing will separate you from God." What would you rather have?

Sometimes the Lord grants both, as in this psalm. But He grants neither unless you choose to live in Him. Have you found that secure place?

An insecure world

As I write this, a person very dear to me waits results from a cancer test. In her early 40s and the mother of three adolescents, she knows something about the unseen harms lurking in the shadows, waiting to destroy.

On my prayer list every day are the names of persons fighting dangerous illnesses or dealing with the aftermath of accidents and tragedies within family. My experience tells me, "Life is not safe."

Variety of dangers (vv. 3–6). In the short span of four verses, the Psalmist thinks through a list of terrors by day or night which we would identify now as a drunken driver, contagious virus, coronary attack, drive-by shooting, domestic violence, etc. Uniting all the dangers is their total unpredictability and suddenness.

God's defenses for us may be as flimsy as the mother bird covering her chicks with feathers or as substantial as shields and ramparts. Of the three, I prefer ramparts—safe thick walls behind which I can be safe from whizzing arrows or speeding bullets.

The point, however, is that for a variety of dangers God has a variety of protections. He may deliver you in a way different from me.

Personal immunity (vv. 7–10). I take malaria medicine when traveling in a country where that disease is prevalent. What antidote is available to counteract all life's ills?

³Surely he will save you from the fowler's snare and from the deadly pestilence. ⁴He will cover you with his feathers, and under his wings you will find refuge; his faithfulness will be your shield and rampart. ⁵You will not fear the terror of night, nor the arrow that flies by day, ⁶nor the pestilence that stalks in the darkness, nor the plague that destroys at midday.

⁷A thousand may fall at your side, ten thousand at your right hand, but it will not come near you. ⁸You will only observe with your eyes and see the

These verses indicate that thousands can be falling around you, but no harm or disaster will come near if you have taken the antidote: You've made the Most High your dwelling place.

The fact "it will not come near you" means that the harm neither hits you nor barely misses you—it comes nowhere near the target.

John the Baptist was decapitated (Matthew 14:1–12), Stephen was stoned to death (Acts 7:54–58), and James was killed with the sword (Acts 12:1,2). None experienced bodily immunity. But nothing destroyed their relationship with God—and that is the deeper immunity which the New Testament insists we overlay on the protections promised in this psalm.

Divine intervention (vv. 1–13). When you dwell within the Lord, He makes unseen messengers available for your protection. However, Jesus did not use these verses as a fallback for disobedience or presumption when tempted by the devil. An angel came into Gethsemane to strengthen but not to rescue Him (Luke 22:43,44). Angels stood by at Calvary but were never summoned (Matthew 26:53). God had a better rescue planned for Jesus when He raised Him from the dead. Will He not do the same for you? Will God not shortly trample Satan underneath your feet also? (Compare v. 13 with Romans 16:20.)

Blessed assurance

The Lord does not help us so we can provide some function or service for Him. "'Because he loves me,' says the Lord, 'I will rescue . . . protect . . . answer . . . be with him . . . deliver . . . and honor

punishment of the wicked. ⁹If you make the Most High your dwelling—even the Lord, who is my refuge—¹⁰then no harm will befall you, no disaster will come near your tent.

¹¹For he will command his angels concerning you to guard you in all your ways; ¹²they will lift you up in their hands, so that you will not strike your foot against a stone.

¹³You will tread upon the lion and the cobra; you will trample the great lion and the serpent.

¹⁴"Because he loves me," says the Lord, "I will rescue him; I will protect him, for he acknowledges my name. ¹⁵He will call upon me, and I will answer him; I will be with him in trouble, I will deliver him and honor him.

him. With long life will I satisfy him and show him my salvation.'"

All these promises need to be understood and interpreted in the light of eternity. A brand-new body, the final benefit conferred by salvation, will not be given until then.

Setbacks, terrible things, even death are all only momentary. It takes resurrection from the dead to realize the worst the devil throws at you never hurts you in the least. Our implicit trust in God brings assurance that the bleeding nail prints of the present moment will become beautiful scars in the future.

> **16With long life will I satisfy him and show him my salvation."**

Prayer of response

Lord Jesus, You never used this psalm as a grant of immunity from danger and suffering. Nor did Your apostles who died for You and Your cause. But like them, I trust in You. Nothing can harm me—not even death—because You are my dwelling place and my protection.

My thoughts on Psalm 91 . . .

Resting, Reflecting

Psalm 92

In his book, *The Gift of Self-Discovery*, Arthur Gordon describes a season of personal burnout. His physician examined him and told him to go to the beach and spend a day without radio, phone, or interruption. The wise old doctor wrote out four prescriptions, folded and numbered them, handed them to the tired Gordon, and said: "Take these at 9, 12, 3, and 6."

Time crawled as Gordon worked on the first prescription: "Listen carefully"—but listen he did for the first 3 hours—to the sounds in waves and within himself. At noon, the second assignment began: "Try reaching back." Events of past years, painful and pleasant, came flooding in. As the tide began receding, the third prescription kicked in: "Reexamine your motives." At first, he felt defensive—nothing was wrong with his motives; but then he realized that if his motives weren't right, nothing can be right.

Finally, as the sun began its descent, he opened the fourth slip: "Write your worries on the sand." He left as the surf washed his words away.

Through a single day of slowing down the pace and reflecting, Gordon reached a healing and turning moment in his life.

This psalm is written for use on the Sabbath, the day of rest. Its words penetrate deeply only when you take the time to stop and listen. Here is its prescription for reflection and renewal.

> [1]It is good to praise the Lord and make music to your name, O Most High, [2]to proclaim your love in the morning and your faithfulness at night,

Take time to worship

Before creation, "the earth was formless and empty" (Genesis 1:2). In 6 days

God worked, changing chaos into matter, life, and order. Then God rested from His creative efforts (Genesis 2:2,3). Have you? Are you too busy to get off the treadmill of activity or worry?

When was the last time you woke up in the morning with good thoughts of God's love and bedded down at night thinking of His faithfulness (v. 2)? Have you lately sung for joy at the works of God's hands (v. 4)? Have you paused to celebrate the sky, birds, flowers, forest, sea, grass, the butterfly as expressions of the Lord's artistry, power, and love of beauty; or gladdened yourself by praising Jesus for what He has done for you (Ephesians 1:3–14)?

Dr. William R. Inge reminds us that "if we spend 16 hours a day dealing with tangible things and only 5 minutes a day dealing with God, is it any wonder that tangible things are 200 times more real to us than God?"

Consider the end

In his best-seller, *The Seven Habits of Highly Effective People,* Stephen Covey suggests each of us write out what we would like said of us at our funeral. His point is that if we have in mind what we want people to think about us after we're gone, we'll begin living that way now.

That suggestion lines up with the counsel of Psalm 92. Only the senseless don't reckon with last things. Their time for flourishing is in the present tense (v. 7), while that of the righteous lies in the future (vv. 12,13).

My devout mother used to remind me, "George, every day is not payday." In other words, don't expect a reward every time you do right. The person who

3to the music of the ten-stringed lyre and the melody of the harp.

4For you make me glad by your deeds, O Lord; I sing for joy at the works of your hands.

5How great are your works, O Lord, how profound your thoughts! 6The senseless man does not know, fools do not understand, 7that though the wicked spring up like grass and all evildoers flourish, they will be forever destroyed. 8But you, O Lord, are exalted forever.

breaks the rules, mistreats people, indulges self, and dishes out hardship on others may indeed prosper for a while.

But God's payday is coming (vv. 7,9). The apostle Paul encourages us while waiting for the Lord to make all things right: "Let us not become weary in doing good, for at the proper time we will reap a harvest if we do not give up" (Galatians 6:9).

Gain the right perspective

I once passed through a season of deep depression. Every night I'd set out for an hour-long walk with my cassette player streaming the majestic strains of the *Messiah* into my ears. No matter how low I felt, I found the music lifting me into the presence of God—"The kingdoms of this world have become the kingdoms of our God, and of His Christ. Hallelujah!" Worship helped me to see that my present despair would one day all be gone, and I had a better future than I knew.

Time for rest and reflection brings self-renewal. Two-thirds into this song of Sabbath, we gain a new self-image.

Do you feel like a defenseless lamb—a victim beholden to another's power or sway over you? Then take time to worship so the Lord can build your confidence that He is making you like a "wild ox" with a powerful "horn"—someone no one ought to mess with (vv. 9–11).

If you've felt yourself unloved and unlovable, through worship God has a fragrance of "fine oil" to pour out on you. He wants you to feel clean from the dirt and grime. His oil brings a pleasant aroma to your person (v. 10; 2 Corinthians 2:14).

Feel like a weed waiting to be stepped

⁹**For surely your enemies, O Lord, surely your enemies will perish; all evildoers will be scattered.** ¹⁰**You have exalted my horn like that of a wild ox; fine oils have been poured upon me.** ¹¹**My eyes have seen the defeat of my adversaries; my ears have heard the rout of my wicked foes.**

on? God wants to make you as graceful and elegant as a palm tree. Do you think of yourself as a tumbleweed—rootless, dead, and driven? Then think again while you worship. God is making you into a cedar: enduring, rooted, tall, stately, and secure (vv. 12,13).

Living in the past? Worship enables you to realize the best is yet to come. God wants you to be vital and fulfilled even in old age. He wants you to stay "fresh and green" (v. 14).

How do we know these things to be true? Because the Lord is completely reliable (our "Rock") and free from evil. He will never lie to us (v. 15).

> [12]The righteous will flourish like a palm tree, they will grow like a cedar of Lebanon;
> [13]planted in the house of the Lord, they will flourish in the courts of our God.
> [14]They will still bear fruit in old age, they will stay fresh and green,
> [15]proclaiming, "The Lord is upright; he is my Rock, and there is no wickedness in him."

Prayer of response

Lord Jesus, I get so busy I fail to take time to renew myself in You. What needless pain I bear because I do not take everything to You in prayer. Slow me down, Lord, in each day for a Sabbath time with You. I need the embrace of Your presence more than accomplishing my list of things to do.

My thoughts on Psalm 92 . . .

Realities

Psalm 93

Things are not always as they appear. It's all well and good to believe the words of Psalm 93 on days when the sun shines, the bills are paid, and life seems like one delicious bowl of cherries.

Can you truthfully say, "The Lord reigns" when your spouse deserted you for someone else? Or when your job of the past 30 years was terminated by a corporate downsizing? Or when your teenage son, whom you dedicated as a baby to the Lord, was picked up for possession of marijuana?

Does the Lord reign when the doctor tells you the cancer is inoperable? Do you think He's in charge of His world even though you made a bad investment and lost your life savings?

What's going on?

[1]The Lord reigns, he is robed in majesty; the Lord is robed in majesty and is armed with strength. The world is firmly established; it cannot be moved.

My friend Ron McManus, pastor of a thriving church in Winston–Salem, North Carolina, recently won a successful fight against lymphoma. The Lord intervened by means of medicine and the prayers of the saints.

In the early days of uncertainty, Ron shared a devotional titled, "Here's What's Happening—But Something Else Is Going On." He illustrated his theme by noting several events from the Bible.

Moses spent 40 years as a fugitive on the backside of the desert—that's what's happening; but what was going

71

on was the preparation of a leader for God's people.

Joseph's brothers sold him—that's what happened. But through that act of treachery God was saving Joseph's entire family, including his brothers. That's what's going on.

You can trace this pattern in story after story: David sinned, but Psalm 51 was written; Stephen was stoned to death, but Saul was being raised to spiritual life; the Roman government exiled John on Patmos, but Revelation flowed from his pen.

Stand at the foot of the cross without knowing the outcome of Easter morning, and the words of this psalm blow back into your face. How can anyone say, "The Lord reigns," when the King of all life hangs bloody and lifeless on a cursed tree? What happened was the violent death of Jesus; what's going on is the salvation of all who let Him bear their sin.

It's no different with you. What is happening in your life right now may be directly opposite to what's really going on—the Lord reigns.

You are not adrift on the wild seas. You are not lost in a trackless desert of need and thirst. You are not abandoned, orphaned, or in exile. You have a Lord who is not only in control of the entire universe—He is in charge of your own personal history. The King has come to live in you and He has brought His kingdom with Him.

How do you see Him?

Our view of God often gets very distorted when we are in crisis. If He doesn't immediately spring to our side, we may falsely assume He is unfair, powerless, or disinterested.

Not so.

Look at how He's dressed. He is "robed in majesty and is armed with strength" (v. 1). Jesus often comes to us in the dress of a servant, taking the towel of humility to serve us—or in the form of a friend, present with us and closer than a brother. But He's far more than that. Before Him every knee will bow.

Have you been making the mistake of projecting your weakness onto Him? Because you're weak, you feel He too is helpless? Not at all.

Is not the Lord, who made the world firmly established so it cannot be moved, able to work out His plan, His creation, His design in your life? Can you not reason from the greater to the lesser—that if He takes care of all things, He can also take care of you? Is it not proper to use this psalm to also say, "I am firmly established. I cannot be moved. God will not let this circumstance destroy me for I am His child, created in His image, redeemed by His love, precious to Him beyond all reckoning"?

How can you be confident of such stability? Look at who is on the throne of heaven and earth, and how long He has occupied the position (v. 2).

How well do you hear Him?

In verses 3 and 4, the Psalmist uses the example of seas and pounding surf to describe his own hour of trial.

Our adversities are like the relentless action of those waves—they never stop coming at us. It's all we hear—their voice, their pounding, the thunder of the great waters. But this psalm reaffirms that God's action for us is more powerful than anything that threatens

²Your throne was established long ago; you are from all eternity.

³The seas have lifted up, O Lord, the seas have lifted up their voice; the seas have lifted up their pounding waves. ⁴Mightier than the thunder of the great waters, mightier than the breakers of the sea—the Lord on high is mighty.

our stability and well-being.

Living in the midst of fierce governmental persecution, the early Christians turned their hearing away from the shouted insults, threats, and hatred— "the seas [which] lifted up their voice." They chose instead to listen to the sounds of heaven: "Hallelujah! For our Lord God Almighty reigns. Let us rejoice and be glad and give him glory!" (Revelation 19:6,7).

At a stop sign the other day a car pulled alongside me, boom box blaring. No other noise had a chance of competing. Where's the boom box in your life? Are the sounds of despair, hurt, and trial the only thing you hear? Or have you tuned your spiritual radio into the tumult of glory surrounding the throne of God? (See Revelation 4 and 5.)

This storm in your life will not last forever; but God will (v. 5).

> [5]Your statutes stand firm; holiness adorns your house for endless days, O Lord.

Prayer of response

Lord Jesus, help me to distinguish between appearances and realities, between what's happening and what's really going on. Let my eyes be upon You rather than my circumstances; let my ears be open to heaven. And, thank You for never letting me out of Your sight or ever turning a deaf ear toward my cry for help.

My thoughts on Psalm 93 . . .

The Spirit of Slap

A new convert asked her pastor if she could replace the wilted old plastic floral arrangement on the Communion table in front of the pulpit. The pastor readily agreed.

The next Sunday the pastor looked out his office window and saw the lady getting out of her car with the new flowers. His office was right off the sanctuary. A few moments later the sound of an awful argument drifted into his office. An older saint had arrived early, saw the younger woman with her fresh bouquet, and vehemently told her the existing flowers were in honor of one of the departed saints of the church and they would be removed over her dead body.

The younger woman tried to explain she had the pastor's permission. Meanwhile, the pastor had the good sense to remain in his office. Suddenly, he heard the sound of a sharp slap, followed by silence.

About 5 minutes later, the new convert appeared at his door, eyes brimming with tears, mascara streaking down her cheeks. "Pastor," she said, "that old lady told me I couldn't put the new flowers on the Communion table. The old ones were in memory of her friend, and I would take them out over her dead body. I explained that you had given me permission, but she kept arguing. Pastor, I don't know what happened, but the spirit of slap came all over me."

Maybe you have felt that way a time or two. Someone unreasonably stands between you and what you want to do.

The writer of this psalm has been on the receiving end of hard slaps against which he has been powerless to defend himself.

How do you pray when you're the victim of another's unjust

treatment and you have neither the opportunity nor the ability to respond? Psalm 94 shows you.

Step 1—God is able to help you.

The Psalmist wants God to slap back. He knows God can if He wants to. After all, He is "the God who avenges," the "Judge of the earth" (vv. 1,2).

The problem lies in the fact God isn't doing anything right away—that's why you're asking Him, "How long?" (v. 3). He seems to be slumbering through your injustice.

Notice carefully, however, that the Psalmist did not misread God's inactivity as inability. Don't mistake God's waiting as weakness. The writer never doubted God's power to deal with the situation; he only remained confused over God's timing.

Don't let the Lord's lack of intervention in your situation sap your confidence in His watchful care over you. Stephen "looked up to heaven and saw the glory of God, and Jesus standing at the right hand of God" at the very moment he was dying from blunt-force trauma in a hail of stones (Acts 7:55). Thrown rocks killed his body but not his faith.

When God delays or declines to act, keep this true confession of the three Hebrew children in your heart: "God is able" (Daniel 3:17,18).

Step 2—Discern which voice you'll listen to.

You can focus on either how bad things appear (vv. 4-7) or on reality (vv. 8-11). The two perspectives always compete in your mind against one another.

¹O Lord, the God who avenges, O God who avenges, shine forth. ²Rise up, O Judge of the earth; pay back to the proud what they deserve.

³How long will the wicked, O Lord, how long will the wicked be jubilant?

⁴They pour out arrogant words; all the evildoers are full of boasting. ⁵They crush your people, O Lord; they oppress your inheritance. ⁶They slay the widow and the alien; they murder the fatherless. ⁷They say, "The Lord does not see; the God of Jacob pays no heed."

⁸Take heed, you senseless ones among the people; you fools, when will you become wise? ⁹Does he who implanted the ear not hear? Does he who formed the eye not see? ¹⁰Does he who disciplines nations not punish? Does he who teaches man lack knowledge? ¹¹The Lord knows the thoughts of man; he knows that they are futile.

When you listen to your circumstances you hear, "The Lord does not see; the God of Jacob pays no heed" (v. 7). Is anyone saying that to you? Their speech is filled with self (v. 4), their actions are heartless (v. 5), and they prey on the weak (v. 6). God never stops them—therefore, they think He doesn't notice.

They just don't get it (v. 8). God, who made ears and eyes, himself hears and sees (v. 9). So, don't be as stupid or misguided as they are. God isn't fooled, and neither should you be (vv. 10,11).

Step 3—Examine yourself.

A wonderful metamorphosis takes place within our spirit as we take the time to pray. When we're in trouble, bothered, or bewildered—we begin our prayers blurting out to God our feelings.

Usually, as in this psalm, you blame others for your own suffering—and you give the Lord all kinds of advice about what He needs to do to this awful other person. But as you stay praying, sooner or later you will sense the Holy Spirit talking to you about your own attitudes.

Instead of sitting in judgment on others, He'll ask you to sit in judgment on yourself (vv. 12–15). When you do that you're "blessed."

Mother Teresa of Calcutta was once asked, "Don't you ever become angry at the causes of social injustice that you see in India or in any of the places in which you work?"

She responded, "Why should I expend energy in anger that I can expend in love?"

Praying well means you are more concerned that God change you than that He judge someone else. As you draw close to

¹²Blessed is the man you discipline, O Lord, the man you teach from your law; ¹³ you grant him relief from days of trouble, till a pit is dug for the wicked. ¹⁴For the Lord will not reject his people; he will never forsake his inheritance. ¹⁵Judgment will again be founded on righteousness, and all the upright in heart will follow it.

¹⁶Who will rise up for me against the wicked? Who will take a stand for me against evildoers? ¹⁷Unless the Lord had given me help, I would soon have dwelt in the silence of death. ¹⁸When I said, "My foot is slipping," your love, O Lord, supported me. ¹⁹When anxiety was great within me, your consolation brought joy to my soul.

²⁰Can a corrupt throne be allied with you—one that brings on misery by its decrees?

²¹They band together against the righteous and condemn the innocent to death.

Him, You experience the warmth of His support and security (vv. 16–19).

Step 4—Choose sides.

It all comes down to what kind of person you choose to be.

God does not ally himself with those who inflict suffering on others (vv. 20,21). If you trust Him, you will always be safe (v. 22). But if you throw your lot in with the victimizers and the heartless, be aware that the Lord himself has the last slap (v. 23).

> [22]But the Lord has become my fortress, and my God the rock in whom I take refuge.
>
> [23]He will repay them for their sins and destroy them for their wickedness; the Lord our God will destroy them.

Prayer of response

Lord Jesus, You know how hard I want to hit back when I am wronged. But You also know how powerless I am to do anything. Deliver me from my compulsion to set others straight. I invite You to work on me instead. And I thank You for the security of Your presence.

My thoughts on Psalm 94 . . .

False Assumptions, Wrong Conclusions

A pastor got wind that the deacons were meeting without him, an action contrary to the church's bylaws.

Why? he wondered. *Are they dissatisfied with my leadership? Do they want me to leave? They have no right to do this,* he thought.

He decided to show up unannounced. "Could I ask why you're meeting without me?" he asked.

An embarrassed deacon answered, "Pastor, your birthday is coming up. And we wanted to plan a surprise party and gift for you."

It was the pastor's turn to be red-faced. His assumptions had been completely false, leading him to the wrong conclusion.

Key words: Today, *if . . .*

In difficult seasons we may think things about God that are not true. Psalm 95 tells us what happens when we do that.

The key to understanding and benefiting from this psalm lies in its crux verse: "Today, if you hear his voice . . ." (v. 7). Those deaf to Him live in the defeat of verses 8 to 11; those tuned to Him take their place as worshipers in verses 1 to 7.

Are you facing a deep trial? You can make one of two assumptions: God will fail you or He will meet your need.

> ¹Come, let us sing for joy to the Lord; let us shout aloud to the Rock of our salvation. ²Let us come before him with thanksgiving and extol him with music and song.

79

Despair

Look first at what happens when you sink into the attitude that the Lord won't come through. The latter part of this psalm (vv. 8–11) describes a key moment for God's people in the wilderness. (See Exodus 17 for background.) They were out of water—no small problem for a host of persons in the desert.

They had already seen firsthand God's mightiest miracles: sending the 10 plagues in Egypt, parting the Red Sea, sweetening the bitter water at Marah, and giving quail and daily manna. What they could not see were the many future miracles God had in store for them.

Would they trust Him one more time? Will you?

They didn't. At the wilderness camp of Rephidim they grumbled and believed the worst. Not brazen enough to criticize God directly, they charged His servant Moses with bringing them into the desert to die of thirst. The place became known as Massah and Meribah, testing and quarreling, "because they tested the Lord saying, 'Is the Lord among us or not?'" (Exodus 17:7).

You will face similar moments in your Christian experience where you too camp in a very dry place. You will be tempted to forget all the Lord has done for you in the past and to believe that God himself has abandoned you (vv. 8,9).

The powerful negative example of Israel, seen in these verses, reminds you to strip yourself of the spiritual mentality that God is against you, or punishing you, or has destructive designs in your life. Don't ever say or think, "Well, I guess the Lord is not with me anymore."

³For the Lord is the great God, the great King above all gods. ⁴In his hand are the depths of the earth, and the mountain peaks belong to him. ⁵The sea is his, for he made it, and his hands formed the dry land. ⁶Come, let us bow down in worship, let us kneel before the Lord our Maker; ⁷for he is our God and we are the people of his pasture, the flock under his care. Today, if you hear his voice,

⁶Come, let us bow down in worship, let us kneel before the Lord our Maker; ⁷for he is our God and we are the people of his pasture, the flock under his care. Today, if you hear his voice, ⁸do not harden your hearts as you did at Meribah, as you did that day at Massah in the desert, ⁹where your fathers tested and tried me, though they had seen what I did.

Trust

Psalm 95 is an attitude check. What kind of spirit will you show in your desert moments? This psalm calls for you to make a clear and complete rejection of the notion that God is not coming through. Don't harden your hearts as at Massah and Meribah—stay tender. Don't stiffen up; don't get into a huff against God or others—lest you spend your remaining years wandering around in circles, never becoming the person God wants or getting where He desired.

If you pick up an ingrained pattern of always challenging God in your trials, thinking dark thoughts about Him, and rebelling against Him, you'll walk down a path that will lead to large failure: "They shall never enter my rest" (v. 11).

How should we then face the moments in life when we've run out of water, or run out of anything? Here's the answer: "Come, let us sing for joy to the Lord; let us shout aloud to the Rock of our salvation" (vv. 1,2).

Do you notice the metaphor—rock? The water produced at Massah/Meribah came out of a stricken rock. All the time the people of Israel complained against God, the answer to their need was beneath the skin of the rock they stood before.

Don't be so busy looking at your rock of obstacle that you don't see your Rock of resource. Come before Him with singing.

What song? That He is barely sufficient for your need? That He is going to be greatly strained in helping you? Oh, no. "For the Lord is the great God" (vv. 3–5).

When we consider who He is, we take action beyond that of praise and wor-

> 10For forty years I was angry with that generation; I said, "They are a people whose hearts go astray, and they have not known my ways." 11So I declared on oath in my anger, They shall never enter my rest."

ship. We yield and humble ourselves, acquiesce and relinquish our own way, submitting to Him: "Come, let us bow down" (v. 6). God seeks for me to kneel not so I can be demeaned, but that I might be surrendered. Only when I am yielded does He pick me up as His lamb, cradle me in His arms, and provide for me in the pasture of His care (v. 7).

The assumption He is going to fail you leads to a lifetime in the wilderness of need, anger, depression, and frustration (vv. 8–11). But the assumption He cares for you and will provide leads you to song, to thanksgiving and joy, and the security of being watched over by the Good Shepherd (vv. 1-7). If false assumptions lead to wrong conclusions, then right assumptions lead to good endings.

Prayer of response

Lord Jesus, forgive me for saying, "I don't think I'll make it this time. I'm completely on empty." I don't want to be a faithless person who says, "My problems are huge, and my god is small." You, Lord, are great—and You will supply all the "water" I need in this desert.

My thoughts on Psalm 95 . . .

Skylight for the Heart

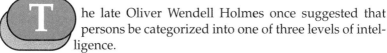

Psalm 96

The late Oliver Wendell Holmes once suggested that persons be categorized into one of three levels of intelligence.

First, there are the one-story people—fact collectors who don't have any aim beyond their facts. Second come the two-story intellects who go beyond the fact collectors by comparing, reasoning, and making generalizations. Finally, three-story people build upon the first two but go higher by idealizing, imagining, and predicting—their best illumination, however, coming from above, through the skylight.

Psalm 96 is for persons whose hearts contain a skylight for receiving encouragement from and giving praise to God. It was first sung in celebration of the bringing of the ark of the covenant into Jerusalem. (See 1 Chronicles 16.) The application of the psalm is timeless for it prepares our hearts for worship. It calls us out of our world into His.

¹Sing to the Lord a new song; sing to the Lord, all the earth. ²Sing to the Lord, praise his name; proclaim his salvation day after day.

Singing to God

When you are tired, discouraged, or depressed, the last thing you want to do is sing. But it's the first thing skylight people do (vv. 1,2).

Why must we sing? Why can't we just say words of praise? Because God knows that words, without music, tend to be flat and expressionless—that most often they touch only the cognitive side and not the deeper intuitive and emotional aspects of our nature. As you sing, a lilt and lift commence in your inmost self. The more you express your song, the more your heart opens wide to Him.

The song is both "new" (v. 1) and "day after day" (v. 2). Has your song become "old"? Are you mumbling mechanically through the words and tune? Or is your walk with the Lord up-to-date and fresh? Do you daily focus only on the things about you that you see, or does your heart go toward those things which are unseen?

There, in His presence, you sing. Yes, He is your audience. It's a stage-frightening experience to stand before a microphone and sing a solo before a distinguished crowd or, for that matter, any audience. Few persons ever solo, although they may have talent. But you are called upon to give a brief concert today for the Maker of Heaven and Earth, Your Redeemer, the Eternal Who Dwells In Light Unapproachable. He has summoned you to come and sing for Him, about Him, to Him—"Sing to the Lord."

Singing about God

Your solo started, He bids you turn around. You do so and find a vast audience: "Declare his glory among the nations, his marvelous deeds among all peoples" (v. 3). When you amplify Him in your heart, you next amplify Him to the world (v. 4). When you really understand who you worship, all the lesser gods (whatever you seek fulfillment from that is outside Him) pale. In such moments, He deals with your priorities. Who are you really trying to please? Does the Lord have first place in your life?

[3]Declare his glory among the nations, his marvelous deeds among all peoples.

[4]For great is the Lord and most worthy of praise; he is to be feared above all gods.

The false gods or idols in life only take from you; they do not give back. They trick you into thinking they'll do something for you—protect you, love you, help you. But your idol can give nothing for it is nothing (v. 5). What a contrast to the splendor, majesty, strength, and glory of the only true God (v. 6)!

Through the portraits of worship in the Bible, especially here in this psalm and the Book of Revelation, you look through the skylight of your heart into the majesty of God's dwelling: to angels in vast battalions, to elders and living creatures, to a glassy shining sea of dazzlement and light before the throne, to the Church in eternal assembly—and, to God himself. Every day, through worship, you can go to heaven and draw strength from the sights and sounds you see and hear there. indeed "glory [is] in his sanctuary."

Therefore, we invite the whole earth to join in as we express worship through praise (vv. 7,8), offering (v. 8), and reverential awe (v. 9).

What offering does He desire me to bring? That of a yielded, surrendered life (Mark 8:34–38), not a gift which costs me little or nothing. The trembling I feel in His presence need never be from terror of Him, but the reverence produced as I realize how unworthy I am to be in His holy presence.

Declaring God's truth

At verse 10, the attention of the Psalmist switches from heaven to earth. The truths we have observed through the heart's skylight into heaven are meant to be declared among the nations: "The Lord reigns" (v. 10).

[5] **For all the gods of the nations are idols, but the Lord made the heavens.**

[6] **Splendor and majesty are before him; strength and glory are in his sanctuary.**

[7] **Ascribe to the Lord, O families of nations, ascribe to the Lord glory and strength.** [8] **Ascribe to the Lord the glory due his name; bring an offering and come into his courts.**

[9] **Worship the Lord in the splendor of his holiness; tremble before him, all the earth.**

[10] **Say among the nations, "The Lord reigns. The world is firmly established, it cannot be moved; he will judge the peoples with equity.** [11] **Let the heavens rejoice, let the earth be glad; let the sea resound, and all that is in it;** [12] **let the fields be jubilant,**

Do you really believe that truth as it pertains to you? Or have you settled into a subtle attitude that He really is not directing the course of your life? Are you permitting Him to reign in your own heart, or are you resisting what He asks of you? If He ultimately "judges the peoples with equity," will He not also be fair with you?

The skylight opened through this psalm lets us look both into heaven (vv. 1–9) and the end of all things—when God acts in judgment on the earth (v. 13). The long view gives us perspective on our present needs, desires, and problems. If you live this day without a skylight into eternal realities, you exist in a small room with four walls closing in on you. With the skylight, you see not only God but the wonderful world He has made— the heavens, the sea, the fields, the trees of the field—all of which exist as praise to Him (vv. 10–12).

and everything in them. Then all the trees of the forest will sing for joy;

¹³they will sing before the Lord, for he comes, he comes to judge the earth. He will judge the world in righteousness and the peoples in his truth.

Prayer of response

Lord Jesus, give me eyes to see beyond my circumstances. Forgive me for looking down or around rather than up, for grumbling when I should be singing Your praises. Help me to get the focus off myself and my problems onto You, Your salvation, and Your glory.

My thoughts on Psalm 96 . . .

The Lord Reigns...Does He?

Psalm 97

It was Sunday and a beloved leader was preparing to announce the monthly prayer emphasis: Thanksgiving. At that moment he learned that two of his pastors had just been martyred in a country where believers face great persecution. He prayed, "Lord, what do You have to say to Your people? How can we continue with thanksgiving? Can we praise You for these murders and martyrdoms? Can we praise You for the injustice? For these families who have lost fathers and husbands?"

He answered his questions this way: "Of course not. How can we praise Him for bad things? We do not praise Him for evil things, but we can praise Him because He is sovereign over whatever happens. Revelation 19:6 says, 'Hallelujah! For our Lord God Almighty reigns.'"

He added, "The situation does not dictate to us what to do. People around us are not the ones directing; it is not enemies who determine what we can and cannot do. What a pitiable person operates like that. We have disciplined ourselves to see martyrdom as does God. When we look through the eyes of God, then we no longer have difficulties. We don't look from down here to up there, but up there to down here. We don't focus on the surrounding difficulties, but to what God says."

¹The Lord reigns, let the earth be glad; let the distant shores rejoice.

Up there

That's the same spirit reflected in this psalm—one alive with the contemplation of God and the fundamental confidence that "the Lord reigns" (v. 1).

87

Too often in our chaotic world, it appears He does not. Just look at the headlines on any day for evidences of evil.

Events in our own lives spin so easily out of control. We are either unsure of what decisions to make or choices are made for us against our own will. We often live with the downside effect of others' actions and decisions.

Is there any sanity in this world? Any design? Anything for sure? Yes. "The Lord reigns." What relief and joy.

But the evidences of His reign are not all that easily observed by sight. The marks of His rule, described in verses 2–5, are visionary in quality. You cannot see them, now with physical eyes.

Oh, I have seen clouds and thick darkness, but not His throne. I have witnessed fire and lightning—but, not as a component of His immediate presence. I have seen mountains—high and hard with stone and earth compacted—but, I have never seen one melt as wax.

When my faith seats me with Christ at the right hand of the Father (Ephesians 2:6), I see all these things, including that Day when the invisible becomes visible (2 Corinthians 4:17,18).

Out there

Through spiritual vision we look into the future when "all the peoples see his glory, and all who worship images are put to shame" (vv. 6,7). Only those who dwell in Zion and the villages of Judah, God's people, know already that He is Most High above the earth (vv. 8,9).

Are you in one of those "villages in Judah" today, a place where you feel disconnected from the mainstream or exiled from where you would rather be? Has

2Clouds and thick darkness surround him; righteousness and justice are the foundation of his throne. 3Fire goes before him and consumes his foes on every side. 4His lightning lights up the world; the earth sees and trembles. 5The mountains melt like wax before the Lord, before the Lord of all the earth.

6The heavens proclaim his righteousness, and all the peoples see his glory. 7All who worship images are put to shame, those who boast in idols—worship him, all you gods!

8Zion hears and rejoices and the villages of Judah are glad because of your judgments, O Lord. 9For you, O Lord, are the Most High over all the earth; you are

the news reached your heart that Jesus is Victor—even over the difficulties in your life? In your small spot on this planet, do you have the big picture that the Lord reigns over all the earth?

exalted far above all gods.

Down here

Christians are like prisoners of war who know their side has won and it's only a matter of time until release. While waiting, we aspire to live in a manner consistent with our status as citizens of heaven—"Let those who love the Lord hate evil" (v. 10).

I admit I have not always hated evil. Sometimes evil comes to us disguised as light and we are not perceptive enough to see that behind the facade, the mask, is the face of Satan himself. We need the Lord's help not only to recognize evil, but deplore it—especially in ourselves: "Light is shed upon the righteous and joy on the upright in heart" (v. 11).

Notice the sequence in this psalm. It does not begin by amplifying life's difficulties, but by magnifying the Lord. Too often we begin our prayers by describing the maze we're in, rather than getting into the spiritual helicopter provided by the Bible and the Holy Spirit. The Lord wants to get us first above the pain, the sorrow, and the questioning by inviting us into His presence.

This psalm and the other songs of Scripture are earphones given to us by the Spirit to let us listen to the music above, to ponder and apprehend truth beyond our immediate experience. The less I listen or enter in, the greater becomes the sorrow in my life. Then, I find it difficult to do what this psalm asks, "Rejoice in the Lord" (v. 12). You are

10Let those who love the Lord hate evil, for he guards the lives of his faithful ones and delivers them from the hand of the wicked.

11Light is shed upon the righteous and joy on the upright in heart.

12Rejoice in the Lord, you who are righteous, and praise his holy name.

not a happy person when you feel defeated.

But when I am "up there," beyond earth and space, I see "out there" to the furthest reaches on the horizon of time. Everywhere I go, up and out, I see God. There's no place "up there" or "out there" where He does not rule.

Finally, I came back to my "real" world of pain and need. But I see things differently. I've learned the truth expressed by the Christian leader in the country where his fellow pastors have been martyred— that I must see things from heaven's rather than earth's vantage point. Through this psalm, I've been above where they're singing praises to the risen Christ, and the joy of that world has moved into mine.

Prayer of response

Lord Jesus, help me to use this psalm to turn up the volume on the music You send me from heaven. I want to be more instant to say, "Jesus is risen," than "I am discouraged"; "God heals," than "I am sick"; and "Jesus is a friend who sticks closer than a brother," than "I am alone." I thank You I am not defeated because You reign.

My thoughts on Psalm 97 . . .

A Frog in My Throat

Psalm 98

Have you ever had something happen to you so bad or hurtful that you simply couldn't do what this song in Psalm 98 asks, "Sing a new song to the Lord"?

I like to compare this psalm with the story of the two downcast followers of Jesus who left Jerusalem on Easter morning believing He was dead. (See Luke 24:13–24.)

Those two disciples were in no emotional shape to sing. When Jesus came to them unrecognized, "they stood still, their faces downcast" (Luke 24:17). The hard reality of death had not destroyed their love for Him, but it had demolished their hope, as indicated by their past-tense statement: "We *had* hoped" (v. 21).

Like them, have you lost hope? A hard experience has slain your expectation of good things, but not your love for God?

This psalm asks you to "sing to the Lord a new song" (v. 1). Why? The psalm answers the question; but before looking at its response, let's probe our own hearts.

How fresh is your experience with the Lord? Do you feel He is not working in your life? Has depression placed a frog in your throat so you don't sing?

Start with an old song

1Sing to the Lord a new song, for he has done marvelous things; his right hand and his holy arm have worked salvation for him.

Before singing to the Lord a new song, perhaps you need to sing an old one. It's appropriate and helpful to meditate upon your own history with God, from the womb to the present.

I have personally found great strength in present trials by rummaging through my past and finding specific instances

91

or processes in which God met me. I remember times I did not think I could make it, but He brought me through. Those experiences of the Lord's help are permanently etched into the pathways of my own personality.

It's today we often have difficulty trusting Him. As Christians we have a wonderful yesterday and a secure tomorrow—but the here and now frequently finds us failing to connect God's past and future help with our present need.

Composing a new song

This psalm is not written by one going through trial. The verbs are past tense—indicating that God's activity in this crisis is now completed (vv. 1–3). We sing other songs and pray other prayers while in the midst of crisis. But this psalm is a reminder that we have a song to sing when God brings us through the hour of difficulty. Your painful experience right now is forming the material from which you will write a new song of praise to God. When this time of peril is over, it will all make sense.

One day you too will look backward over the trail of your climb out of a lonesome, deep valley and sing full-heartedly all the words of these verses.

The reason for singing the new song is "the Lord has done marvelous things." Marvelous may be the last word you would have used to describe God's dealings with you while in the midst of your fight for survival. In such a time, God does not appear to know what He is doing—and, for our part, we may feel He is leading us to complete ruin.

But trust Him. The day will come when you look back over your shoulder

²The Lord has made his salvation known and revealed his righteousness to the nations. ³He has remembered his love and his faithfulness to the house of Israel; all the ends of the earth have seen the salvation of our God.

and honestly say to the Lord, "What You did was marvelous." Let, therefore, the future theme of joy celebrated in this psalm be an encouragement for you today—let it be a tuning instrument of the Spirit for the out-of-tune sorrow now in your heart.

The Lord's activity, however, is far more than just personal to me. He works on behalf of His people. In Jesus Christ, God has provided the most vital thing we need—salvation. And the work of His right hand and holy arm in raising Jesus from the dead is now being revealed to the nations, to all the ends of the earth (vv. 2,3).

The fact that God remembers His love and faithfulness assures us He is the one constant in our lives that cannot be taken from us. He can be depended upon absolutely. And He seeks to incorporate the characteristics of His personality into our own so we too can have a faithful and enduring love.

Let everybody sing!

In celebration of His marvelous salvation, the choir (v. 4) and orchestra (vv. 5, 6) are ordered to strike up the music. Then, nature in personification also joins in (vv. 7,8). When everything is right with us, it seems like everything is right with the world as well. It's like walking through a park with the one you love—even the rivers "clap their hands" and the "mountains sing together for joy" (v. 7).

As you consider the outcome of God's dealings with you, it becomes apparent that He is a far better decision-maker than you. He operates on fixed principle (v. 9), whereas we often act from emotions and whim. His fairness in "judg-

⁴Shout for joy to the Lord, all the earth, burst into jubilant song with music;

⁵make music to the Lord with the harp, with the harp and the sound of singing, ⁶with trumpets and the blast of the ram's horn—shout for joy before the Lord, the King.

⁷Let the sea resound, and everything in it, the world, and all who live in it. ⁸Let the rivers clap their hands, let the mountains sing together for joy;

⁹let them sing before the Lord, for he comes to judge the earth. He will judge the world in righteousness and the peoples with equity.

ing" gives us the assurance that all humans will be handled with "equity."

If you have allowed bitterness, resentment, self-pity, or blame into your spirit so that there's a frog in your throat keeping you from singing this psalm, the same risen Lord who appeared to the two disciples on the road to Emmaus desires to come to you today and open your heart to understand the Scriptures. Jesus is very much alive and you have a glorious future.

Prayer of response

Lord Jesus, there's so much joy in Your presence, and I needed to hear the music of heaven in my heart today. I look forward to the Day when I see the whole picture, but I won't let a frog in my throat prevent me from already praising You today for how You will bring my life to a perfect completion.

My thoughts on Psalm 98 . . .

God Forever

Recently I watched an old black-and-white television rerun of *I Love Lucy*. The program, a mainstay on American television in the 1950s and 60s, featured the madcap adventures of Lucille Ball and her ever-tolerant husband, Desi Arnaz.

They are both gone now—a poignant reminder of life's brevity.

The good news of the Bible is that in the midst of our own mortality and transience, we may come to the Eternal. He will not be off the scene in a few decades nor is He up for election every 4 years. He has no plans of retiring from office or dying.

Psalm 99 commences with the abrupt declaration, "The Lord reigns." No doubt about it—an even greater certainty than two plus two equals four.

God rules

¹The Lord reigns, let the nations tremble; he sits enthroned between the cherubim, let the earth shake.

In 1997, the United States National Aeronautics and Space Administration landed the *Pathfinder* rover on the planet Mars unleashing a flood of speculation as to whether life exists elsewhere or how life on earth began. One news report devoted a major clip to speculating that life on our planet may have resulted from a tiny microbe hidden deep into a rock which bounced off Mars through space to earth. Ultimately, the microbe crawled out of the rock—and poof—the evolutionary trail to man had begun.

95

All those lines were delivered by a reporter with a straight, serious face.

However, believers in the God revealed in the Bible have always known how life on earth began, and that life does exist outside planet Earth. The place is called heaven—the dwelling place of God free from all moral, ethical, and ecological contaminants—where no microbes of disease or death or decay exist.

This news, "the Lord reigns," should "make the nations tremble." Obviously, the nations would tremble if the science fiction writers' dreams of alien invasion came true. So why should we not tremble at the news that One exists so powerful that any nightmares of aliens landing would seem like a pleasant dream compared to meeting Him unprepared—"let the earth shake" (v. 1).

The enthroned Lord, surrounded by spectacular heavenly life-forms called cherubim, is not the meaningless or powerless deity imagined by popular culture which says, "All belief systems are equal. Pick the god you want." Rather, the One True God has revealed himself as "great in Zion" (v. 2). Indeed in Zion or Jerusalem, city of David, our Lord suffered, died, and rose again. Jesus, David's Son, is the one exalted over the nations (Philippians 2:5–11). His awesome greatness merits our praise (v. 3), not indifference.

²**Great is the Lord in Zion; he is exalted over all the nations.**

³**Let them praise your great and awesome name—he is holy.**

How does God rule?

It's one thing to believe God exists; it's quite another to profess you know God personally—that you are aware of God's likes and dislikes, of His personality, and the words He has spoken in self-disclosure to the people of earth.

1. *He is great and good* (v. 4). "The King is mighty, he loves justice." Evil human dictators act tyrannically because they separate power from goodness. God is not a despot. His deeds are never unjust nor capricious. In Jesus we see God's power momentarily stripped away from His love. In dying on the cross, the Son of God functioned from goodness alone; God's power withheld from any rescue effort. But power is not absent from Him for long. In His resurrection He openly triumphed over death and evil.

Such goodness/greatness in God summons me to humility. Perhaps before we learn to reign with Him or appreciate we are seated with Him in the heavenly places (Ephesians 2:6), we do well to kneel or fall prostrate at His footstool (v. 5).

There is really no intimacy of relationship pictured in this psalm. God is holy. Before I am invited to be His friend, I must willingly become His subject.

2. *He listens to His people* (vv. 5–7). God not only speaks, He hears. The Psalmist cites three of God's servants—Moses, Aaron, and Samuel—who knelt at God's footstool, who drew close enough to hear God's voice and know Him clearly.

We have even greater access now than they, because rather than hearing God speak through a pillar of cloud or statutes carved on stone, He has spoken in the person of Jesus Christ. In Him, we are given not only laws but the grace to keep them.

3. *He forgives* (v. 8). In "punishing their misdeeds," the Psalmist shows us that God does not always let us escape the bad consequences of our wrongful decisions. But the good news of God's love means that punishment is never His last

⁴The King is mighty, he loves justice—you have established equity; in Jacob you have done what is just and right.

⁵Exalt the Lord our God and worship at his footstool; he is holy. ⁶Moses and Aaron were among his priests, Samuel was among those who called on his name; they called on the Lord and he answered them. ⁷He spoke to them from the pillar of cloud; they kept his statutes and the decrees he gave them.

⁸O Lord our God, you answered them; you were to Israel a forgiving God, though you punished their misdeeds.

word for those who desire a restored relationship with Him.

The story is told of a diamond badly nicked by an incompetent jeweler. The stone was given to an expert who used imperfection to create a beautiful and valuable rose etching. When we bring to the Lord our own marred lives, He takes us in His skilled hands, forgiving us the imperfection and sin, reworking the mar to become the centerpiece of His grace and redesign of our lives.

This short psalm ends with a powerful shout of joy (v. 9). That should be our normal and natural reaction when we reflect on the Lord and all He has done for us.

⁹Exalt the Lord our God and worship at his holy mountain, for the Lord our God is holy.

Prayer of response

Lord Jesus, I don't have access today to the rich or powerful people of this world. But in Your great love and mercy, You have granted me access to You. I feel so unworthy I fall down in front of You. But You are so gracious You pick me up and embrace me. How can I ever find the right words to say, "Thank You"?

My thoughts on Psalm 99 . . .

Joy, Pure Joy

What's the difference between happiness and joy? The word *happiness* has as its root the old English word *hap*, from which comes the related word *happened*. If, therefore, a good thing happens, you feel *happy*.

But what about the times when difficulties or losses occur? If you're not happy, can you still have joy? Hard to believe, but the answer is yes. Psalm 100, affectionately known as "Old One Hundred," shows us how.

Shout for joy

¹Shout for joy to the Lord, all the earth. ²Worship the Lord with gladness; come before him with joyful songs.

The Psalm begins with an invitation to worship God: "Shout . . . all the earth" (v. 1). The "all" does not grant an exception for you or me—it embraces everyone.

But shouting is not your current mood. You review your calendar for the days past or ahead and it does not contain any shouting events. Maybe you feel more like shouting from pain or boredom. But this psalm summons you out of grief, sadness, or depression by saying, "Shout for joy . . . worship the Lord with gladness; come before him with joyful songs" (vv. 1,2).

Lord, I don't feel like doing that today. I'm more in the mood to sing a dirge, to wallow in the Pathos of Psalm 88, to sit on the dung hill with Job, or recite the alphabet of Lamentations—my woes from A to Z— with Jeremiah. I feel more like Gethsemane evening than Resurrection morning. How can I turn off the faucet of sorrow and wash instead from the spigot of unrelenting joy?

Four reasons for joy

The Psalmist has an answer to your question of how. "Know that the Lord is God. It is he who made us, and we are his; we are his people, the sheep of his pasture" (v. 3).

Four fundamental realities serve as the sources for the fountain of joyous worship.

1. *The Lord is God.* Underlying the universe and your own personal world is His reality. You have a floor of hope, a foundation of sureness. No matter what stage you are passing through, whether you are at the peak or in the pit, the Lord reigns eternal.

2. *He made you.* God never does anything without purpose, and that includes making you. Please don't limit the word *made* to your birth as a baby. True, you were *made* then; but, God is not finished *making you* until your last breath.

3. *You are His.* You are God's possession and far more. You are also in His family. Even as a husband says of his wife, or a mother says of her daughter, "She is mine," so God affirms without hesitation our relationship to Him.

4. *You belong to God's community.* You are not simply a solitary soul valiantly struggling alone through life. You are one among "his people, the sheep of his pasture" (v. 3). You are in His flock, not the only sheep, but one nevertheless. He knows you by name, leads you to green

³**Know that the Lord is God. It is he who made us, and we are his; we are his people, the sheep of his pasture.**

pastures, rests you by quiet waters, protects you from ravaging animals, finds you when you are lost, holds you when you are wounded, and places you secure in His fold against the elements and the night.

Acting with joy

No wonder at public worship the Psalmist can't contain his enthusiasm (v. 4). You won't find him mumbling through the congregational singing or passively watching others express their love for God. He has reasons for thanksgiving and praise—as do you.

Using temple language, the psalm writer describes a visit to the temple. What an exciting moment as he approaches the gate. He's reviewed his understanding of and relationship to God, so he is ready to enter with joy.

When our hearts fill up with the contemplation of the Lord and His watchful care over us, thanksgiving rather than complaint or confusion expresses itself from our hearts. Often when you are in pain, you become overly focused on the world within you rather than the realities outside you. That's why it's so important to begin your day with a visit to His sanctuary, and to frequently return to that sanctuary during the day to lift your voice and heart in thanksgiving for His watchful care over you, and for placing persons and circumstances in your life to help you.

A few moments later, beyond the gates and inside His courts, you feel calm and security. You know that "the Lord is good and his love endures forever; his faithfulness continues through all generations" (v. 5).

4Enter his gates with thanksgiving and his courts with praise; give thanks to him and praise his name.

5For the Lord is good and his love endures forever; his faithfulness continues through all generations.

Prayer of response

Thank You, Lord, for Your goodness. That means there is no deceit in You. You will never tell me something untrue about yourself. I will never discover in You a flaw that will rock me to my foundations. And I can always count on Your love. There will never be a moment when I am not loved by You—even when I fail You.

Your love endures—endures during all my neglect, carelessness, and rebellion. You will never abandon nor betray me, for You are faithful throughout all generations. So Lord, I will go ahead and join the other worshipers today who understand Your truth: I too will shout for joy and worship You with gladness.

My thoughts on Psalm 100 . . .

Noble Ideals

Psalm 101

O n August 22, 1949, *Time* magazine reported on the rising popularity of a beautiful 17-year-old actress whose career to that date had involved her playing roles of youthful innocence.

The interview revealed her inner world as far different from the screen images she had portrayed. "She pretends to no more learning than she needs," wrote *Time*, "reads little besides movie magazines, hates school, loves ice cream sodas, convertibles, swimming pools and admires big strong men."

Asked about her future in movies, she gasped excitedly, "What I'd really like to play is a monster—a hellion."

As her life evolved, she went from one big strong man to another and had opportunity to play the hellion role she coveted as a teen. Her name? Elizabeth Taylor.

Life sometimes does give you what you ask for.

In Psalm 101, David sets forth wonderful ideals by which he purposed to live.

The psalm forces this question upon us personally: "Am I living in the humdrum of the day-to-day without good aspirations for my conduct or with a clean heart filled with noble goals?"

Absence of guilt

1I will sing of your love and justice; to you, O Lord, I will sing praise.

When you live rightly, you have inner freedom. God puts a song in your heart. When you act outside God's will, morally or ethically, you substitute self-fulfillment for true love, and justify wrong conduct by saying, "I'm the exception." But, when you walk in the sunlight of God's will you can sing unhindered praise to the God of love and justice (v. 1).

When Isaiah focused upon God in His holy temple, the Lord immediately drew Isaiah's attention to his own personal standard of conduct (Isaiah 6). The same movement occurs in this psalm—serving a moral God forces us to consider our own code of behavior: "I will be careful to lead a blameless life" (v. 2).

Self-inventory for a blameless life

David's desire to live nobly includes specific pinpoint applications to the everyday. We do poorly if we relegate our spiritual life to broad generalizations rather than focusing on exact instances of attitude and conduct.

1. *"In my [own] house."* Let's start by asking, "What kind of person will I be in my own house?" David answers: "I will walk in my house with blameless heart" (v. 2).

Your real identity is found not in public, but in your own home. Who are you there? Are you considerate, cheerful, faithful, seeking to serve rather than being served, loving rather than waiting to be loved?

2. *"Before my eyes."* David purposes to set no "vile thing" before his eyes (v. 3). How about you? What magazines, books, movies, Internet material, or live events do you permit into your field of vision? Choose carefully what you look at lest your walk with God becomes diluted. If you let the eye-gate fall into disrepair, the enemy will storm your life and wreak havoc on the inside.

²I will be careful to lead a blameless life — when will you come to me? I will walk in my house with blameless heart.

³I will set before my eyes no vile thing. The deeds of faithless men I hate; they will not cling to me. ⁴Men of perverse heart shall be far from me; I will have nothing to do with evil.

3. *"Deeds of faithless men I hate.* "As Christians we are uncomfortable with the word "hate." After all, Jesus taught us to love. However, this psalm calls us not to hate people—just "the deeds of faithless men" (v. 3).

Who are faithless people? I saw this sign recently on a restaurant board: "He was as good as his word, and his word wasn't any good." How about you?

4. *"Far from me."* David not only disavows the deeds of the faithless, he pledges to keep far away from people with a perverse heart. And who are they? Those whose thinking is so twisted they call evil good and good evil. They say, "The end justifies the means." You'll stay a thousand miles away from such attitudes if you make decisions from this question: "What would Jesus do?"

5. *"Slanders . . . put to silence."* What kind of speech do you permit in your presence? David acted to protect the character of others by not allowing gossip or smears to be spoken when he was in the room. He vowed not to get caught up in the same attitudes as the proud (v. 5). Rather he purposed to keep as his closest associates those whose lives were worthy of imitation (v. 6).

You are known by the company you keep—don't develop a tolerance for liars (v. 7).

Making resolute choices

Verse 8 strikes a modern audience as intolerant behavior. David, however, had the responsibility of governing: punishing evildoers and rewarding those who do good. (See Romans 13:1–7.) You may not run the government but God lets you make decisions affecting yourself and others.

5Whoever slanders his neighbor in secret, him will I put to silence; whoever has haughty eyes and a proud heart, him will I not endure. 6My eyes will be on the faithful in the land, that they may dwell with me; he whose walk is blameless will minister to me. 7No one who practices deceit will dwell in my house; no one who speaks falsely will stand in my presence.

8Every morning I will put to silence all the wicked in the land; I will cut off every evildoer from the city of the Lord.

Whom have you allowed into your life today? Have you kept a sensitive heart so you can recognize what or who is wicked? Are you willing to make difficult choices to remove yourself from situations or persons that bring harm to your walk with God?

In this psalm David stated the best of intentions. With Bathsheba and Uriah, he failed catastrophically. But he did not permit that failure to finish him. He repented and made a fresh start in pursuing noble ideals. Indeed, as someone has said, if you reach for the stars you may not get there; but at least you won't end up with a handful of mud.

Prayer of response

Lord, I began this psalm with singing and close it with a determination to act against evil. Forgive me for false worship when I sing and then go through the day unchanged. I seek a genuine worship which alters my lifestyle.

My thoughts on Psalm 101 . . .

Deep Hurt

Psalm 102

The superscription to Psalm 102 identifies it as the "prayer of an afflicted man when he is faint and pours out his lament before the Lord." No other psalm has such a heading.

You know the cry is authentic when you see the word "faint" following that of "affliction." Weakness, not strength, describes the person lashed with adversity. In such a season you really can't start your prayer with high praise. A cry for help is much more appropriate (v. 1). If there were immediate answers for your desperate dilemma, you wouldn't be distraught as you begin your prayer.

¹Hear my prayer, O Lord; let my cry for help come to you. ²Do not hide your face from me when I am in distress. Turn your ear to me; when I call, answer me quickly.

The cry for help

You hope God hasn't turned His back on you and that He will answer quickly (v. 2).

When you hurt badly, time drags. The Greeks had two words for time: *chronos* and *kairos*. *Chronos* time is the endless tick-tick-tick of the clock, chronological progression, the long wait for something wonderful or dreadful.

But *kairos* time is a season. It can be so enjoyable you lose track of *chronos* time altogether. When you are in emotional pain, there's no *kairos*—your life is so burdened that each second seems as an hour, each minute a day, each day a month, and each month a year. That's why the Psalmist asks God to do something quickly—*chronos* time is a terrible burden and tedium.

Feeling awful

The Psalmist, like Hannah in the sting of her broken circumstances (1 Samuel 1:15), pours out the anguish of his soul to God (vv. 3–11). Have you felt similar pain?

- A sense of accomplishing nothing—"days, vanish like smoke."
- Deep bodily aches from the trauma—"bones that burn as glowing embers."
- A Sahara-desert condition in your emotions, intellect, and will—"a blighted heart as withered grass."
- No appetite, followed by weight loss—"forgot to eat . . . reduced to skin and bones."
- Sleeplessness alongside a sense of desolation—"an owl among ruins . . . a bird alone."
- Acute sense of hurt over what someone else has done to you—"enemies taunt me . . . rail against me."
- Meals are tasteless and the dinner table is depressing—"I eat ashes as food and mingle my drink with tears."
- Feeling even God has turned against you—"because of your great wrath . . . you have . . . thrown me aside."
- Gloom and personal darkness—"my days are like the evening shadow; I wither away."

How awful to be in such desolation of soul and brokenness in spirit.

Exercising faith

You must not end your prayer at verse 11 when you hurt. Look at the next seg-

³For my days vanish like smoke; my bones burn like glowing embers. ⁴My heart is blighted and withered like grass; I forget to eat my food. ⁵Because of my loud groaning I am reduced to skin and bones. ⁶I am like a desert owl, like an owl among the ruins. ⁷I lie awake; I have become like a bird alone on a roof. ⁸All day long my enemies taunt me; those who rail against me use my name as a curse. ⁹For I eat ashes as my food and mingle my drink with tears ¹⁰because of your great wrath, for you have taken me up and thrown me aside. ¹¹My days are like the evening shadow; I wither away like grass.

¹²But you, O Lord, sit enthroned forever; your renown endures through all generations. ¹³You will arise and have compassion on Zion, for it is time to show favor to her; the appointed time

ment of this psalm (vv. 12–22). Your pain is real, but so is God's power; your time is short, but God reigns eternal (v. 12). He's not unfeeling toward you (vv. 13,14). Surely He who holds power over the nations (v. 15) and rebuilds Zion (v. 16) will also respond to your personal need (v. 17).

Take a long look down the road. What will the final chapters of your life say? That God failed you? Oh, no. Decades later your biography will contain the testimony of how God kept and delivered you in this time of profound vulnerability (vv. 18–22).

Faith allows you to skip ahead and see that glorious day when you are no longer in the tunnel.

Dealing with the relapses

From his expression of strong confidence in God, the Psalmist plunges straight back into the pit of depression. Don't be surprised about your vacillating feelings when you hurt. Pain will keep slicing into praise. You may even blame God for what happened to you (v. 23).

Learn from the Psalmist. In those moments of despair, keep talking to the Lord. You'll be absolutely amazed at the words of powerful faith the Holy Spirit puts in your heart immediately following your own statement of hopelessness. The feeling of being "cut off" (v. 24) actually springboards the Psalmist into making one of the most memorable statements of God's eternity ever expressed (vv. 25–27).

Sometimes false counsel is given believers who are struggling with hurts. You may have been told to repress your pain or deny it: "Just praise God and everything will be all right." But there

has come. ¹⁴For her stones are dear to your servants; her very dust moves them to pity. ¹⁵The nations will fear the name of the Lord, all the kings of the earth will revere your glory. ¹⁶For the Lord will rebuild Zion and appear in his glory. ¹⁷He will respond to the prayer of the destitute; he will not despise their plea.

¹⁸Let this be written for a future generation, that a people not yet created may praise the Lord: ¹⁹"The Lord looked down from his sanctuary on high, from heaven he viewed the earth, ²⁰to hear the groans of the prisoners and release those condemned to death." ²¹So the name of the Lord will be declared in Zion and his praise in Jerusalem ²²when the peoples and the kingdoms assemble to worship the Lord.

²³In the course of my life he broke my strength; he cut short my days. ²⁴So I said: "Do not take me away, O my God, in the midst of my days; your years go on through all generations. ²⁵In the beginning you laid the foundations of the earth, and the heavens are the work of your

are days when that advice seems glib and superficial. Are you therefore condemned because you don't have enough faith?

Not at all. This psalm shows you that God permits you to be human. You are free to tell Him how badly you really feel. You can also tell Him your doubts. He'll even let You blame Him for your problems. As you continue to talk with Him, He'll be talking with you. The Holy Spirit will intersect your words of despair with the language of faith and hope.

Ultimately, He will bring you to a final position of confidence. The Psalmist closes not with the thought of days "cut short" (v. 23), but of an enduring posterity (v. 28). The last bounce of the ball is up.

hands. 26They will perish, but you remain; they will all wear out like a garment. Like clothing you will change them and they will be discarded. 27But you remain the same, and your years will never end. 28The children of your servants will live in your presence; their descendants will be established before you."

Prayer of response

Lord Jesus, I feel so safe with You. I can blurt out my hurt and tell You that I don't see a good personal ending. You listen to me without condemnation. You put hope into my heart by reminding me who You are, and assuring me that the final chapter will have a good ending. Thank You, loving Lord.

My thoughts on Psalm 102 . . .

Deep Healing

Have you ever heard a healing take place? I have. I listened to an audio tape of Duane Miller teaching his Sunday school class from the text of Psalm 103 at the First Baptist Church in Brenham, Texas, on January 17, 1993. Duane prematurely retired from pastoring three years earlier because of a virus which penetrated the myelin sheath around the nerves in his vocal cords, reducing his speech to a raspy whisper.

He experienced firsthand the awful distress described in Psalm 102, the counterpoint to the joy found in Psalm 103.

Teaching his class that day with a special microphone resting on his lips, he reaffirmed his belief in divine healing and that miracles had not ended with the Book of Acts. Listening to the tape, at times you can barely understand his weakly spoken wheezy words of faith. The miracle happened at verse 4 when he said, "I have had and you have had in times past pit experiences."

On the word "pit," Duane's life changed—the word was as clear as a bell, in contrast to the imperfect enunciation of the preceding word "past." He paused, startled; began again and stopped. He said a few more words—all in a normal clear tone—and stopped again. The class erupted with shouts of joy, astonishment, and sounds of weeping. God completely healed him as he was declaring the truth in this psalm. (You can read the full account in Miller's book, *Out of the Silence*, Nelson Publishers.)

¹Praise the Lord, O my soul; all my inmost being, praise his holy name. ²Praise the Lord, O my soul, and forget not all his benefits —

Consider His benefits

Like Duane Miller, perhaps you have spent a lengthy time in the despair found in Psalm 102; but Psalm 103 shows that the Lord has a deep healing to match your deep hurt. Psalm 102 ended with a sense that God's blessings would skip over you (v. 23) and benefit instead your children and their descendants (v. 28). Psalm 103 says God will not forget you.

No wonder the psalm begins with gratitude (vv. 12). Look at what the Lord has done (vv. 3-5).

1. *He forgives all your sins.* Sins, like legal wrongs, are of two kinds: those arising from intention and those stemming from negligence. God forgives both our acts of commission and omission. He frees you to start over after failure, cancels all indictments against you, and discharges all your debts.

2. *He heals all your diseases.* The sticking point for many is that they have not yet experienced a healing like Duane's nor that assured in this psalm. But as believers in Jesus, we must take the long view when miracles do not immediately occur—that ultimately in Christ healing will come even if you must wait for the glorification of your body at the resurrection. God is committed to stamping out all disease; but in His providence, He has not yet banished death nor the instruments of illness which lead toward it.

Please broaden the definition of disease to include any deterioration which diminishes your well-being and wholeness. A disease can just as easily be a bad attitude, an unforgiving spirit, a bitter heart, an eruptive and angry tongue, a fundamentally flawed will that does not resist addictions. In Jesus, the good news of the gospel works to liberate us from these deformative and degenerative diseases so that on the inside our personali-

³who forgives all your sins and heals all your diseases, ⁴who redeems your life from the pit and crowns you with love and compassion, ⁵who satisfies your desires with good things so that your youth is renewed like the eagle's.

⁶The Lord works righteousness and justice for all the oppressed.

⁷He made known his ways to Moses, his deeds to the people of Israel: ⁸The Lord is compassionate and gracious, slow to anger, abounding in love. ⁹He will not always accuse, nor will he harbor his anger forever; ¹⁰he does not treat us as our sins deserve or repay us according to our iniquities. ¹¹For as high as the heavens are above the earth, so great is his love for those who fear him; ¹²as far as the east is from the west, so far has he removed our transgressions from us.

ty and disposition increasingly resemble that of Jesus.

3. *He redeems your life from the pit.* The pit represents the abyss from which you cannot escape. God reaches His long arm into the pitch-dark hole of depression or despair where you lie helpless and imprisoned, grabs you strongly, pulls you up, and sets your feet on solid ground in the sunlight of His presence.

4. *He crowns your life with love and compassion.* A crown of righteousness, life, and glory waits for you in heaven (2 Timothy 4:8; James 1:12; 1 Peter 5:4). Right now, the Lord wants you to wear a crown of love and compassion. Let others seek the crown of success, riches, or power. God has a better gift for you.

5. *He satisfies your desires with good things.* The principal horror of depression is its total lack of hope. But God is committed to bringing good into your life— no matter what. The subtlety of temptation is that it bids you to believe you are headed down into the pit of nonfulfillment if you obey God, when the opposite is true: "At his right hand are pleasures for evermore" (Psalm 16:11). There's no disappointment in Jesus.

6. *He renews your life like the eagle's.* Trap an eagle and confine him to a dark cage. He won't live long. He lives best when he flies free. You're no different—and that's why the Lord has provided "all his benefits" (v. 2) for "all the oppressed" (v. 6). Note the word "all." Our Lord is not a God who has pets nor is He a respecter of persons. His favor applies to all who call upon Him.

Our basis for confidence

How can we be sure God is like this? We have the records of generations to

13As a father has compassion on his children, so the Lord has compassion on those who fear him; 14for he knows how we are formed, he remembers that we are dust. 15As for man, his days are like grass, he flourishes like a flower of the field; 16the wind blows over it and it is gone, and its place remembers it no more. 17But from everlasting to everlasting the Lord's love is with those who fear him, and his righteousness with their children's children — 18with those who keep his covenant and remember to obey his precepts.

19The Lord has established his throne in heaven, and his kingdom rules over all. 20Praise the Lord, you his angels, you mighty ones who do his bidding, who obey his word. 21Praise the Lord, all his heavenly hosts, you his servants who do his will.

whom He has revealed himself (v. 7). His character is seen in how He helped Israel and what He's done for you (vv. 8–12). And if that's not enough to convince you, observe His tender parenting (vv. 13–18). Your life has a fixed center of stability because the Lord reigns (v. 19).

> **22Praise the Lord, all his works everywhere in his dominion. Praise the Lord, O my soul.**

Prayer of response

Lord Jesus, there's only one thing left to do—end the psalm the way it began, with praise. I ask the angels to praise You, along with all the heavenly hosts and all Your works. But I too will join in: "Praise the Lord, O my soul." Earth's song to You is not complete without my verse of personal testimony. Thank You for including my voice in the anthem of eternal praise to You.

My thoughts on Psalm 103 . . .

The Big Picture

Do you take the creation for granted? The splendor of a sunrise, the haunting glow of a new moon suspended without ropes or supports against a dark sky, dew glistening on a grass blade, a butterfly darting past morning glories—these awesome scenes of visual delight can be missed by the dulling of our hearts in the midst of life's humdrum or pain.

But imagine you could go back to the dawn of creation and become the first man or woman. Picture yourself with a heart unfettered by sin or disguise in Eden's paradise; endowed with the skill of a master artist and wordsmith so that through drawing and verbal expression you could adroitly describe exactly the perfect and awesome grandeur laid out before you.

¹Praise the Lord, O my soul. O Lord my God, you are very great; you are clothed with splendor and majesty. ²He wraps himself in light as with a garment; he stretches out the heavens like a tent ³and lays the beams of his upper chambers on their waters. He makes the clouds his chariot and rides on the wings of the wind.

That's the spirit in Psalm 104: the breathless freshness of wonder in viewing God's handiwork. There are no words of response more appropriate than these: "Praise the Lord, O my soul" (v. 1).

Where's your focus?

Maybe you don't feel like praising Him this day. Your life seems more like a desolation than a creation. You are tired, dejected, defeated. Experience has hammered you, and a hurricane has blown through your heart toppling every tree and power line, ripping off your roof of protection, blowing out your windows, knocking down your

115

walls, and lifting you off your foundations. And after the violent storm passed, a dark night has come—with electrical power gone and stars hidden as though the lights in heaven themselves puffed out as a candle in the wind.

The psalmist takes us by the hand and walks us back in time when all was fresh and pure. He draws open the shutters of heaven and lets us look in on God at His workbench—designing and building His master work of earth and sky. In such a setting you become still and hushed, reverent again—your mind off the terrible storm that brought you such devastation. You are now outside your own pain-filled world of sorrow and loss, caught up in God's activity, recognizing that He who creates also desires to make all things bright and beautiful for you. If He does such wonders in hanging universes and worlds in place—will He not also perform His creative work in living flesh like yours?

Why not take a step back from your despondency and get perspective by joining an anthem in praise to God for His creation? Can you offer up your heart to God by also saying, "Praise the Lord, O my soul" (v. 1). Turn your focus heavenward and in your inward self of emotions, will, and intellect, consciously praise Him. Elect not to wallow in despair nor complain against His ways. Don't demean His providence toward you. Acquiesce and say, "O Lord my God, you are very great; you are clothed with splendor and majesty" (v. 1).

Look what the Lord has done.

With broad brush strokes, as a painter would commence to fill a canvas with

4He makes winds his messengers, flames of fire his servants. 5He set the earth on its foundations; it can never be moved. 6You covered it with the deep as with a garment; the waters stood above the mountains. 7But at your rebuke the waters fled, at the sound of your thunder they took to flight; 8they flowed over the mountains, they went down into the valleys, to the place you assigned for them. 9You set a boundary they cannot cross; never again will they cover the earth. 10He makes springs pour water into the ravines; it flows between the mountains. 11They give water to all the beasts of the field; the wild donkeys quench their thirst. 12The birds of the air nest by the waters; they sing among the branches. 13He waters the mountains from his upper chambers; the earth is satisfied by the fruit of his work. 14He makes grass grow for the cattle, and plants for man to cultivate — bringing forth food from the earth: 15wine that gladdens the heart of man, oil to make his face shine, and bread that sus-

the blues, greens, and browns of sky and earth, the psalmist first quickly brushes in the vast expanses in creation's tapestry (vv. 2–4). Then, swiftly moving downward in bold strokes he fills in the world with waters, mountains, and valleys (vv. 5–8). Remember, as God fashions your own existence, that He has boundaries for the waters (v. 9)—your rivers, oceans, springs, or wells of sorrow cannot flow beyond the limits He ordained.

Next, the psalmist takes a finer brush and etches in individual scenes and specific vignettes of creation's morning (vv. 10–18). Before humans are introduced (v. 22) God already is thinking of you—providing resources for you to have: (1) a gladdened heart, (2) a shining face, and (3) a sustained heart—one that makes it through the long haul (v. 15).

The psalmist rapidly completes added details on the canvas of creation (vv. 19–22) consistent with the sequence of creation days given in Genesis 1 and 2, the creation of man coming last (v. 23). How fascinating that man is introduced to the scene as working, not at play nor at rest. It's as though the whole of life can be summed up in a day—we can only do our work until evening, and then the night comes when no man can work (John 9:4). When we stay busy, rather than idle, the roaring lions of doubt or depression steal away, lie down, and sleep (v. 22 compared to v. 23). Your response, please (vv. 24–35)!

God's creation completed (v. 24), the psalmist draws our attention to the vast and spacious sea where "ships go to and fro" (v. 26). The sea is a most fitting metaphor of life itself, a journey from one shore to another across an unknown

tains his heart. ¹⁶The trees of the Lord are well watered, the cedars of Lebanon that he planted. ¹⁷There the birds make their nests; the stork has its home in the pine trees. ¹⁸The high mountains belong to the wild goats; the crags are a refuge for the coneys.

²³Then man goes out to his work, to his labor until evening.

²⁴How many are your works, O Lord! In wisdom you made them all; the earth is full of your creatures. ²⁵There is the sea, vast and spacious, teeming with creatures beyond number — living things both large and small. ²⁶There the ships go to and fro, and the leviathan, which you formed to frolic there. ²⁷These all look to you to give them their food at the proper time. ²⁸When you give it to them, they gather it up; when you open your hand, they are satisfied with good things. ²⁹When you hide your face, they are terrified; when you take away their breath, they die and return to the dust. ³⁰When you send your Spirit, they are created, and you renew the face of the earth. ³¹May the glory of the Lord endure forever;

expanse filled with the unpredictability of the suddenness of a storm (Mark 4:35–41) or an unknown lurking danger (v. 26)—a leviathan frolicking who with a capricious flick of his tail can make your smooth sailing a nightmare of broken relations and shattered hopes.

But the Lord does not send us out on this voyage absent of His own presence. He remains involved in our rhythms of hunger and sustenance, dread and fulfillment, death and life (vv. 27–30).

Stand back now and look at the big picture of God's creation. Are you a critic of His art? Not the psalmist. Nor the person who truly comprehends the magnitude of God's great acts. It's time for praise, awe, and adoration (vv. 31–34). All others disappear (v. 35).

may the Lord rejoice in his works — ³²he who looks at the earth, and it trembles, who touches the mountains, and they smoke. ³³I will sing to the Lord all my life; I will sing praise to my God as long as I live. ³⁴May my meditation be pleasing to him, as I rejoice in the Lord. ³⁵But may sinners vanish from the earth and the wicked be no more. Praise the Lord, O my soul. Praise the Lord.

Prayer of response

Lord Jesus, I confess I have intently looked at my problems for so long that they have become huge and You have become small. Forgive me for my obsession with self and for losing sight of the big picture. Open my eyes to Your greatness, and I too will "praise the Lord, O my soul. Praise the Lord" (v. 35).

My thoughts on Psalm 104 . . .

The Long View

It looked like an abstract painting. A notation on the easel invited the viewer to find the face of Abraham Lincoln.

I stared at the painting for a long time, observing it close up and from different angles. It baffled me. "There's no Abraham Lincoln there," I said resignedly and headed for the exit.

But at the door, I turned for one last look. I saw him. From 100 feet away, he stood out clearly. The face of Lincoln filled the canvass. I had given up because I had been too near. I saw only when I had distance and perspective.

¹Give thanks to the Lord, call on his name; make known among the nations what he has done. ²Sing to him, sing praise to him; tell of all his wonderful acts. ³Glory in his holy name; let the hearts of those who seek the Lord rejoice. ⁴Look to the Lord and his strength; seek his face always. ⁵Remember the wonders he has done, his miracles, and the judgments he pronounced, ⁶O descendants of Abraham his servant, O sons of Jacob, his

The promise

Your circumstances may be as confusing to you this day as that abstract painting. The Bible and your faith tell you there is a pattern somewhere in the drawing of your life, but you can't see it. You're too close to the hurt to view the healing and too near the pain to figure out the plan.

Psalm 105 recalls all the wonderful things God did for Israel as an encouragement for you to not lose heart. It encourages you, like Israel, to take the long view and say, "Give thanks to the Lord . . . sing to him . . . tell of all his wonderful acts . . . Remember the wonders he has done, his miracles" (vv. 1–7).

119

He is the God who does not forget His promises (vv. 8–11). He wants your heart to be saturated with the understanding that He is absolutely faithful—"He remembers his covenant forever" (v. 8).

Remembrances

God doesn't forget, but we do. You will be tempted constantly in your present trial to forget God's care for you in the past. That's why the rest of the psalm focuses on all the things God did for His people, from the migrations of their forefathers, the patriarchs (vv. 12–15), to the descent into slavery in Egypt (vv. 16–25), to the deliverance under Moses from bondage (vv. 26–38), to His care for them in wilderness wanderings (vv. 39–41), and to joyous entry into the land of promise (vv. 42–45). In each epoch, God was with them—as He is with you.

Nomads (vv. 12–15). God cared for His people even before He brought them into a land of their own. Perhaps you feel like a nomad. Others have stable positions or families and blossoming careers. But you don't know where you're going next. Your life at this moment is not stable, and everything is uncertain.

Can God be with you in such a time? He was with Abraham—described as a "stranger" and one who "wandered" (vv. 12,13). In your weak and vulnerable times, God protects you (vv. 14,15).

Hard times (vv. 16–25). Both in famine (vv. 16–22) and slavery (vv. 17–25), the Lord provided for the needs of His people.

Famines aren't limited to the physical. You may be famished for acceptance, love, wholesome relationships, or physical health. But God is already working out a plan so you won't starve, so you'll

chosen ones. 7He is the Lord our God; his judgments are in all the earth.

8He remembers his covenant forever, the word he commanded, for a thousand generations, 9the covenant he made with Abraham, the oath he swore to Isaac. 10He confirmed it to Jacob as a decree, to Israel as an everlasting covenant: 11"To you I will give the land of Canaan as the portion you will inherit."

12When they were but few in number, few indeed, and strangers in it, 13they wandered from nation to nation, from one kingdom to another. 14He allowed no one to oppress them; for their sake he rebuked kings: 15"Do not touch my anointed ones; do my prophets no harm."

26He sent Moses his servant, and Aaron, whom he had chosen. 27They performed his miraculous signs among them, his wonders in the land of Ham. 28He sent darkness and made the land dark — for had they not rebelled against his words? 29He turned their waters into blood, causing their fish to die. 30Their land

have plenty. He did that for Israel with Joseph.

Have you noticed God "sent" Joseph into Egypt? Joseph, at the time his brothers sold him into slavery, surely didn't feel like God was "sending" him. It was his worst nightmare come true. Only by gaining the distance of time did everyone, including Joseph, understand that God engineered the whole thing.

God also knew your famine was going to occur. Just as He sent Joseph down into Egypt years in advance to prepare for Israel's future well-being, so He has anticipated your needs and instituted His rescue plan before your trouble ever began. As a bonus, in the place of difficulty, He also can make you very fruitful (vv. 24,25).

Escape (vv. 26–38). You probably would never select the means God chooses to get you out of a jam. If you had been in Egypt, would you have chosen the self-effacing, unarmed, 80-year-old fugitive Moses as deliverer? What a laugh. He had no power to throw against the might of Egypt.

Don't demand God use your solutions. He'll use things you never thought of. He'll cause you to emerge from adversity laden down with resources (v. 37) rather than impoverished.

Transition (vv. 39–41). From Egypt, Israel went into wilderness. The psalmist remembers, however, only the good things—omitting any mention of Israel's complaints about hunger and thirst, or rebellions against God and His leaders.

How good the Lord is. He allows us to exercise a selective memory in which we recount what He did while forgetting all our own back talk and grumbling. You won't have any complaints when God

teemed with frogs, which went up into the bedrooms of their rulers. ³¹He spoke, and there came swarms of flies, and gnats throughout their country. ³²He turned their rain into hail, with lightning throughout their land; ³³he struck down their vines and fig trees and shattered the trees of their country. ³⁴He spoke, and the locusts came, grasshoppers without number; ³⁵they ate up every green thing in their land, ate up the produce of their soil. ³⁶Then he struck down all the firstborn in their land, the first-fruits of all their manhood. ³⁷He brought out Israel, laden with silver and gold, and from among their tribes no one faltered. ³⁸Egypt was glad when they left, because dread of Israel had fallen on them.

³⁹He spread out a cloud as a covering, and a fire to give light at night. ⁴⁰They asked, and he brought them quail and satisfied them with the bread of heaven. ⁴¹He opened the rock, and water gushed out; like a river it flowed in the desert.

⁴²For he remembered his holy promise given to his

has finished with you—so why gripe today?

Fulfillment (vv. 42–45). If today is not one of joy, God's tomorrow will be. The Lord will never leave or abandon you in "Egypt" or "wilderness." He intends to bring you into a place where the ecstasy far outweighs the agony. (See Romans 8:18–25.) He has all eternity to make good His promise.

servant Abraham. [43]He brought out his people with rejoicing, his chosen ones with shouts of joy; [44]he gave them the lands of the nations, and they fell heir to what others had toiled for — [45]that they might keep his precepts and observe his laws. Praise the Lord.

Prayer of response

Lord, I too join this song of holy history. I am one of those You remember. I feel so forgotten today, so I have to rely upon Your Word that You always know where I am—whether in hard times or transition. It's good you know where I am because I've momentarily lost the map. But I'm not lost because You are with me—and one day I'll be able to look back and see how You fit everything together for my good. So I myself join the psalmist's conclusion: "Praise the Lord."

My thoughts on Psalm 105 . . .

No Bottom

A testimony from the Azusa Street revival in 1906 told of a missionary being attacked by the enemy with the suggestion she was forsaken by God and had committed the unpardonable sin. "God hates you—drown yourself," he repeatedly urged. She almost did.

She returned to her room from the river, threw herself down, fell asleep, and dreamed. She seemed to be in a boat on which all the people but herself were rejoicing and praising God. She heard the captain call out to the pilot, "Sound the depths and compare it with the love of God." The depths were sounded, and the call came back, "No bottom. No bottom."

She awoke in an ocean of God's love, all darkness past and the cry ringing in her ears, "No bottom."

That's the spirit of Psalm 106 which, like Psalm 105, reviews God's acts on behalf of Israel—except this psalm does not skip over the record of human failures.

> ¹Praise the Lord. Give thanks to the Lord, for he is good; his love endures forever. ²Who can proclaim the mighty acts of the Lord or fully declare his praise? ³Blessed are they who maintain justice, who constantly do what is right. ⁴Remember me, O Lord, when you show favor to your people, come to my

Their history, my history

Too often church folk fail to be honest about their own faults.

Not so this psalmist. In advance of describing Israel's long and deep plunge into disobedience and rebellion, he places himself in their company by saying, "We have sinned, even as our fathers did" (v. 6). That's why he can begin the psalm by praising the Lord not because he is good, but that God is good (v. 1). The heart of a God-seeking person desires to do right (vv. 2,3) but honestly admits personal failure and the need for God's help (vv. 4,5).

Whom do you identify with? Those religious types who act like they've never done anything wrong; or the humble, vulnerable, poor, and sinful, who say, "I have done wrong. Please, Lord, help me."

Falling away from God

The bulk of this psalm is an album detailing one photo after another in Israel's descent away from the one who called, delivered, sustained, and loved them.

Snapshot 1: Failure in Egypt (vv. 7-12). When Israel found themselves at the cul-de-sac of the Red Sea, they had already forgotten the miracle of the 10 plagues. They failed to connect God's past help with their present need.

Are you, like them, resentful and rebellious that God permitted a Red Sea in your life?

God keeps helping you anyway—just as He did with Israel. He leads through depths (v. 11) and deserts (v. 14). You feared the waves would drown you, but your enemies perished instead. Can you give God a hand for that (v. 12)?

Snapshots 2–7: Failures in the wilderness (vv. 13-33).

One problem in wilderness living is the sameness of the daily diet—you resent the *monotony* of the routine and crave something more fulfilling. Israel hated its plain morning/evening menu of manna and wanted more tasty food. God sometimes gives you what you want, and to your surprise, it makes you sick (vv. 13–15).

aid when you save them, ⁵that I may enjoy the prosperity of your chosen ones, that I may share in the joy of your nation and join your inheritance in giving praise.

⁷When our fathers were in Egypt, they gave no thought to your miracles; they did not remember your many kindnesses, and they rebelled by the sea, the Red Sea. ⁸Yet he saved them for his name's sake, to make his mighty power known. ¹²Then they believed his promises and sang his praise.

¹³But they soon forgot what he had done and did not wait for his counsel. ¹⁴In the desert they gave in to their craving; in the wasteland they put God to the test. ¹⁵So he gave them what they asked for, but sent a wasting disease upon them.

²³So he said he would destroy them — had not Moses, his chosen one, stood in the breach before him to keep his wrath from destroying them.

²⁴Then they despised the pleasant land; they did not believe his promise. ²⁵They grumbled in their tents and did not obey the Lord. ²⁶So he

Another problem in wilderness living is the temptation to *mutiny* when things aren't going your way by listening to people who tell you what you want to hear rather than what is right (vv. 15–18). Don't resent spiritual authority in your life: the authority of Jesus, of the Bible, of godly counsel.

Impatience is also a problem in the wilderness. Israel stopped still for 40 days while their leader Moses disappeared up on a mountain. Don't you hate doing nothing but waiting? Will you also make your own god, your own solution (vv. 19–23)?

Next comes *unbelief* with its horrendous consequences. When you are tempted for the umpteenth time to lash out at God, why not instead hand over to Him your bad attitude and ask Him to give you a right heart about His purposes for you in the wilderness (vv. 24–27)?

Resist the Lord over long periods of time and the unthinkable can happen: *moral disintegration.* Numbers 25 spells out the full story summarized in vv. 28–31 of this psalm: seduction, flagrant immorality, and idolatry. You are capable of more evil than you think. Will you draw personal and public lines of loyalty as did Phinehas?

Finally, the perpetual ever-present wilderness test is to *mistrust* God, to suppose He's abandoned you in the desert of life and will provide no resource to sustain you (vv. 32,33). Are you grousing with the untruth that God doesn't care about you?

Snapshot 8: Failure in the land of promise (vv. 34–39). Centuries of living in Canaan, summarized in these verses, show God's people going from bad to worse—becoming so vile that the holy

swore to them with uplifted hand that he would make them fall in the desert, [27]make their descendants fall among the nations and scatter them throughout the lands.

[28]They yoked themselves to the Baal of Peor and ate sacrifices offered to lifeless gods; [29]they provoked the Lord to anger by their wicked deeds, and a plague broke out among them. [30]But Phinehas stood up and intervened, and the plague was checked. [31]This was credited to him as righteousness for endless generations to come.

[32]By the waters of Meribah they angered the Lord, and trouble came to Moses because of them; [33]for they rebelled against the Spirit of God, and rash words came from Moses' lips.

[34]They did not destroy the peoples as the Lord had commanded them, [35]but they mingled with the nations and adopted their customs. [36]They worshiped their idols, which became a snare to them. [37]They sacrificed their sons and their daughters to demons. [38]They shed innocent blood, the blood of their sons and daughters, whom

land was stained with the blood of their children whom they sacrificed to idols. How can anyone get so far from God? It begins with disobedience (v. 34) and ends with not a shred of difference between you and the worst pagans.

Snapshot 9: Disinheritance (vv. 40–43). God wanted His people to be fulfilled. They chose instead to reject His love. When you do that, here's what happens: You fall away from freedom into bondage and oppression, and "waste away in [your] sin."

God's great and marvelous grace

After such a record of failure, does God wipe His hands clean of His people? Not so. He heard their first cry in Egypt centuries earlier (Exodus 3:7) and their most recent (v. 44).

He hears yours also. You have not yet exhausted His grace—but don't try to find the bottom.

they sacrificed to the idols of Canaan, and the land was desecrated by their blood. [39]They defiled themselves by what they did; by their deeds they prostituted themselves. [40]Therefore the Lord was angry with his people and abhorred his inheritance. [41]He handed them over to the nations, and their foes ruled over them. [42]Their enemies oppressed them and subjected them to their power. [43]Many times he delivered them, but they were bent on rebellion and they wasted away in their sin. [44]But he took note of their distress when he heard their cry.

Prayer of response

Thank You, Lord Jesus, that my failures do not doom me. Your love endures against all my "noes" and flirtations with evil. No matter how far I've traveled from You, You are ready at my cry to resume the relationship I had broken. Your mercy lasts forever.

My thoughts on Psalm 106 . . .

No Greater Love

Psalm 107

A college student brought a framed picture of his girl-friend to a photographic studio for duplication. In removing the photo from the frame, the studio owner saw this inscription on the back: "Dearest Tommy, I love you with all my heart. I love you more and more each day. I will love you forever and ever. I am yours for all eternity."

The note was signed, "Dianne," and contained this P.S., "If we should ever break up, I want this picture back."

That's a striking contrast to Psalm 107, which begins with "his love endures forever" (v. 1) and ends with "consider the great love of the Lord" (v. 43).

You will find yourself in at least one of the four groups of people considering that love: the lonely (vv. 4–9), the trapped (vv. 10–16), the sick (vv. 17–22), and the adventuresome (vv. 23–31). The praise of all four joins together in verses 1–3 prior to their individual testimonies. Have you also found God's love reaches longer than your ability to outrun it—east or west, north or south?

Each life story of the redeemed contains four parts.

¹Give thanks to the Lord, for he is good; his love endures forever. ²Let the redeemed of the Lord say this — those he redeemed from the hand of the foe, ³those he gathered from the lands, from east and west, from north and south. ⁴Some wandered in desert wastelands, finding no way to a city where they

First, a description of the need

Lonely people wander in dry and barren places—sites without any resources to meet needs. You wander when you lack direction, cut off from community ("the city"). Your appetites remain unrelentingly unmet. You feel life slipping away (vv. 4,5).

127

Are you trapped by alcohol, drugs, perversion, chaining habit, or destructive relationships? Then you know what darkness, gloom, iron shackles, bitter labor, and stumbling around are all about. Is it your own fault? Did you say no to God (vv. 10–12)?

Is your body sick because you sinned? Can that happen? By all means. In every community you'll find people suffering or dying because they insisted on smoking, drinking, overeating and lack of exercise, destructive attitudes which poisoned them physically, immoral relationships that produced sexually transmitted diseases. Looking back, you see how foolish you were (vv. 16–18).

Then there are the adventuresome. Are you among those who risk in order to gain? Could it be that you've even embarked on some great venture for God? You also are not immune from peril (vv. 23–27). If God didn't spare the apostle Paul shipwrecks, He may not spare you either (2 Corinthians 11:25; Acts 27:13–44).

Second, a cry for help

Lonely, trapped, suffering, and adventuresome people in trouble must cry to the Lord in order to be rescued (vv. 6,13, 19,28).

A cry is nothing fancy. You don't have to collect a bunch of words or memorize a prayer. When you're in trouble, God doesn't require anything thought-provoking from your lips. A cry will do—a cry to the Lord.

Third, God's response to the cry

God delivers. He brings the lonely into community (vv. 7,8), the trapped into

could settle. ⁵They were hungry and thirsty, and their lives ebbed away.

¹⁰Some sat in darkness and the deepest gloom, prisoners suffering in iron chains, ¹¹for they had rebelled against the words of God and despised the counsel of the Most High. ¹²So he subjected them to bitter labor; they stumbled, and there was no one to help.

¹⁷Some became fools through their rebellious ways and suffered affliction because of their iniquities. ¹⁸They loathed all food and drew near the gates of death. ¹⁹Then they cried to the Lord in their trouble, and he saved them from their distress.

²³Others went out on the sea in ships; they were merchants on the mighty waters. ²⁴They saw the works of the Lord, his wonderful deeds in the deep. ²⁵For he spoke and stirred up a tempest that lifted high the waves. ²⁶They mounted up to the heavens and went down to the depths; in their peril their courage melted away. ²⁷They reeled and staggered like drunken men; they were at their wits' end.

freedom (vv. 13,14), the sick into wellness (vv. 19,20), and the sinking adventurer into safe harbor (vv. 28–30).

The Lord totally changes our condition of helplessness either all at once or over time.

"Over time" may bother you (as it does me) because you want God's deliverance instantly. I had a friend who felt that way. He'd belonged to the category of the trapped, bound by an addiction over years.

When he gave his life to the Lord, he prayed for and anticipated that his addictive thirst would pass immediately. Instead, he felt the Lord say to him, "You took time to fall into this, and you will need time to repattern your thought life." I must add he immediately quit the addictive behavior; the Lord, however, worked over time in renewing his mind.

Fourth, our response to God's help

How about an ovation? When God delivers you from anything, take time to give Him thanks (vv. 8,9; 15,16; 21,22; 31,32). But there is an additional response God seeks—that we learn our spiritual lessons well (vv. 33–43).

There's a price to be paid for doing wrong (vv. 33,34,39,40) and a reward for doing right (vv. 35–38,41,42). In this psalm's Old Testament setting, the payback came in the material realm—serve God and prosper, or forget God and suffer. Job and Joseph and a handful of others in the Old Testament introduced the exception—that hardship is not always the evidence of disobedience. Jesus carried this further by announcing that suffering would be part and parcel of living

28Then they cried out to the Lord in their trouble, and he brought them out of their distress. **29**He stilled the storm to a whisper; the waves of the sea were hushed. **30**They were glad when it grew calm, and he guided them to their desired haven.

31Let them give thanks to the Lord for his unfailing love and his wonderful deeds for men. **32**Let them exalt him in the assembly of the people and praise him in the council of the elders.

33He turned rivers into a desert, flowing springs into thirsty ground, **34**and fruitful land into a salt waste, because of the wickedness of those who lived there. **35**He turned the desert into pools of water and the parched ground into flowing springs; **36**there he brought the hungry to live, and they founded a city where they could settle. **37**They sowed fields and planted vineyards that yielded a fruitful harvest; **38**he blessed them, and their numbers greatly increased, and he did not let their herds diminish. **39**Then their numbers decreased,

for Him (Mark 8:34–38). Our paycheck doesn't come until the end (Matthew 25:21,23), although the Lord gives many wonderful installments along the way—Christ acting for us (1 Thessalonians 1:4) and living in us by the Spirit (Galatians 5:22,23; Ephesians 5:17-20).

The psalm closes by inviting us, in reviewing our own testimony and that of others, to "consider the great love of the Lord" (v. 43). How much better we should be able to do that than even the psalmist, for we now have what he did not—the New Testament record of how much God loved us in sending Jesus to suffer for us and save us from our sins.

This psalm deserves the P.S. of 1 John 3:1: "How great is the love the Father has lavished on us, that we should be called children of God!"

and they were humbled by oppression, calamity and sorrow; 40he who pours contempt on nobles made them wander in a trackless waste. 41But he lifted the needy out of their affliction and increased their families like flocks. 42The upright see and rejoice, but all the wicked shut their mouths. 43Whoever is wise, let him heed these things and consider the great love of the Lord.

Prayer of response

I'm considering Your great love for me today, Lord, and I admit it's way over my head. You heard my cry when I was lonely, trapped, sick, and in a storm. My unworthiness didn't stop You for a moment. You, who touch untouchables, also took firm hold on me and I thank You.

My thoughts on Psalm 107 . . .

Getting Out of Bed

Psalm 108

Mhen you're depressed, about the last thing you want to do is get out of bed and rise to face the morning.

Here's a psalm to counteract hopelessness and help you welcome a new day with courage.

If you think the words of Psalm 108 sound familiar—they are. Look back to Psalm 57 (vv. 7–11) and Psalm 60 (vv. 5–12) and you will find Psalm 108 simply repeats the endings to these two earlier psalms. Psalm 57 begins with David hunted; the setting for Psalm 60 is David defeated. Yet, both psalms end, not in despair, but in confidence that God has a brighter day ahead. It's those positive endings that are joined together in this psalm.

Aren't you glad to know that tough moments in your life, when you feel trapped or beat up, don't last forever—that later you'll focus upon God's promises fulfilled rather than your present pain?

¹**My heart is steadfast, O God; I will sing and make music with all my soul.** ²**Awake, harp and lyre! I will awaken the dawn.** ³**I will praise you, O Lord, among the nations; I will sing of you among the peoples.**

A wake-up song

Are you so excited about living that you can't wait for the dawn of a new day? David is. He's up and singing, musical instruments in hand (v. 2), expressing the sentiments, "When morning gilds the skies, my heart awaking cries, may Jesus Christ be praised!"

Maybe you don't face your days like that. You had a sleepless or troubled night, filled with dread or anxiety. The last thing on your mind is cheerfully getting up.

You really need to tune in to the fun-

131

damental truth conveyed in this psalm and all of Scripture. Your day will go better if you begin with praise to the Lord who made and redeemed you.

Remember the apostle Paul? In prison he wrote, among other things, the letter to the Philippians. It's a letter of abounding joy and the assurance that he could do all things through Christ who strengthened him (4:13). I used to be troubled by that phrase "all things," thinking maybe Paul was using a cliché. After all, what could he "do" in prison—no preaching, church planting, mentoring of pastors. In fact, he could do very little within the confines of his cell. Then it dawned on me one day—the toughest, most difficult thing God ever asked him to "do" was prison. And through Christ, he found he could "do" even that. Surviving unjust incarceration was one of the "all things."

Are you going to compound your misery by having a miserable attitude or will you decide to sing instead (vv. 1,2; Philippians 4:4)?

What's there to sing about? That you're not lost or alone in God's great universe today, that you are part of a vast assembly on earth who lift their voice to praise Him (v. 3). The Lord has not permitted you to fall outside His grace by your own weakness, stubbornness, or rebellion. He folded you to himself even as you ran from Him—otherwise, how would you know His love reaches to the heavens and His faithfulness to the skies (v. 4)?

Jesus' love is no come-on. He didn't cross His fingers behind His back when He said it. At no point has He considered retracting His love for you or breaking the bad news to you that He doesn't love you anymore. He loves you today. He

4For great is your love, higher than the heavens; your faithfulness reaches to the skies. 5Be exalted, O God, above the heavens, and let your glory be over all the earth.

loved you yesterday. He will love you tomorrow.

Why not open your heart and voice to God in response: "Be exalted, O God, above the heavens, and let your glory be over all the earth" (v. 5).

Confidence for the day

What gives you hope to live this day? Is it not God's past performance? Isn't the best predictor of what a person will do in the future what he has done in the past?

The psalmist reviews God's track record with geographical references to camping places (Shechem and Succoth) where the Lord sustained Abraham and Jacob (v. 7), as well as the names of a sampling of the tribal territories of Israel (v. 8) and historic enemies God has defeated (v. 9). All these references relate not only to God's past deeds but also constitute promises of present and future aid. With confidence David can ask for help because of what the Lord has already done (v. 6). The Lord's consistent character can be relied upon.

⁶Save us and help us with your right hand, that those you love may be delivered. ⁷God has spoken from his sanctuary: "In triumph I will parcel out Shechem and measure off the Valley of Succoth. ⁸Gilead is mine, Manasseh is mine; Ephraim is my helmet, Judah my scepter. ⁹Moab is my washbasin, upon Edom I toss my sandal; over Philistia I shout in triumph."

Challenges to meet

David ends the psalm by recounting the most difficult task facing him—the fortified city of Edom (v. 10). Such a place lay impregnable because of its walls, battlements, and defenses.

You may have your own Edom—an absolutely impossible situation. You don't have a clue as to how you can crack through the fortifications of your problem. David didn't know the "how" either, but he knew the "who." The Lord himself.

¹⁰Who will bring me to the fortified city? Who will lead me to Edom?

But, here's the catch. What if the Lord says, "Not you. You failed Me. You didn't listen to Me, so why should I pay any attention to you?" David faced that prospect head on (v. 11), but did not let it deter him from asking the Lord for help anyway (v. 12). The very God who refuses to assist you when you are stubborn, rebellious, and self-willed turns toward you when you are vulnerable, humble, and penitent.

He'll give you strength to make it through this day (v. 13).

> ¹¹Is it not you, O God, you who have rejected us and no longer go out with our armies?
>
> ¹²Give us aid against the enemy, for the help of man is worthless. ¹³With God we will gain the victory, and he will trample down our enemies.

Prayer of response

Lord Jesus, I remember that "while it was still dark" Your followers came grieving to Your tomb (John 20:1). I also know what it's like to be sad when something or someone precious to me lies dead. But let me never forget You awakened the dawn with Your resurrection, tearing open fortifcations far stronger than Edom's—death, hell, and the grave. If You can destroy defenses like that, then I can trust You to help me all through this day. So I welcome the daylight with song and praise to You.

My thoughts on Psalm 108 . . .

Getting Even

Newspaper columnist and minister George Crane tells of a wife who came into his office full of hatred toward her husband. "I do not only want to get rid of him, I want to get even. Before I divorce him, I want to hurt him as much as he has me."

David feels just like her in this psalm.

> ¹O God, whom I praise, do not remain silent, ²for wicked and deceitful men have opened their mouths against me; they have spoken against me with lying tongues. ³With words of hatred they surround me; they attack me without cause. ⁴In return for my friendship they accuse me, but I am a man of prayer. ⁵They repay me evil for good, and hatred for my friendship.
>
> ⁶Appoint an evil man to oppose him; let an accuser stand at his right hand.
>
> ⁷When he is tried, let him be found guilty, and may his prayers condemn him.

Lord, here's the problem

Perhaps like David you never anticipated rejection or betrayal from a person close to you. David begins his prayer with a gush of anguish that we might paraphrase: God, please don't let them get away with this. I've been wronged, lied to, and lied about. It's not fair. I gave love and got used" (vv. 1-5).

Lord, here's my delicious solution

Appoint a prosecutor (v. 6). When you've been harmed, it's normal to want justice. David doesn't want some rookie or softie to handle his case, but a prosecutor as crooked as the guy who wronged him.

Get a guilty verdict (v. 7). You would like to hear the other person admit his or her wrong or be held responsible.

135

David Augsburger tells the story of the wife who said, "Sure I'll forgive him, but not until he's paid for all he's dragged me through." Years later the husband said, "You can keep your phony forgiving. I've paid through the nose for what I've done. Who needs forgiveness when he's already paid?"

Make 'em suffer (vv. 8–15). The Old Testament law of retaliation (eye for eye, tooth for tooth) was given to limit vengeance. If someone, for example, knocked out your tooth you should not be able to extract their tooth plus cut off their hands. But in this prayer David's anger leaps over all stop signs. He asks God to cut short the former friend's lifespan and get him fired, ruin his family, and wreck his ancestors and descendants.

God, they deserve it (vv. 6–20). You have good rationale in asking for payback time. David notes how hard-hearted and verbally destructive his former friend was.

Lord, I just need help

David closes the psalm by shifting the focus back to himself (v. 21).

Why should God act on his behalf? He was helpless—that's why (v. 22). Like David, do you just want to lie down and die (vv. 23,24)? Have you worn your pain so visibly and vocally that others now treat you with clucking pity (v. 25)?

When everyone quits listening, there's One who still welcomes your voice (v. 26). Calmer with that thought, David closes his prayer more with a request for vindication than vengeance (vv. 27–29) and a powerful statement of trust in God (vv. 30, 31). Will you do the same?

8May his days be few; may another take his place of leadership. 9May his children be fatherless and his wife a widow. 10May his children be wandering beggars; may they be driven from their ruined homes. 11May a creditor seize all he has; may strangers plunder the fruits of his labor. 12May no one extend kindness to him or take pity on his fatherless children. 13May his descendants be cut off, their names blotted out from the next generation. 14May the iniquity of his fathers be remembered before the Lord; may the sin of his mother never be blotted out. 15May their sins always remain before the Lord, that he may cut off the memory of them from the earth.

21But you, O Sovereign Lord, deal well with me for your name's sake; out of the goodness of your love, deliver me. 22For I am poor and needy, and my heart is wounded within me.

26Help me, O Lord my God; save me in accordance with your love.

Remember the wife that came to George Crane wanting to get even? He advised her to go home and act as if she really loved her husband and when she had him thoroughly hooked, dump him.

She gleefully left his office to implement the fiendish plan of revenge. Two years later when she still had not returned, Dr. Crane called her, "Are you ready now to go through with the divorce?"

"Divorce?" she exclaimed. "Never. I discovered I really do love him."

There is a higher way than getting even. Jesus calls you to forgive and do good. Will such action restore the relationship? There's no guarantee for that. But, forgiveness will always make you a better person, and it may even make room on some future day for the one who wronged you to say, "I'm sorry."

30With my mouth I will greatly extol the Lord; in the great throng I will praise him. 31For he stands at the right hand of the needy one, to save his life from those who condemn him.

Prayer of response

Lord Jesus, help me to never treat another so badly that they would think of me as David did his former friend. Lift me to a higher moral ground where I would rather be the wounded than the wounder. And help me to get where David ended (vv. 30,31)—full of healing rather than hurt, confident of Your help rather than drowning in my own despair.

My thoughts on Psalm 109 . . .

Highest Honor

Several weeks ago we waited with our daughter Evangeline and her husband Rick in a hospital birthing room for the arrival of our grandson Jacob George Zorehkey. In the long hours prior to his delivery, the fetal monitor sounded out the presence of little Jacob through the constant swoosh-boom, swoosh-boom of his beating heart.

I felt a sense of sacred awe in realizing that, although I could not yet see my grandson, he was living and near.

David must have felt that way. In Psalm 110 he's waiting the arrival of his great grandson, to the 40th great. (See genealogy in Luke 3:23-32.) From a millennium away, David, through the enlightenment of the Holy Spirit, put his stethoscope on the future and listened to the fullness of Christ.

Jesus, as Lord and King

¹The Lord says to my Lord: "Sit at my right hand until I make your enemies a footstool for your feet."

Jesus used the opening words of this psalm to stump His religious opponents: "How is it that the teachers of the law say that the Christ is the son of David . . . David himself called him 'Lord.' How then can he be his son?" (See Mark 12:27–37.)

The antagonists to Jesus wouldn't answer His question because it compelled a response that united the truths of Psalm 110 (as David's Lord, Jesus is divine) with 2 Samuel 7:12,13,16 (as David's descendant, Jesus is human).

139

Think what this psalm meant to the first followers of Jesus. They witnessed the disgraceful and vile treatment He received in the miscarriage of justice which nailed Him to the cross. Opposed to the unjust verdict of men is the honor given Jesus by God himself.

David prophesied of that moment when Jesus' redemptive mission on earth would be completed and the Father would welcome His return into heaven with the words, "Sit at my right hand" (v. 1). Jesus has done everything He can to save you, so He sat down (Acts 5:31; Romans 8:34; Ephesians 1:20; Colossians 3:1; Hebrews 10:12).

You then enjoy the benefits of His victory (v. 2) and join His army as one of His "troops" depicted in dress parade, fresh as the dawn or glistening dew (v. 3). Indeed, we are His soldiers (2 Timothy 2:3), but our weapons are not of this world (2 Corinthians 10:4).

Jesus, as Priest

The purpose of a priest is to make intercession. No king in Israel held the role also of priest. One of David's descendants, King Uzziah, tried to take both responsibilities and was severely judged by God (2 Chronicles 26:16–21).

Only one of David's descendants, according to the flesh (Romans 1:3), has been anointed by God to be both our King and Priest. His priesthood is not after the order of Levi, but Melchizedek— king of righteousness. (See Genesis 14:18–20 and Hebrews 5:5–10; 6:19–7:28.) A priest forever, without beginning or end.

²The Lord will extend your mighty scepter from Zion; you will rule in the midst of your enemies.

³Your troops will be willing on your day of battle. Arrayed in holy majesty, from the womb of the dawn you will receive the dew of your youth.

Jesus, as Conquering Hero

David's stethoscope reaches all the way to the end of time when his Lord, King Eternal and Priest Eternal, has subdued all enemies.

As a prophet, David knew a "day of wrath" was coming (v. 5) in which God would settle all accounts with evil.

There's no doubt about final outcomes—at the end of the age the Lord serenely refreshes himself when all foes have been vanquished (v. 7).

Hands of love

On that first day of my grandson Jacob's life, everyone who held him did so with care and love. I want Jacob to accomplish the purposes for which God sent him; however, I cannot foretell his future. Who of us can predict what our descendants will do?

That's what makes this psalm so extraordinary. One thousand years before Bethlehem and Calvary, David received revelation from God about the identity and mission of Jesus.

God himself has exalted Jesus to the highest place and given Him the name that is above every other (Philippians 2:9). Have you told Jesus that He has the highest place of honor in your life?

4The Lord has sworn and will not change his mind: "You are a priest forever, in the order of Melchizedek."

5The Lord is at your right hand; he will crush kings on the day of his wrath. 6He will judge the nations, heaping up the dead and crushing the rulers of the whole earth.

7He will drink from a brook beside the way ; therefore he will lift up his head.

Prayer of response

Lord Jesus, I welcome You today as my Lord and King. I submit every area of my life to Your control and direction. Your will be done in me. Thank You for Your ministry as priest on my behalf in dying for my sin and interceding for me at the right hand of God.

My thoughts on Psalm 110 . . .

How Big
is God?

Imagine that you are at the mercy of 25- to 30-foot giants who speak a language you cannot understand, pick you up with ease, and swing you high over their heads. While you're screaming, they're laughing.

When they are tired of playing with you they drop you in a stockade called a crib or playpen where you can entertain yourself with only things the giants choose. You eat when they decide, with foods of their choice; and if you find something you like, they may forcibly remove it from your mouth.

Your house is gigantic: stairs with steps more than 2 feet high, doors reaching up to 40 feet, and the doorknob way beyond your reach. You're not even tall enough to look out a window.

What I've just described are the proportions that exist between a toddler and a parent. To the child, Mom or Dad is great. It's tragic when they are not also good.

The greatness of God

¹Praise the Lord. I will extol the Lord with all my heart in the council of the upright and in the assembly.

Think of the immense house we live in—the universe. The $3 billion Hubble telescope recently spotted a black hole (a collapsed star so dense that not even light can escape its gravitational pull) in the heart of galaxy M84, at least 300 million times the mass of the sun. And that's only one black hole among how many?

Just how big is the God who made all this?

Perhaps as a child you prayed the mealtime prayer, "God is great; God is good." This psalm shows us that God's greatness is irrevocably married to His goodness: His deeds are glorious and majestic, but also His righteousness endures forever. In other words, this giant God can be trusted.

The goodness of God

This psalm portrays God's greatness through His goodness to us, His people. Here's how God uses His power for our well-being.

God is very kind to you (v. 4).

What would you do if you had everything? Would you let little people, poor people, unimportant people, needy people, or sick people get anywhere near you?

God does. Why? He's gracious and compassionate.

God sustains you (v. 5).

Israel never forgot that the Lord daily gave them manna in the wilderness. Jesus also taught us to pray for our "daily bread" (Matthew 6:11).

It's scary living on just enough to make it through today. I fear the provision will run out, and the next morning I'll have less or nothing.

But because God remembers your hunger—for food, security, relationship, or fulfillment—He will provide the "bread" on the day you need it. Don't panic that tomorrow's bread is not yet on your plate.

God enlarges you (v. 6).

In Him, you are never diminished. He expands the territory of your life, enlarging your sphere of influence. In temptation, the enemy whispers to you that if you obey God you will have less. Not so.

²Great are the works of the Lord; they are pondered by all who delight in them. ³Glorious and majestic are his deeds, and his righteousness endures forever.

⁴He has caused his wonders to be remembered; the Lord is gracious and compassionate.

⁵He provides food for those who fear him; he remembers his covenant forever.

⁶He has shown his people the power of his works, giving them the lands of other nations.

The reliability of God

You can depend on what He says. He's not fickle. He won't turn on you, manipulate, or deceive you (v. 7). He won't tease or tantalize you with promises of illusory love (v. 8).

He is rock solid dependable. And more than that, He provides redemption for His people (v. 9). His love for you is so deep He died to save you even when you were indifferent or opposed to Him (Romans 5:8).

Application

The starting place for wisdom must always be Him. If you do not have awe or respect for His great power and love toward you, you'll not make right decisions. A God who loves you so much deserves a response of praise, yieldedness, and joyful submission to His will.

⁷The works of his hands are faithful and just; all his precepts are trustworthy.

⁸They are steadfast for ever and ever, done in faithfulness and uprightness.

⁹He provided redemption for his people; he ordained his covenant forever — holy and awesome is his name.

¹⁰The fear of the Lord is the beginning of wisdom; all who follow his precepts have good understanding. To him belongs eternal praise.

Prayer of response

Lord Jesus, I so easily forget to extol You with all my heart. Forgive me for the times I have permitted depression, discouragement, or unmindfulness to rob me from adoring You. In giving Your life for me, You demonstrated there is no limit to either Your goodness or Your greatness.

My thoughts on Psalm 111 . . .

The Good Life

Psalm 112

T he story is told of a Montana sheepherder who became enormously rich when oil was discovered on his ranch. He promptly bought a Rolls Royce limousine, the kind where the driver sits in front of a glass partition.

A friend asked, "What do you like best about it?"

"Well," he drawled, "I can take my sheep to market now without having them lick my neck."

What would change in your life if you had the money?

This psalm talks about gaining prosperity—financial advantage is only part of the story. All the qualities presented in Psalm 112 form a picture of the ideal life.

A close relationship with the Lord

To build a good life you start with God. Prayers are not something to mumble; nor worship a routine to be endured; nor obedience to God an act to be resisted.

Is your ever-present response to Him one of indifference or complaint? Not so the psalmist. He's full of praise to the Lord.

When you have Jesus, you have everything; and if you have everything without Jesus, you have nothing.

We don't have a problem praising

1Praise the Lord. Blessed is the man who fears the Lord, who finds great delight in his commands.

147

someone who loves us and whom we love. But sometimes we do struggle with obeying God.

If you do not feel like the psalmist who takes "great delight" in doing God's will, be honest with Him about your resistance: *Lord, I want to be more than just an obedient soldier snapping to attention and performing my duty just because it's an order. Help my response to be from my heart.*

²His children will be mighty in the land; the generation of the upright will be blessed.

Children of strength

A home in which a mom or dad serves the Lord with earnest delight yields children who emerge into adulthood with spiritual force and vigor. They have not been crippled by the poor patterning of wounded, indifferent, or rebellious parents.

Of course, even in such homes, children do not always turn out well—as the caring father of the prodigal discovered (Luke 15). This psalm doesn't seek to deal with the exception to the rule but the general rule itself—that parents who love the Lord without hypocrisy beget well-adjusted children.

True riches

The gospel of Jesus Christ does raise the living standard, for it instills an ethical response to life and work. A truly converted person is no longer lazy, self-indulgent, wasteful, or foolish with money.

Even at that, the Christian's riches are not the size of his paycheck; but the wealth and riches "*in* his house."

As I write this, the news is dominated by stories of a divorce where a wife successfully won a $20 million marital set-

³Wealth and riches are in his house, and his righteousness endures forever. ⁴Even in darkness light dawns for the upright, for the gracious and compassionate and righteous man. ⁵Good will come to him who is generous and lends freely, who conducts his affairs with justice.

tlement rather than the $8 million proposed by the husband. They were poor for they had no wealth in their "house."

Living for Jesus brings a dramatic improvement in how well you live—even if that improvement is not reflected in your bank balance.

Generosity

The believer has a "light" in personal dark times, for the Holy Spirit has helped him to develop a response of never retreating completely into self. The Christian's life gaze involves both an upward (to God) and outward (to others) look. Thus, a generous person gets through night seasons a lot better, for he has not abandoned compassion or practical concern for others with hurts and needs.

Security

Look at the images of security—never shaken, remembered forever, no fear of bad news, steadfast heart, trusting in the Lord, no fear, triumph over foes. And ultimately, a horn lifted high—imagery likening you to a great bull raising its head in a sense of power and indestructibility.

The psalm closes with a look at the life that is not good, one marked by anguish and unfulfillment (v. 10).

Which life describes you?

6Surely he will never be shaken; a righteous man will be remembered forever. 7He will have no fear of bad news; his heart is steadfast, trusting in the Lord. 8His heart is secure, he will have no fear; in the end he will look in triumph on his foes. 9He has scattered abroad his gifts to the poor, his righteousness endures forever; his horn will be lifted high in honor.

10The wicked man will see and be vexed, he will gnash his teeth and waste away; the longings of the wicked will come to nothing.

Prayer of response

Loving God, help me to measure wealth by Your standards. Let me not despair if my outward circumstances seem not to be as prosperous as another's. Teach me anew that the good life lies not in what I have, but whose I am; not in what I keep, but what I give away.

My thoughts on Psalm 112 . . .

High and Low

Mark's Gospel tells us that after Jesus had taken the Passover with His disciples "they sung a hymn" and went out to Gethsemane (Mark 14:26).

In all likelihood, the hymn came from the collection of six psalms known as the *Hallel* (praise), Psalms 113–118. These psalms were traditionally sung by a Jewish family as it partook of and completed the Passover meal.

Thus, if you want to know the portion of Scripture which sustained Jesus as He entered the most difficult hours of His life, you will find it here—beginning with Psalm 113.

If you were facing a garden of sorrow and a hill of crucifixion, would you have felt like beginning and ending your prayer with praise to the Lord (vv. 1,9)? Jesus did. Why?

¹Praise the Lord. Praise, O servants of the Lord, praise the name of the Lord. ²Let the name of the Lord be praised, both now and forevermore.

God on high

As Jesus entered the dark clouds of Gethsemane and Calvary, He fell back on what is always true. The seemingly out-of-control things happening to Him did not mean that God had lost track of Him.

You must learn to distinguish how you feel from what you know. You will not always feel God's presence. Your emotions may tell you God has abandoned you. You don't feel like praising the Lord. Yet, five times in the first three

151

verses of this psalm, we are invited to praise the Lord—not blame Him, fuss at Him, or accuse Him—but praise Him.

There is a breathtaking sweep to the praise for it is: eternal—"now and for-evermore" (v. 2); global—"from the rising of the sun to the place where it sets" (v. 3).

Jesus approached His dying hours in trust that what He did for us would produce a ceaseless and worldwide praise from His church on earth.

Never project your weakness onto God. You may be powerless but He is powerful; you may be confused but He is not; you may be knocked off your feet but He sits enthroned on high (vv. 4,5).

God bending low

The latter half of this psalm reminds us that God above also "stoops down to look" (v. 6).

There are two kinds of looks: The priest and the Levite looked at the man lying wounded on the roadside of life but passed on without helping. The Good Samaritan looked, and his look produced the action of help. (See Luke 10:31–33.)

In Jesus Christ, God has stooped to look you in the face and help you.

Two groups benefit from the Lord's caring look.

1. *The poor or needy* (vv. 7,8). Jesus came with good news for the poor. (See Luke 4:18.) In fact, the kingdom of God is open only to those who say, "I need help." (See Matthew 15:25.) Jesus came not only for the poor in spirit, but also those lying on the pile of burned-out dreams and hopes, feeling worthless and used. He com-

3From the rising of the sun to the place where it sets, the name of the Lord is to be praised.

4The Lord is exalted over all the nations, his glory above the heavens. 5Who is like the Lord our God, the One who sits enthroned on high,

6who stoops down to look on the heavens and the earth?

7He raises the poor from the dust and lifts the needy from the ash heap; 8he seats them with princes, with the princes of their people.

pletely restores your value.

2. *The barren* (v. 9). In many cultures, a childless wife is looked upon as an unproductive member of society. Hannah represents a host of women who have cried their eyes out in anguish and grief, praying to conceive a child. (See 1 Samuel 1:8,16.)

No matter what the nature of your barrenness—these words remind you that God is committed to helping you.

Think of how this psalm must have fortified Jesus as He prepared to leave the Upper Room where He had taken the Passover with His disciples. The opening half refreshed His confidence in the greatness of His Father; the latter half deeply reminded Him of why He had come.

⁹He settles the barren woman in her home as a happy mother of children. Praise the Lord.

Prayer of response

Lord Jesus, when I face hard moments I so easily get depressed rather than rising up to trust You. Help me to pass through my own Gethsemanes with confident faith in You. You are not only high and mighty, but You stoop down to help me when I am in the dust and ash heap. You are bringing me to fullness and fruitfulness, to palaces and pleasures of Your choosing,

My thoughts on Psalm 113 . . .

Look What the Lord Has Done!

W hen a contemporary Jewish family sits down together to take the Passover *(Seder)*, the written liturgy they recite through the meal will include reference to four kinds of children: the wise, the wicked, the simple and the one who has no capacity to inquire.

The second son—the wicked one—asks, "What mean you by this service?"

As commentary on the wicked son's unthinking use of "you," the family reads this response: "By the word 'you' it is clear he doth not include himself, and thus hath withdrawn himself from the community; it is therefore proper to retort upon him by saying, 'This is done because of what the Eternal did for me when I went forth from Egypt; for me and not for him; for had he been there, he would not have been thought worthy to be redeemed.'"

Many ways

Psalm 114 is the second of six *Hallel* (Praise) psalms, which would have been sung by Jesus and His disciples at the conclusion of Passover meal immediately prior to Gethsemane. Jesus used that occasion to inject the truth of the greater redemption than Israel's exodus

¹When Israel came out of Egypt, the house of Jacob from a people of foreign tongue, ²Judah became God's sanctuary, Israel his dominion.

155

from Egypt—a redemption He brought through His broken body and shed blood by which we are freed from the slavery of sin and brought into the glorious land of new birth and eternal life.

Thus, this psalm may be sung with multidimensional meaning. First, we sing it, as did Jesus, to remember Israel's deliverance by God from Egypt. Second, we sing it to remember what Jesus did for us in bringing us out of bondage and into His kingdom.

Third, we sing it when we remember the times God has met us personally and delivered us from difficult, oppressive, or hurtful situations—our individual Egypts.

Many times

Maybe you are in your own Egypt today—not the literal country but the same kind of circumstance Israel found itself in. Someone near you has become like the Pharaoh, "who did not know about Joseph" (Exodus 1:8). The person or circumstance you were very comfortable with has now become intolerable and cruel. You're being spoken to with a "foreign tongue" (v. 1)—the words are cold and harsh.

You feel more like a ruin than God's sanctuary, more decimated than a part of God's dominion (v. 2).

Our life experience often replicates that of ancient Israel. We need to move from captivity of Egypt to the Promised Land but our trek is filled with seemingly insurmountable obstacles: a Red Sea (v. 3), a Jordan River (v. 5) and a stretch of dry wilderness in between (v. 8).

The question is: Will you be like the wicked son who asks, "What mean you

³The sea looked and fled, the Jordan turned back; ⁴the mountains skipped like rams, the hills like lambs.

⁵Why was it, O sea, that you fled, O Jordan, that you turned back, ⁶you

by this?" Or will you see yourself singing this psalm as one of those included in the Israel who "came out of Egypt"?

Many assurances

For the people of ancient Israel, the partings of the Red Sea and the Jordan River were earthshaking events (vv. 4,6,7). So also at the death of Jesus the ground shook (Matthew 27:51); and a violent earthquake accompanied His resurrection from the dead (Matthew 28:2).

Jesus sang this psalm the night before He faced the cross. It would be his "hard rock" (v. 8). But He knew from the experience of Israel what God does in difficult or impossible situations. These verses must have filled our Lord with strength and confidence on the night in which He was betrayed.

They're intended to give you peace and hope as well. God will also part obstacles before you and sustain you in desert-like places.

mountains, that you skipped like rams, you hills, like lambs? [7]Tremble, O earth, at the presence of the Lord, at the presence of the God of Jacob, [8]who turned the rock into a pool, the hard rock into springs of water.

Prayer of response

Lord Jesus, I do not want to be the wicked son who excludes himself from what You have done. I thank You for the Red Seas You part in my own life, for the Wildernesses in which You give me water, and for the Jordans You open in order that I might enter a place of promise and potential.

My thoughts on Psalm 114 . . .

The Lord Remembers

I was a gangly 16-year-old when our large church got a new pastor, J.L. McQueen. As I exited the sanctuary, he asked my name and I told him.

Several Sundays later I headed out a different door, and there was the new pastor. Several hundred other young people were in the church; I knew he wouldn't remember my name. With a friendly voice and firm grip, he shook my hand and said, "Hi, George."

How did he remember my name? I asked myself, and then I asked my friends. They all reported the same experience. Pastor McQueen remembered everybody's name.

Almost 30 years went by. I was back in the church of my teen years for a homecoming. Pastor, now retired, had come back. After his sermon that morning, I watched an old couple with walkers edge their way through the crowd to greet him.

The little old man lifted his bent head and in a quavering voice said, "Pastor, you probably don't remember us—"

Before he could say another word, Pastor McQueen folded them both into his long arms and endearingly said, "Oh, Bill and Mary, how could I ever forget you?"

The way Pastor related to Bill and Mary—that he had not forgotten them—is how Psalm 115 tells us God relates to us.

¹Not to us, O Lord, not to us but to your name be the glory, because of your love and faithfulness. ²Why do the nations say, "Where is their God?"

The taunts and doubts

The first eight verses of the psalm respond directly to the question, "Where is your God?" (v. 2), as though

159

God has forgotten His people.

That question doesn't faze you when everything's going well. It does bother when you are in distress and need, vulnerable and seemingly powerless. You may feel the Lord is not doing much for you. You suffer the same outrageous blows of misfortune and fate as those who do not know or love Him.

The enemies of Israel evidently have a momentary upper hand as this psalm was written and are taunting Israel about its loyalty to an unseen God. Buttressed by the security of gods (idols) they could see, they throw the insinuation, "If you are so sure God loves you, why are you suffering? Why doesn't your God make himself visible?"

This third of the *Hallel* (praise) psalms, which in all likelihood Jesus sang in the Upper Room before He went to Gethsemane, makes this powerful answer: "Our God is in heaven; he does whatever pleases him" (v. 3). Is it any wonder, that fresh from reciting this psalm, Jesus was able to say yes to "Thy will be done" (Matthew 6:10).

The psalmist turns the argument of his enemies against them by saying, in effect, "So you want me to serve visible gods? Well, why don't you take a closer look? My God, who is unseen, is alive. Your gods, which you can see, are dead!" (vv. 4–8).

Trust and blessing

From verse nine to the conclusion, this psalm calls upon you to deepen your walk with God by depending wholly upon Him.

Do you need assistance or protection? Whether you are an ordinary believer

³Our God is in heaven; he does whatever pleases him.

⁴But their idols are silver and gold, made by the hands of men. ⁵They have mouths, but cannot speak, eyes, but they cannot see; ⁶they have ears, but cannot hear, noses, but they cannot smell; ⁷they have hands, but cannot feel, feet, but they cannot walk; nor can they utter a sound with their throats. ⁸Those who make them will be like them, and so will all who trust in them. ⁹O house of Israel, trust in the Lord — he is their help and shield. ¹⁰O house of Aaron, trust in the Lord — he is their

("house of Israel") or a priest ("house of Aaron"), three successive verses remind you He is your help and shield (vv. 9–11).

The Lord never forgets you—He is committed to blessing you (v. 12). Whether you are well-known or unknown, you have His favor when you reverence Him (v. 13).

On the night He was betrayed, Jesus could have read into the events of that evening the idea that the Father had abandoned Him. However, our Lord did not take His cue from the external but from the Eternal.

The blessed person does not shrink or shrivel away (vv. 14,15). The Cross did not diminish Jesus. He emerged from death, himself blessed and blessing us with the gift of eternal life. Likewise, God wants you to emerge from taunts and doubts with such strength you will be a marvelous resource and encouragement to others.

The highest heavens belong to Him (v. 16), but your feet are still on earth. If the dead don't praise Him (v. 17), then you establish the fact you are alive by extolling Him "now and forevermore" (v. 18).

help and shield. [11]You who fear him, trust in the Lord — he is their help and shield.

[12]The Lord remembers us and will bless us: He will bless the house of Israel, He will bless the house of Aaron, [13]he will bless those who fear the Lord — small and great alike.

[14]May the Lord make you increase, both you and your children. [15]May you be blessed by the Lord, the Maker of heaven and earth.

[16]The highest heavens belong to the Lord, but the earth he has given to man. [17]It is not the dead who praise the Lord, those who go down to silence; [18]it is we who extol the Lord, both now and forevermore. Praise the Lord.

Prayer of response

Lord Jesus, thank You for remembering me. I am so tempted to interpret You by my circumstances and to falsely think that hardship means You're down on me as well. I receive the encouragement that You know fully who I am and remain committed to blessing me.

My thoughts on Psalm 115 . . .

When the Trial is Over

A little girl asked her Sunday school teacher why Jesus first came to His disciples in the garden and said, "Watch and pray," but the last time He just said, "Sleep on and take your rest." (See Matthew 26:41–45.)

The teacher did not immediately respond. Then the child spoke again. "I think I know. It was because Jesus had seen the face of His Father and He didn't need their help anymore."

In Psalm 116, this fourth of the *Hallel* (praise) psalms—which Jesus most likely sang with His disciples after the Last Supper—fervent thanksgiving is offered to the Lord for a recent deliverance from trial. As Jesus entered His deepest valley of suffering, this testimony of the psalmist served as an encouragement that all will end well also for Him.

If you believe the Scripture that endurance, character, and hope issue from suffering (Romans 5:3–5) and that God works good in all things (Romans 8:28), then let this psalm encourage you even if you are in a severe personal trial. The psalm tells how you'll feel when you're on safe ground again.

Desperate need

¹I love the Lord, for he heard my voice; he heard my cry for mercy. ²Because he turned his ear to me, I will call on him as long as I live.

You cry when you hurt so badly you don't have words to describe the pain. You never cry alone. God listens to your grief. You will always love best the One who stands with you in your moment of greatest need (vv. 1,2).

163

Jesus experienced the powerful entangling pull of death into the grave (v. 3). Your trial may be dragging you into a grave of depression and hopelessness. Keep taking the antidote: "Then I called on the name of the Lord: 'O Lord, save me!'" (v. 4).

The Lord may not save you from your dilemma all at once. (See Exodus 13:17; 23:29,30.) He may untie the knots of entangling cords one at a time. But because He is gracious, righteous, and full of compassion, you can count on His help (vv. 5,6).

Wonderful deliverance

Affliction brings disquiet. When the storm is over, like the psalmist, you may talk to yourself in an atmosphere of peace (v. 7; see also Mark 4:39).

The psalmist looks back upon his harrowing passage. Death stared him in the face. He wept, lost his footing, knew great affliction and didn't trust anyone (vv. 8–11).

Too often we look to human resources for answers to our dilemmas. Today the Lord is calling you to trust Him and Him alone. You know your trial is deep if the Lord is the only One who could pull you out.

Will you imitate the psalmist by placing the words "I believe" before your lament, "I am greatly afflicted" (v. 10)? Then, look to the face of the Father.

Promises remembered

How do we thank God after He brings us out of a tough spot (v. 12)?

The psalmist keeps the promises he made to the Lord while he was in trial.

³The cords of death entangled me, the anguish of the grave came upon me; I was overcome by trouble and sorrow. ⁴Then I called on the name of the Lord: "O Lord, save me!"

⁵The Lord is gracious and righteous; our God is full of compassion. ⁶The Lord protects the simplehearted; when I was in great need, he saved me.

⁷Be at rest once more, O my soul, for the Lord has been good to you.

⁸For you, O Lord, have delivered my soul from death, my eyes from tears, my feet from stumbling, ⁹that I may walk before the Lord in the land of the living.

¹⁰I believed; therefore I said, "I am greatly afflicted." ¹¹And in my dismay I said, "All men are liars."

¹²How can I repay the Lord for all his goodness to me? ¹³I will lift up the cup of

Thus, he goes to the temple for presentation of the drink and meat offerings of thanks (vv. 13-19).

As followers of Jesus, we bring a different kind of sacrifice: the continual offering of our life to the Lord, our praise, and doing good to others (1 Peter 2:5; Hebrews 13:15,16).

One phrase, often lifted from this section for comfort at funerals, is, "Precious in the sight of the Lord is the death of his saints" (v. 15). The more likely translation is, "Costly in the sight of the Lord is the death of his saints." If this is the meaning intended, it's the psalmist's way of linking us with the Lord's purposes by stating that our removal from the human scene is costly to God's work on earth. It's a supporting argument for our plea of rescue to God, "Please let me live a while longer because there's work I have to do for You that won't get done without me."

When God delivers us, it is appropriate to consider ourselves as freed from chains that we might be more effectively God's servants (v. 16). A grateful heart of surrender to the Lord leads to freely flowing praise and thanksgiving (vv. 17–19).

salvation and call on the name of the Lord. [14]I will fulfill my vows to the Lord in the presence of all his people. [15]Precious in the sight of the Lord is the death of his saints. [16]O Lord, truly I am your servant; I am your servant, the son of your maidservant; you have freed me from my chains.

[17]I will sacrifice a thank offering to you and call on the name of the Lord. [18]I will fulfill my vows to the Lord in the presence of all his people, [19]in the courts of the house of the Lord — in your midst, O Jerusalem. Praise the Lord.

Prayer of response

Lord Jesus, You pay attention to my cry for help. You mount a rescue operation. When I have no one else to trust, You do not fail me. As Your servant, I relinquish my life to You. Let my living have purpose—for Your good pleasure.

My thoughts on Psalm 116 . . .

Love and Faithfulness

A television talk show host recently interviewed a bride who was stood up at the church on her wedding day, with 250 guests waiting. Now months downline from being stood up, the jilted bride hesitated when asked, "Do you still love him?"

With a tear or two she admitted she still had feelings for him, but didn't know if she could ever trust him again.

The host advised: "Listen the first time to what a person tells you, not by what they say—but what they do. For what they do is what they really are."

Here's the shortest chapter in the Bible—Psalm 117—and it tells us who God is by what He does.

> ¹Praise the Lord, all you nations; extol him, all you peoples.

The psalm invites all the nations to praise and extol the Lord. He's not the God limited to one family, clan, tribe, or nation. His love and faithfulness–two aspects of His character celebrated in this psalm—are for all.

God's love is great

Some things seem too good to be true, but remain true nevertheless. That's the way it is with God's love.

For many years I could not really believe God loved me personally. He was too holy and I too sinful. My service to Him came from a sense of duty.

167

I rationally believed Christ truly died for my sins and rose again from the dead, but I was utterly confounded at the notion He loved me as an individual. I could envision His love more as a general disposition toward all people, but the thought of Him singling me out as the object of His love remained outside my emotional comprehension.

Thus, the psalm bids us to consider the greatness of His love, a theme fulfilled in the New Testament when we are invited to exclaim, "How great is the love the Father has lavished on us, that we should be called the children of God" (1 John 3:1).

His love is immediate. Jesus does not stand you in a corner and say, "I want to look you over. Can you do Me any good? Are you worth My love? Let me think awhile before I decide whether I should love you."

Oh, no. Whether you're a rich young ruler, a woman with a checkered past, a young person with a future, an old woman with a need; whether you have or lack potential, whether your personality sparkles or fizzles, whether you're colorful or bland; whatever your age, gender, race, culture, or politics—He loves you without hesitation.

His love endures. God doesn't fall in love with you only to fall out again. The word "great" (v. 2) in the Hebrew carries this connotation: "The love of God prevails." It never wavers, tires, or gives up on you. Peter denied Him and all the others forsook Him, but Jesus never stopped loving them. He loves even His enemies. You don't hear Him say on the cross, "I'll get even with you"; but, rather, "Father, forgive them" (Luke 23:34).

2For great is his love toward us, and the faithfulness of the Lord endures forever. Praise the Lord.

God's faithfulness is eternal

Derek Kidner, in his commentary on this psalm, explains the phrase, "God's faithfulness is eternal." He says, "God's plans and promises are as fresh and intact now as on the day they were made, and they will remain so."

A raft of New Testament passages flesh out the many dimensions of the Lord's faithfulness. Because He is faithful, He can be relied upon

- To strengthen and protect you from the evil one (2 Thessalonians 3:3).
- To not let you be tempted beyond what you can bear (1 Corinthians 10:13).
- To remain faithful even when you're not (2 Timothy 2:11–13).
- To forgive you when you sin (1 John 1:9).
- To present you blameless on the day of our Lord Jesus Christ (1 Corinthians 1:8,9; 1 Thessalonians 5:23,24).

We should take this advice when it comes to the Lord: "Listen the first time to what a person tells you, not by what they say—but what they do. For what they do is what they really are."

God is love. God is faithful. Everything He does tells you who He is.

Prayer of response

Lord Jesus, You do not leave me when I am no longer charming or scintillating; when I am ill or in distress; when pot holes crop up in my personality. You do not love me because I am flawless—You and I both know better. You love me through all my imperfections and in spite of them. You are ever faithful to me, dear Lord.

My thoughts on Psalm 117 . . .

Straight Ahead!

As the last psalm in the *Hallel* series, Psalm 118 provides us the text of the last words of corporate worship Jesus shared with His disciples before His death.

At any time prior to His arrest that evening, Jesus could have fled up and over the Olivet hill and lost himself in the Judean desert, but He had long ago resolutely set His face toward the cross (Luke 9:51; Revelation 13:8).

Perhaps today you have a choice between running away or advancing straight ahead into the most difficult situation you have ever faced. If the Lord is directing you to go forward, then let the mind of Jesus—reflected in this psalm—be in you.

Confidence in God

> [5]In my anguish I cried to the Lord, and he answered by setting me free. [6]The Lord is with me; I will not be afraid. What can man do to me? [7]The Lord is with me; he is my helper. I will look in triumph on my enemies.

In the hours ahead of Him, Jesus faced the betrayal of Judas, the listlessness and apathy of the disciples, their flight from danger, Peter's denial, flogging and insult, horrific despondency (Luke 22:39–46; Psalm 88), a total miscarriage of justice, the torture of crucifixion, the agony of sinbearing, and feeling forsaken by God.

This psalm tells us that Jesus' circumstances did not alter His faith. God is good. His love endures forever.

171

God, our only hope

In Gethsemane, Jesus sought the comfort of His disciples and was keenly disappointed they would not watch with Him for even an hour.

When you cry, no other human may be listening. Like Jesus, you must take comfort and assurance from the fact God hears you (vv. 5–7). As the Lord continues to pray through this psalm, He contemplates the advantage of trusting in God rather than others (vv. 8,9).

Victory rather than defeat

In Gethsemane, Jesus told His disciples He was surrounded with sorrow (Mark 14:34). Perhaps the concept of encirclement was fresh on His mind because this theme dominates verses 10 through 12.

Three times He describes himself as surrounded. The imagery is of an army positioned on all sides against Him or a swarm of bees stinging Him. However, for every mention of the word "surrounded" there is the counterblow of faith. "In the name of the Lord I cut them off" (v. 10).

When you move forward into crises, a season of deep vulnerability or trial, the enemy wants you to think, *I'll never survive this.* Why not take instead these Spirit-inspired words:

"The Lord helped me" (v. 13);

"The Lord is my strength and my song" (v. 14);

"The Lord's right hand is lifted high" (v. 15);

"I will not die but live" (v. 17);

"I will enter [the gates of righteousness]" (v. 19);

"You answered me" (v. 21).

8It is better to take refuge in the Lord than to trust in man. 9It is better to take refuge in the Lord than to trust in princes.

10All the nations surrounded me, but in the name of the Lord I cut them off.

13I was pushed back and about to fall, but the Lord helped me. 14The Lord is my strength and my song; he has become my salvation. 15Shouts of joy and victory resound in the tents of the righteous: The Lord's right hand has done mighty things!

17I will not die but live, and will proclaim what the Lord has done. 19Open for me the gates of righteousness; I will enter and give thanks to the Lord. 21I will give you

Vindication

Jesus knew that the rejection from others was part of the Father's plan to elevate Him. Thus, He could say, "This is the day the Lord has made; let us rejoice and be glad in it" (v. 24).

Finally, this psalm ends with the theme of procession. On the eve of Calvary, Jesus looked forward to the future procession into heaven itself (v. 28; Ephesians 4:7–10).

The final words of worship spoken in the Last Supper are these: "Give thanks to the Lord, for he is good; his love endures forever" (v. 29). Will you go straight ahead into your trial with these words on your heart and lips?

thanks, for you answered me; you have become my salvation.

²⁴This is the day the Lord has made; let us rejoice and be glad in it.

²⁸You are my God, and I will give you thanks; you are my God, and I will exalt you.

²⁹Give thanks to the Lord, for he is good; his love endures forever. Aleph

Prayer of response

Lord Jesus, I so easily permit entrance into my mind thoughts that are not from You. Help me to learn from Your example that I must fill my heart with right words from Your Word. When dark thoughts assail me or sadness fills me up, grant me perspective to meditate upon and declare the everlasting truth of Your goodness and love.

My thoughts on Psalm 118 . . .

A Fixed Reference Point

O n April 13, 1970, the flight of the moon-bound Apollo 13 suffered an onboard explosion, crippling the spacecraft.

The astronauts' survival depended on correcting a return trajectory that doomed them to skip earth and perish in space. With insufficient battery power, Commander Jim Lovell could not rely on the sophisticated computerized navigational instruments to realign Apollo 13. He had to fly the ship for a 14-second manual burn while keeping the distant marble of Planet Earth in the crosshairs of his small spacecraft window.

During the burn, Apollo 13 jumped and jittered while the crew finessed the engine thrusters so Lovell could keep earth in view. The maneuver worked. The astronauts returned home because Lovell kept his eye on the fixed reference point.

Psalm 119, the longest chapter in the Bible, tells us that our journey through life must similarly be lived by looking at a fixed reference point—God' s Word.

Each of the psalm's 22 stanzas begins with a succeeding letter of the Hebrew alphabet, the A to Z in why and how the Bible forms the basis for our trajectory through life. As an acrostic, the psalm resembles more a strand of equal-sized pearls than a spiral staircase where one step builds upon another.

You will find in each stanza at least one problem, distress, or need—life's "onboard explosions "—and the remedy theme, too.

Aleph (vv. 1–8). You look at God's standards and honestly know you don't measure up (v. 5). Keep reaching to live the ideals given in the Bible.

Beth (vv. 9–16). Are you young (v. 9)? Don't let your friends dictate how you act—take God's advice instead.

Gimel (vv. 17–24). Don't permit the bad example of a leader (v. 23) to become your excuse for not seeking or loving God's way.

Daleth (vv. 25–32). When depression overwhelms you (v. 28) keep coming to the Word for strength.

He (vv. 33–40). Reexamine your priorities and goals (vv. 36,37). Living by the Book will keep you from treasuring selfish gain or pursuing worthless things.

Waw (vv. 41–48). When someone verbally denigrates you (v. 42) keep in mind God's love. Gain the freedom that comes from doing right. Let God-talk come out of your mouth.

Zayin (vv. 49–56). Find comfort in God's promises when you are made to feel like a nobody (v. 53).

Heth (vv. 57–64). Whose anger or injustice has tied you up in knots (v. 61)? Sing God's truth even at the midnight hour.

Teth (vv. 65–72). Has your good reputation been smeared (v. 69)? Don't be distracted from serving God and loving His Word.

Yodh (vv. 73–80). Have you been cheated, taken advantage of without cause (v. 78)? Don't live that way yourself.

Kaph (vv. 81–88). Discouraged because you've prayed, waited, and God still hasn't acted (vv. 81,84)? Don't give up on God's promises—they'll save your life.

Lamedh (vv. 89–96). Problems so heavy you feel you won't make it (v. 92)? A determined enemy (v. 95)? Delight in God's Word as a ballast against the pressure.

Mem (vv. 97–104). Resist the temptations to make choices that put you on the wrong path (v. 101). Cherish what God wants. Let His counsel be as tasty as your favorite candy bar.

⁵Oh, that my ways were steadfast in obeying your decrees!

⁹How can a young man keep his way pure? By living according to your word.

²³Though rulers sit together and slander me, your servant will meditate on your decrees.

²⁸My soul is weary with sorrow; strengthen me according to your word.

³⁶Turn my heart toward your statutes and not toward selfish gain.

⁴²I will answer the one who taunts me, for I trust in your word.

⁵³Indignation grips me because of the wicked, who have forsaken your law.

⁶¹Though the wicked bind me with ropes, I will not forget your law.

⁶⁹Though the arrogant have smeared me with lies, I keep your precepts with all my heart.

⁷⁸May the arrogant be put to shame for wronging me without cause; but I will meditate on your precepts.

⁸¹My soul faints with longing for your salvation, but I have put my hope in your word.

⁹²If your law had not been my delight, I would have perished in my affliction. ⁹⁵The

Nun (vv. 105–112). You don't see any overnight solutions to a long-range problem (v. 107)? Trust God anyway.

Samekh (vv. 113–120). Bothered by people who say one thing and do another (v. 113)? Don't become like them. Love God's Word and live without deceit.

Ayin (vv. 121–128). Concerned you won't be rewarded for doing right (v. 121)? Never mind—keep your eye instead on what God wants you to do.

Pe (vv. 129–136). Has a particular sin acquired power over you? Pray for God to break its rule (v. 133), that your longing to do right will far outstrip your urges to do wrong.

Tsadhe (vv. 137–144). You've been unselfish with your time and talent and now feel worn out (v. 139) and unappreciated (v. 141)? Draw fulfillment from living the way God wants.

Qoph (vv. 145–152). Who's cooking up plans to cheat you or is out to get you (v. 150)? Depend on God's Word and presence when others have been proven wholly unreliable.

Resh (vv. 153–160). Don't let the bad times (v. 153) or the disobedience of others (v. 158) destroy your hope in God's help or determination to follow God's words.

Sin and Shin (vv. 161–168). Persecuted for your faith? Consider what you still possess: God's promises and great peace.

Taw (vv. 169–176). You never intended to backslide or turn away from God? Like a sheep, you carelessly strayed from the Shepherd and His flock (v. 176)? Come back to your senses and live like God wants you to.

wicked are waiting to destroy me, but I will ponder your statutes.

¹⁰¹I have kept my feet from every evil path so that I might obey your word.

¹⁰⁷I have suffered much; preserve my life, O Lord, according to your word.

¹¹³I hate double-minded men, but I love your law.

¹²¹I have done what is righteous and just; do not leave me to my oppressors.

¹³³Direct my footsteps according to your word; let no sin rule over me.

¹³⁹My zeal wears me out, for my enemies ignore your words.

¹⁴¹Though I am lowly and despised, I do not forget your precepts.

¹⁵⁰Those who devise wicked schemes are near, but they are far from your law.

¹⁵³Look upon my suffering and deliver me, for I have not forgotten your law. ¹⁵⁸I look on the faithless with loathing, for they do not obey your word.

¹⁶²I rejoice in your promise like one who finds great spoil.

¹⁷⁶I have strayed like a lost sheep. Seek your servant, for I have not forgotten your commands.

Prayer of response

Lord Jesus, thank You for Your Word which gives me a fixed reference point, keeping me on course with a right heart, right attitudes, and right conduct.

My thoughts on Psalm 119 . . .

Too Long in the Wrong Place

A young couple, fresh in the ministry, sat at their piano and composed the melody and words to this well-known and loved invitational hymn, "Room at the Cross."

The husband, Ira Stanphill, went on to write many gospel songs; but, the bride who sat with him that day, Zelma—herself a preacher's daughter—soon began frequenting nightclubs. Five years after leaving Ira, driving with her manager after a late nightclub singing engagement, she was killed in an auto accident.

We don't know if, in her dying moments, she made it back to the Cross, the place "where there's still room for one." From all appearances, she stayed too long in the wrong location.

Psalm 120 is the first of 15 psalms of ascent—the songs pilgrims sang during festival seasons as they made the steep climb up the Jericho road from 1,200 feet below sea level to the 2,400-foot-high city of Jerusalem.

These ascent psalms begin with the words of one who decided he had stayed too long in the wrong place, and the time had come for him to embark on the journey back to God.

The psalmist tells us what triggered his decision to begin the pilgrimage home.

> [1]I call on the Lord in my distress, and he answers me.

Personal pain

How blessed we are when God permits enough spiritual discomfort that we are ready to decide to get out of the place we're in. The prodigal son never started toward Father until the pain of remaining became greater than the pain of going home (Luke 15:17-20).

Martin Luther reminds us the central mission of Jesus is to help us in such a moment: "Jesus never gave himself for our righteousness, but He did give himself for our sins. The first link between my soul and Jesus Christ is not my goodness, but my badness; not my merit, but my misery, not my standing, but my fallings; not my riches, but my need. He comes to visit His people, not to admire their beauties, but to remove their deformities; not to reward their virtues, but to forgive their sins."

Disappointment with others

Whom did you place your confidence in only to find out later it was all a trick? Is your life messed up because that trusted person lied to you and for a good period of time pulled the wool over your eyes? You never spotted their duplicity. You were so naive.

The psalmist knows the path back to personal spiritual health lies in asking God for help (v. 2). A victim often never gets to "unload" on the one who hurt him or her, so the only alternative is to engage the victimizer in imaginary conversation (v. 3). In the flush of anger, you may also wish God would stick and burn your antagonist (v. 4).

You'll do better if you turn that anger into forgiveness (Matthew 6:14,15).

A decision to move on

Jesus said that no one can serve two masters (Matthew 6:24). You can't alter-

²Save me, O Lord, from lying lips and from deceitful tongues.

³What will he do to you, and what more besides, O deceitful tongue? ⁴He will punish you with a warrior's sharp arrows, with burning coals of the broom tree.

nate between the old life one moment and the new life the next. The psalmist rues the length of time he lived with a split personality, "Woe to me that I dwell in Meschech, that I live among the tents of Kedar!" (v. 5).

Actually Meschech and Kedar form two geographical polarities in the dispersion of the Jews: Meschech to the far north (Ezekiel 39:1); and Kedar, the second born to Ishmael who settled to the south near the border of Egypt—a clan described as "living in hostility toward all their brothers" (Genesis 25:13,18; compare with vv. 5,6).

The psalmist wanted to let go of his Ishmaelite split personality which put him in a location halfway between the Jerusalem of promise and the Egypt of bondage.

Are you having a terrible time getting unified again? The world pulls you in one direction, and the Holy Spirit tugs at you in another? It's your choice which pull prevails.

The pilgrim's journey begins with this psalm. Whether you are far north or far south, you must decide to leave the place of pain or compromise. The poet said it well:

> There is a place I know not where
> A time I know not when
> Which marks the destiny of men
> To heaven or despair

You're "valley low" when you begin. How will you ever get up the hill, on top? Follow the example of this psalmist. He began his ascent by letting God know he wanted out. He put his heart in the right direction even before his feet had climbed the first step upward.

5Woe to me that I dwell in Meshech, that I live among the tents of Kedar! 6Too long have I lived among those who hate peace. 7I am a man of peace; but when I speak, they are for war.

Prayer of response

Lord Jesus, I too have pitched my tent in the wrong place. No matter how far away or low down I am today, I'm choosing to move toward You. I can't continue living as I have. I need Your help to change.

My thoughts on Psalm 120 . . .

Four Fears

Psalm 121

With my daughter and son, then ages 14 and 12, we set out for a brief summer morning stroll down a path from the southern rim into America's Grand Canyon. So rapid and enjoyable was our descent that before we knew it we had reached Indian Gardens—a drop of 4,000 feet on four-and-one-half miles of switchback trails.

We should have paid attention to all the hikers struggling on the upward climb; instead, we bantered among ourselves about how out of shape they were.

How foolish. By the end of the afternoon my wife, who had remained behind, was just about to call for the rescue squad when we rounded the final bend.

I learned two lessons that day: it's easier to go down than up; never underestimate the difficulty of the climb.

The psalmist had no such miscalculation. In Psalm 120 he began his pilgrim journey of ascent to Zion by deciding he had remained too long in the wrong place. Now in Psalm 121, he stood in the Jericho Valley 1,200 feet below sea level and gazed upward to the mountains around Jerusalem. A long, tough climb lay ahead.

You are no match for the difficulty

¹I lift up my eyes to the hills — where does my help come from?

The psalmist immediately concludes he can't make the ascent on his own power. So, he asks, "Where will my help come from?"

183

Don't make the mistake of thinking verse 1 teaches your help comes from the hills. Not so. The hills are against you—they're the problem, not the solution.

Perhaps you face an insurmountable obstacle today. Your problems appear as big as a mountain; your answers, the size of a molehill. Don't let the difficulty become bigger than God. Instead, declare your faith, "My help comes from the Lord" (v. 1).

²My help comes from the Lord, the Maker of heaven and earth.

You won't make it

The psalmist worries about his foot slipping. Such could be a momentary setback, resulting in a serious injury, or far worse, a fatal fall.

Are you slipping today? Into grief? Depression? Feelings of worthlessness? Are you saying to yourself, *What's the use? I've tried and tried and it doesn't make any difference. I might just as well give up.*

From his exile as a prisoner on the island of Patmos, the apostle John keys in on the same concept as the psalmist. John sees the Lord Jesus securely holding the "angels" (i.e., messengers or leaders) of the Church (Revelation 1:20). Jesus will not let go of you (v. 3). He's on guard round the clock. When you sleep, He doesn't (v. 4).

³He will not let your foot slip — he who watches over you will not slumber; ⁴indeed, he who watches over Israel will neither slumber nor sleep.

You are vulnerable and unprotected

Five times in this short psalm the word "watch" is used of God's care for you. It means far more than the Lord looking *at you.* He's looking *out* for you, guarding and protecting you from the hardships and terrors of the trail, including exposure to sun and moon.

He knows when the sun, the heat of circumstances, is too much for you. He will give you shade. But, He also knows when the moon tears at your viscera— when it brings you haunting memories of an action which caused you great injury, of someone close who shattered your love and trust or preceded you in death. He won't let that "moon by night" harm you.

You ask yourself if God will really come through

The potential disasters on the pilgrim climb to Zion are: the difficulty of the ascent itself (v. 1), a slip or fall (v. 3) and exposure (v. 6). Lest any danger be omitted, the psalm closes with a promise the Lord will keep you from *all* harm (v. 7) at *all* times (v. 8).

You may not understand how the Lord spared you from harm until you have gained the perspective that can only come through time and distance. Remember, it wasn't until Easter morning that the preceding Friday was called good.

⁵The Lord watches over you ⁶the sun will not harm you by day, nor the moon by night.

⁷The Lord will keep you from all harm — he will watch over your life; ⁸the Lord will watch over your coming and going both now and forevermore.

Prayer of response

Lord Jesus, I am having trouble on the climb. If You do not help me, I won't make it. My fears often overwhelm my faith. I know it should be the other way around. I take this moment to still my heart and honestly say, "I trust You." I hear You answer, "I am with you."

My thoughts on Psalm 121 . . .

Dream City

I n the seventh of his Chronicles of Narnia, a book entitled *The Last Battle,* C.S. Lewis closes with this observation:

"The things that began to happen after that were so great and beautiful that I cannot write them. And for us this is the end of all the stories, and we can most truly say that they all lived happily ever after. But for them it was only the beginning of the real story. All their life in this world and all their adventures in Narnia had only been the cover and the title page; now at last they were beginning Chapter One of the Great Story, which no one on earth has read: which goes on forever: in which every chapter is better than the one before."

Just as C.S. Lewis transported his characters from time into eternity, so Psalm 122, this third psalm of ascent imaginatively helicopters us from our struggle on the trail far below directly into the city where "every chapter is better than the one before."

¹I rejoiced with those who said to me, Let us go to the house of the Lord."

If the 15 psalms of ascent were recited sequentially by pilgrims on the two-day climb from the Jordan Valley up to Jerusalem, then this psalm comes long before the city was entered or even lay in view.

Why then is this psalm here, near the beginning of the psalms of ascent rather than the end? Because if you are going to reach the top, you must keep alive the faith of actually getting there.

I call this a dream psalm because, although the psalmist is just starting the

187

difficult upward trail, in spirit he's already been to the top of the mountain. He's refreshing himself in the present toil by drawing from the well of future gladness (v. 1). He's stabilizing his slipping feet (Psalm 121:3) by visioning the coming time when he will stand safe within the gates of God's own city (v. 2).

Here's what life in that city is like:

Security and a strong sense of community

Jerusalem is closely compacted together, making it easy to defend. It's not like the wilderness or the suburbs, where you're either alone or don't know the person living next door.

Although we often picture heaven as a renewed Eden, it's biblical also to envision it as a city (Revelation 21:2). In that glorious urban environment we'll never be lonely or vulnerable again. The comradeship begun in the old Jerusalem with the Early Church, where they "devoted themselves . . . to the fellowship" (Acts 2:42), will be complete in the new Jerusalem.

Unity of worship

"The tribes go up" (v. 4). Shall we also say that those belonging to different denominations, the "tribes" in Jesus' kingdom, also go up?

I may walk today with a limited number of brothers and sisters under our church banner, but in that day all God's people will be waving the same flag.

There, the Lord's name is praised. There'll be no reserve or ingratitude, just thanksgiving and adoration for the One

²Our feet are standing in your gates, O Jerusalem.
³Jerusalem is built like a city that is closely compacted together.

⁴That is where the tribes go up, the tribes of the Lord, to praise the name of the Lord according to the statute given to Israel.

who saved us by His blood.

Justice

Thrones are there—not just any throne, but those of David. The Son of David, Jesus Christ our Lord, sits on that glorious throne (Matthew 19:29), never to be toppled by another (Hebrews 1:8). His throne of judgment (Revelation 20:11) becomes a throne of grace (Hebrews 4:6) to all those who believe in Him.

Prayer for that city

What's the use of climbing the trail to Jerusalem if, during the course of your pilgrimage, the city fell to its enemies?

Pilgrims to the New Jerusalem don't need to pray for that city. It's secure. Neither sin, death, nor the devil can ever get inside.

As citizens of the heavenly Jerusalem, we pray instead that the peace, security, and prosperity of our eternal dwelling place will come to us while we remain on the trail below.

⁵There the thrones for judgment stand, the thrones of the house of David. ⁶Pray for the peace of Jerusalem: May those who love you be secure. ⁷May there be peace within your walls and security within your citadels." ⁸For the sake of my brothers and friends, I will say, "Peace be within you." ⁹For the sake of the house of the Lord our God, I will seek your prosperity.

Prayer of response

Lord Jesus, let the peace of Jerusalem enter me today. Take away the stress and distress. Let me be as whole today down here as Jerusalem is above. Thank You for preparing and bringing me to a city that is even better than my dreams.

My thoughts on Psalm 122 . . .

Right Focus

Psalm 123

A farmer and his 16-year-old son were plowing when a bullhorn from the house summoned with an urgent message. The boy begged to operate the tractor alone. Dad relented with this clear instruction: "Son, the key to plowing a straight furrow lies in picking out an object across the field, then steadily driving the tractor in that direction."

When the father returned 20 minutes later, he was horrified at the squiggly s-shaped furrows. "Son," he remonstrated, "I told you the key to plowing straight furrows was keeping your eye on a distant object and plowing straight toward it."

Tearfully the boy answered, "Dad, I did just what you told me, but there was no way I could get that cow to stand still."

Perhaps along with that teenager, and the psalmist, you are finding it difficult to stay focused on the right thing.

Which direction are you looking?

1I lift up my eyes to you, to you whose throne is in heaven.

You're on the pilgrim trail of ascent to Zion, but periodically you look down on the valley floor and think about turning back to the old places you chose to leave (Psalm 120:5,6). Then, when you look up, the difficulties looming over you are formidable and, without God's help, insurmountable (Psalm 121). You take a momentary flight of fancy into your final goal (Psalm 122) but quickly find yourself again toiling on the upward climb, still far below your ultimate destination (Psalm 123).

The psalmist knows he's having trouble with a fixed gaze. He needs an anchoring orientation. He began the second psalm of ascent by lifting his eyes to the hills (Psalm 121:1). He quickly determines to transfer his gaze from the difficult circumstances to God himself. He repeats that lesson here in beginning the psalm by focusing not on the mountains, but the Lord.

How closely are you looking?

Because the psalmist worships, however, his heart does not look at God through a telescope. The Lord is not a distant object, but a Presence so near that he can read God's intentions for him as clearly as a slave or maid reads the body language of owner or employer (v. 2). A familiar gesture is given—a clapped or clenched hand, a pointing finger—and instantly the master communicates nonverbally what he wants.

Is that how you are in regard to the Lord? Or are you so rebellious, stubborn, or distant that He has to shout at you? Are you looking to God's hand . . . His quiet nonverbal inner ways of ordering your life?

How long will you look?

Notice the phrase, "till he shows us his mercy" (v. 2). Do you work hard for the Master? Your eyes stay glued on Him, and you remain sensitive to the slightest nuance of His day-to-day direction?

Evidently the pilgrim has gone a long period without a break. His endurance and stamina depleted, he gives up wait-

[2]As the eyes of slaves look to the hand of their master, as the eyes of a maid look to the hand of her mistress, so our eyes look to the Lord our God, till he shows us his mercy.

ing for a hand signal to indicate time-out. He asks for it (vv. 3,4).

You might think, based on verses 1 and 2, that the weariness arose because of constant readiness to serve the Lord even as a slave serves a master or a maid serves her mistress. Not so.

Rather, the exhaustion comes from the proud and arrogant. The pilgrim's lament reveals his inner plight: "We have endured much" (v. 4). The Lord's yoke is easy and His burden, light (Matthew 11:30). It's the oppression of burdens or adversaries that wears you down.

The pilgrim does not turn to the afflicting persons or circumstances and request they back off. They wouldn't listen anyway. He asks the Lord for mercy. He does not dictate to the Lord what should be done; he prays only that some relief be given.

Not a word of praise or thanksgiving is found in this psalm. Have some days been like that for you?

It's an effort to move upward and forward. The best you can do is tell the Lord you still have your eyes on Him and need mercy. You feel harassed and your energy depleted. You don't even pray with much faith. You're worn out.

Why not follow the psalmist's example and resolve to keep focused on the Lord "until he shows us his mercy" (v. 2)?

Are you in the Christian journey for the long haul? You'll make it if you keep your eyes on the Lord. (See also Hebrews 12:1,2.)

[3]Have mercy on us, O Lord, have mercy on us, for we have endured much contempt. [4]We have endured much ridicule from the proud, much contempt from the arrogant.

Prayer of response

Thank You, Lord, for giving me psalms of ascent rather than descent. Your pull takes me upward in spite of the strong emotional and spiritual gravitational forces which seek to drag me to the bottom. I may be far down on the trail today, long days of steep climbing before me, but You've got me going in the right direction. I'll do more than look up; I'll look to You.

My thoughts on Psalm 123 . . .

Stark Terror

As a 10-year-old, I dreamed the Lord came and I was left behind. The experience frightened me into asking Jesus into my life.

However, for years after, I lived with a distorted view of His return. The Bible teaches that His coming is our hope. Instead, it was my fear. I knew that salvation was by grace, but I thought Rapture was by works—and I didn't measure up.

Four decades later I dreamed again that the Lord returned. Only this time, I began to lift off. *A mistake has been made,* I thought. *I'm not good enough. The drop to the ground will hurt when the error is discovered.* But, I kept rising—above the tree line and into the deep blue sky. *Oh,* I despaired, *I'm so high now that when they find the mistake, the fall will kill me.*

But, I continued to ascend until the houses below were little dots. There had been no mistake. I woke myself up shouting at the top of my lungs, "I made it! I made it!"

The psalmist in Psalm 124 anticipates declaring that same testimony as he pens this fifth psalm of ascent.

The pilgrim climb from Jericho to Jerusalem held great dangers. Robbers lurked, ready to strip a traveler of clothes, beat him, and leave him for dead. (See Luke 10:30.)

I see the ascent psalms as an encour-

¹If the Lord had not been on our side — let Israel say — ²if the Lord had not been on our side when men attacked us, ³when their anger flared against us, they would

195

agement for all those on their way from spiritual Jericho to spiritual Jerusalem. You'll never make it to the top if the Lord is not on your side.

The psalmist testifies to surviving four stark terrors.

1. Swallowed alive

Peter identifies our real enemy as the devil who "prowls around like a roaring lion looking for someone to devour" (1 Peter 5:8). Our adversary actively seeks opportunity to overwhelm us. His aim is to get us to stop believing, to stop trusting.

We rarely see him as the roaring lion. He comes most often as an angel of light, smiling rather than roaring. However, the Bible tells us that we must not forget his true nature. In contrast to the Lord, he does not care for you. (See 1 Peter 5:7.)

2. Swept away

From his vantage point higher on the trail, the psalmist looks down on the deep *wadi* (ravine) where a flash flood almost cost him his life. What unexpected torrent almost swept you away? You couldn't run fast enough. You had no chance to prepare for what hit you, and no defenses against it.

You made it to safety only because the Lord himself reached in and grabbed you. Perhaps He did not bring you out of the waters all at once. Since He is stronger than the flood, He can remain in it endlessly while holding you. He forced you to learn how to swim, to use spiritual muscles you never knew existed. He made you develop coping skills for sur-

have swallowed us alive; [4]the flood would have engulfed us, the torrent would have swept over us, [5]the raging waters would have swept us away.

viving violent undertows, powerful currents, and towering waves.

3. Chewed on

Picture a child in the grip of a mad dog. What a miracle if that child escapes without dog teeth ever breaking into flesh.

The psalmist recounts the terror of such a moment of vulnerability in his own life.

God controls the jaws gripping you. He won't let them tear you apart.

6Praise be to the Lord, who has not let us be torn by their teeth.

4. Trapped

Famed escape artist Harry Houdini used to boast he could break out of any locked jail cell in the country. Then one day he found himself in a cell he couldn't open. After two hours of intense effort to pick the lock, he slumped against the door in defeat and it swung open. It had been locked only in Houdini's mind.

Are you also mistakenly thinking you are in circumstances with no options and no exit? Then, look again. You have the strongest help possible (v. 8), and He is opening a way of escape (1 Corinthians 10:13).

7We have escaped like a bird out of the fowler's snare; the snare has been broken, and we have escaped. 8Our help is in the name of the Lord, the Maker of heaven and earth.

Prayer of response

Lord Jesus, I am praying today that You will help me emotionally to realize I will not be gulped down, swept away, torn apart, or trapped by any of the dangers facing me. You are stronger than all the terrors of the trail. I'm going to make it because You're not going to drop me.

My thoughts on Psalm 124 . . .

Faith Unshaken

Psalm 125

Anna Spafford stood with her four daughters on the deck of the sinking French liner S.S. *Ville du Havre,* November 22, 1873. Only moments before, on a clear midnight, the English ship *Lochearn* struck and clawed a 30-foot-long and 18-foot-deep hole in the *du Havre.* From impact to sinking, the elapsed time was 12 minutes. Two hundred and twenty-six lives were lost—87 survived.

The 31-year-old mother had immediately headed for a lifeboat with her girls, ages 2 through 11. Panic reigned. She hesitated to race against the others and paused. She asked herself, *Would I be willing to meet these people before the judgment bar of God if I and the girls were to take the seats of those who would never have another chance to hear the gospel?*

At that moment, the main mast crashed down on the lifeboat she would have entered, killing those in it. The *du Havre* began to break up. Annie, the oldest, helped her mother support Tanetta, the youngest, who had her arms wrapped around her mother's neck. Bessie, the second youngest, clutched her mother's knees. Maggie, the second oldest, calmly stood beside her mother and said, "Mama, God will take care of us." Annie added, "Don't be afraid. The sea is His and He made it." Then the water engulfed them.

Anna Spafford's last memory was of her baby being torn violently from her arms by the force of the waters. A plank floated beneath Anna's unconscious body and propelled her to the surface

[1]Those who trust in the Lord are like Mount Zion, which cannot be shaken but endures forever.

where a lifeboat picked her up. But her daughters were gone.

Her first reaction was complete despair. Then, she felt a voice speak to her, "You were spared for a purpose." And immediately she thought of the advice a friend had given her many times, "It's easy to be grateful and good when you have so much, but take care that you are not a fair-weather friend to God."

Nine days later she reached Cardiff, Wales, and cabled back to her lawyer husband in Chicago these two words: "Saved alone."

He immediately boarded a ship to join her in Europe. One night the captain called him to his private cabin. "A careful reckoning has been made," he said, "and I believe we are now passing the place where the *du Havre* was wrecked. The water is three miles deep."

Horatio Spafford went back to his cabin, and on those high seas that night, near the place where his children perished, wrote the hymn later set to music by Dwight Moody's song leader, P.P. Bliss. It begins: "When peace, like a river, attendeth my way, When sorrows like sea billows roll; Whatever my lot, Thou hast taught me to say,'It is well, it is well with my soul.'"

Sometimes we falsely think that the Christian life should carry immunity from disasters like that recounted in the Spafford story. However, shipwrecks, auto crashes, tornadoes, hurricanes, earthquakes, cancer, and the whole host of accidents and illnesses fall upon both believer and unbeliever.

How do you deal with such losses?

In Psalm 125, this sixth psalm of ascent up to Jerusalem, the writer lets us know

[2]As the mountains surround Jerusalem, so the Lord surrounds his people both now and forevermore.

his faith has struggled with that question and prevailed.

Verse 3 telegraphs his trial. A foreign invader now ruled over the land of the righteous. Evil has the upper hand and people of faith waver (i.e., "might use their hands to do evil").

What difficulty seems to have advantage over you?

The psalmist sandwiches his problem (v. 3) in between great affirmations of trust in God (vv. 1,2,4,5). It's always good to put your need, fear, or worry smack-dab in the middle of a prayer which starts with faith and closes with confidence and peace.

This pilgrim prayer provides grips for your faith.

1. *What shakes you up will not shake you apart* (v. 1). When you trust the Lord in the midst of your trial, God will make you as solid as Mount Zion.

2. *Nothing can penetrate God's inner ring of protection for you* (v. 2). Adversity and sorrow can form only the outer circle. God himself becomes your inner perimeter of care and protection. His constant close surrounding is more permanent than even the mountains around Jerusalem.

3. *Watch for the good God will do* (v. 4). I can't explain tragedies like the drowning of the Spafford girls. But I know because Horatio and Anna continued trusting, God gave them a song to bless believers in trial for all time; and, He gave them decades of faithful ministry to the peoples of Jerusalem where they lived the balance of their lives. God will help you overcome evil with good. (See Romans 12:21.)

4. *Bad times must not become an excuse*

³The scepter of the wicked will not remain over the land allotted to the righteous, for then the righteous might use their hands to do evil.

⁴Do good, O Lord, to those who are good, to those who are upright in heart.

for bad conduct (v. 5). It's important to continue living right when everything is going wrong.

Keep these principles of faith and the peace God promised Israel, that He gave the Spaffords and all who trusted Him, will be yours as well.

> ⁵But those who turn to crooked ways the Lord will banish with the evildoers. Peace be upon Israel.

Prayer of response

Lord Jesus, I find it easier to say, "It is well with my soul" when peace like a river attendeth my way than when sorrows like sea billows roll. May I not be a fair-weather friend of Yours. Thank You for stabilizing me when I am shaken and surrounding me when I am defenseless. Help me to go on doing good while I trust You that You always work for my good.

My thoughts on Psalm 125 . . .

Keeping Hope Alive

Psalm 126

As one very nauseated passenger leaned over the rail of the cruise ship, a steward walked by, sized up the situation, and offered encouragement: "You'll be okay. Just remember, no one's ever died yet of seasickness."

The ashen-faced man looked up and replied, "Oh, don't say that. It's only the hope of dying that's keeping me alive."

This psalm is the seventh in a series of 15 psalms of ascent, a collection of prayers by pilgrims on their way up the difficult climb to Jerusalem. Their prayers in upward toil become models for our own struggles to surmount life's difficulties.

Let's face it. Sometimes you are worn out from the struggle of trying to make progress. You feel like the seasick passenger— "When will this be over?"

Don't forget the past

¹When the Lord brought back the captives to Zion, we were like men who dreamed.

I picture the original psalmist writing this prayer about halfway on his climb up to Jerusalem. He's tired and winded, so he walks off the trail a few paces and seats himself on a large boulder. He takes in the panoramic view of the Jordan Valley below, directly east, and remembers those who have made the climb before him.

The psalmist particularly remembers the Jewish exiles who returned from captivity. On their way back to Jerusalem, they had climbed the very same trail. Only a few weeks before their release they languished in Babylon, helpless and perhaps hopeless. Their freedom seemed like a dream (v. 1) that quickly turned to the reality of joy (v. 2) and grateful recognition of what the Lord had done (v. 3).

You can hear the psalmist thinking, *If God did that for them, won't He do the same for me?*

That sort of reflection doesn't seep into our emotions unless we take time to let God's Word speak to us about what God does for His people. He delivers. By faith, you place yourself within the company of those who belong to God, and you say, "He did not release only them. My day is coming."

As a Christian, I find myself on occasion in stark emotional contrast to the joy experienced by those first disciples to whom the risen Jesus appeared. Like the psalmist, I need to find a rock to sit on and view the panoramic sweep of holy history. I have much better vantage than the psalmist because I live A.D. rather than B.C.

Far down below and across the plain I see and hear the distant shouts of joy unspeakable in the tumultuous celebration of those proclaiming the dawn of Grace's golden age, "He is risen!" I see the joy of holy fathers and mothers defiantly shouting their faith out of flaming and consuming fire. The whole plain below fills up with the cries of saints whose victory is won: apostles, evangelists, pastors, doctors, missionaries, healers, teachers, and servants. They are the company of God's liberated men and women. Pain, sorrow, night, anguish— all such is now gone. The sound of their shouts reaches me today. I feel their joy, and it fills me as well.

²Our mouths were filled with laughter, our tongues with songs of joy. Then it was said among the nations, "The Lord has done great things for them." ³The Lord has done great things for us, and we are filled with joy.

There is no night so dark, no pit so deep, no cell so secure that Christ is not in it.

Do remember the future

At the end of the psalm you see the contrast between the present and the promise of things to come. Now the desert—the Negev—the period of desperate thirst. Then streams will flow in the very place where you are now parched.

Now you're not seeing the results of prayer, labor, and continuing to do your best in a tough situation. You presently are limited to sowing, but harvest is coming. Jesus himself tells you that "your grief will turn to joy" (John 16:22).

You are in the moment between "great things He has done" (vv. 1–3) and "songs of joy" (vv. 4–6). Get back on the trail. Continue the upward climb. Now is no time to quit.

4Restore our fortunes, O Lord, like streams in the Negev. 5Those who sow in tears will reap with songs of joy. 6He who goes out weeping, carrying seed to sow, will return with songs of joy, carrying sheaves with him.

Prayer of response

Lord Jesus, I confess I sometimes do not remember well what You have already done for me, nor do I fill up with anticipation over the good things You have in store yet for me. Such forgetfulness only intensifies the emotional and spiritual nausea of the present. Forgive me, Lord. Grief and sorrow are but for a season; the glory You give is eternal.

My thoughts on Psalm 126 . . .

Help From Outside Yourself

Psalm 127

Bart Starr was a great quarterback for the pro football champion Green Bay Packers. When his son, Bart Jr., brought home schoolwork which was well done or a report card with good grades, Bart Starr would tape a dime to the corner as a reward and write next to it, "Good work . . . I believe in you!"

Then the day came when Bart Sr. had a terrible game against a leading opponent. It was one of his all-time worst performances. When he got home from the game that night, he found a note from Bart Jr. with a dime taped to the corner. It simply read, "Dad, I believe in you."

In this eighth of 15 psalms of ascent we are midway on the climb up to Jerusalem. Your geographical location today may be different from the psalmist's; but if you have been journeying upward for some time out of a deep personal valley, you may just want to lie down and quit. You've gone too far to turn around and go back, but you don't think you have the stamina to make it the rest of the way. You won't survive unless help comes from outside yourself.

Who is going to put a note on your heart that says, "I believe in you"?

¹Unless the Lord builds the house, its builders labor in vain. Unless the Lord watches over the city, the watchmen stand guard in vain.

Help from above

The opening verses of this psalm refer to the occupations of builder, watchman, and general laborer. They describe you.

With great effort and skill, you seek

207

to build a life of value. With keen sensitivity to dangers lurking in the distance and the dark, you remain alert. With diligence and long hours, you work hard to make a living. But will you succeed?

Halfway up the trail you honestly don't know. Will there ever be a time when you feel secure and sleep a good night's rest?

I am reminded of the man who sold his property to a developer. After the transfer of title, the new owner showed up with bulldozers, a crane and wrecking ball. "What are you doing?"asked the former owner. "I thought you wanted this."

"Oh," the new owner replied, "I didn't want the buildings, just the land. I'm going to put up something better."

Have you reconciled yourself to the idea that what you wanted built on your life may not come to pass? In fact, what you tried to build may have been demolished by events you had no control over. The important thing is that you are still here even though what you tried to create is not. As an empty lot you may have trouble envisioning the beauty that God will yet place on the property called your life.

This psalm tells you three vital truths about God's personal care: (1) He builds your life. (2) He watches over you. (3) He provides for you.

The encouragement in these first two verses is for you to avoid thinking and acting as though everything depended on you. It doesn't. The Lord is helping you.

²In vain you rise early and stay up late, toiling for food to eat — for he grants sleep to those he loves.

Help from alongside

Even though the Lord loves you, you can still feel very alone and isolated. God knew that when He said of the first human that loneliness was not good.

Pilgrims to Jerusalem traveled together. We get a glimpse of this family event and group travel in the story of Jesus' visit with His parents to Jerusalem at the age of 12 (Luke 2:41–51). The trip gave opportunity for a father to reflect on the blessings of his children as they scampered about him on the journey.

Perhaps you do not have sons or daughters, or your children have not been your "arrows"—i.e., weapons useful against the discouragements of the outside world. Maybe your kids have become more like daggers aimed against your own soul.

How do you apply verses like this when you're childless or your children are distanced from you? Lift your eyes off the word "sons" or "children" and substitute the word "friends" or "family."

The Christian life was not meant to be lived alone. You need the companionship, encouragement, and support of others.

Just as Bart Starr's son said, "I believe in you," so family and friends are weapons ("arrows") helping us defeat discouragement and difficulty. The more "arrows," the better.

³Sons are a heritage from the Lord, children a reward from him. ⁴Like arrows in the hands of a warrior are sons born in one's youth. ⁵Blessed is the man whose quiver is full of them. They will not be put to shame when they contend with their enemies in the gate.

Prayer of response

Lord Jesus, thank You for those special people who are with me and understand the struggle, hardship, and danger of my upward climb. While encouragement comes from them, my real security is in You. Give me strength to take a few more upward steps today.

My thoughts on Psalm 127 . . .

Personal Wellness

Several years ago the syndicated comic strip Frank & Ernest depicted two vagrants sifting against a wall, talking. "Do you believe in fate?" one asked. The second replied, "Sure. I'd hate to think I turned out like this because of something I had control over."

In Psalm 128, this ninth psalm of ascent, the pilgrim is almost two-thirds of the way up the mountain trail to Jerusalem. In the climb of life, he's already grappled with negative circumstances over which he had no control: poor treatment from others (120:2), personal vulnerability (121), blows to self-worth (123:4), danger that threatened survival (124:3–5), and oppression (126:1).

Unlike the Frank & Ernest character, he chose to become a victor rather than a victim. In this psalm he shares principles for personal wellness.

God-centeredness

The starting place and fundamental essential for good living lies in the quality of your relationship with the Lord. People and things may drop in and out of your life, but at your invitation He remains.

Thus, this psalm begins with an expression of reverence and obedience to God himself—"fear the Lord" and "walk in his ways" (v. 1).

The ancient Egyptian astronomer Ptolemy conjectured that the earth was the center of the universe and the heav-

> ¹Blessed are all who fear the Lord, who walk in his ways.

211

ens rotated around it. Twenty centuries later the Polish astronomer Copernicus looked into the heavens through a telescope and announced the earth rotated around the sun. Many persons live with an outdated spiritually Ptolemaic view: "I am the center of all things. They exist to serve me." The Christian ideal expresses itself this way: "Jesus is at the center of my life. I exist to love and serve Him."

Productive behavior

When my daughter left home and moved into her own apartment, she called me one day to come and inspect the window blinds she had installed. She was so proud of handling a new task.

The psalmist knows how rewarding it feels to accomplish something—to "eat the fruit of your labor" (v. 2).

Mentally and spiritually healthy people stay active. A vital key to fighting depression or the doldrums is to do today whatever you would have done had you not been feeling low.

Wholesome core relationships

God-centered and productive people often have the wholesome marriages and families depicted in this psalm. Their children are both "arrows" (Psalm 127:4) and "olive shoots"—eager to conquer what lies before them, but needing tender nourishment all the while.

This psalm doesn't deal with the many exceptions to the rule. Saintly Eli had sons who were scoundrels (1 Samuel 2:12-17,22-25). Godly Hosea had a wife who took up the lifestyle of an adulteress who "never stayed at home," rather than

²You will eat the fruit of your labor; blessings and prosperity will be yours. ³Your wife will be like a fruitful vine within your house; your sons will be like olive shoots around your table. ⁴Thus is the man blessed who fears the Lord.

the faithful mate in this psalm who remained "within [his] house" (Proverbs 7:11; Hosea 3:1).

The Christian life is not designed to be lived alone. Whether it's your biological kin or the body of Christ, pursue close and caring relationships.

As an unmarried person, the apostle Paul never experienced the blessings outlined in these verses. Since he had no children, he couldn't lay claim to an expectation of living long enough to see his grandchildren (see v. 6). But that did not keep him from having a "dear son" in the faith (2 Timothy 1:2) or a core circle of believers for mutual strength and encouragement (see Romans 16).

Optimism about the future

Healthy persons look toward tomorrow with hope. This psalm expects three things: God's blessing, their community's prosperity, and the safe arrival of grandchildren. The New Testament expands our horizon to include eternity, recognizing that some good things we desire may not happen to us on earth.

The apostle Paul wrote his last letter to Timothy while facing imminent execution, most likely through decapitation. There's not a single hint of pessimism in his letter. He might lose his head, but not his crown (2 Timothy 4:8).

What's your outlook on this life and what lies beyond? Even if your circumstances fall far short of the idyllic experience described in this psalm, you can still live with personal wellness and hope.

5May the Lord bless you from Zion all the days of your life; may you see the prosperity of Jerusalem, 6and may you live to see your children's children. Peace be upon Israel.

Prayer of response

Lord Jesus, Your will for me is that I live in shalom (peace)—Your wonderful word for a life that is complete and whole. Mend empty and broken places in me. Grant me the wellness of Your Spirit in my inner being and in my relationships.

My thoughts on Psalm 128 . . .

Outlasting the Adversity

Psalm 129

T he late great American preacher Clarence McCartney recounted ministering at the funeral of a young husband. He stood by the coffin and listened as the young widow poured out her soul in grief. Finally he said to her: "God will give you strength and faith, and out of this will come good."

"No," she answered, "good will not come out of this."

McCartney later reflected that no matter how much God wills it, good would never come to that widow unless she also willed it.

In Psalm 129, this 10th of 15 psalms of ascent, two-thirds of the way up to Jerusalem, the psalmist considers the long-enduring adversity suffered by the people of God from their enemies. Perhaps you are in the same situation—what Eugene Peterson calls "a long obedience." You have found no quick answers or short-cut solutions for an ever-present problem, and you doubt good will ever arrive.

Surviving

Some things are so hard that you find it difficult not to repeat how hurt you feel. That's what the psalmist does. He opens, "They have greatly oppressed me from my youth"; then stops and asks for his listeners to join in, "Let Israel say—they have greatly oppressed me from my youth" (vv. 1,2).

The refrain, "Let Israel say . . ." hearkens back to an earlier psalm of ascent when Israel had been asked to say, "If

¹They have greatly oppressed me from my youth — let Israel say — ²they have greatly oppressed me from my youth, but they have not gained the victory over me.

215

the Lord had not been on our side" (124:1).

Life is often lived out between the bookends of these realities: "They have greatly oppressed me," and, "If the Lord had not been on our side." Phrase one describes the hurt; phrase two, the help. In between lies the battle for survival.

Maybe your trial isn't over. You've not yet gotten to the top of the mountain. Like the psalmist, perhaps the best thing you can say is, "They have not gained the victory over me" (v. 2). You haven't won, but neither has the adversary.

Escaping

The psalmist employs a horrific analogy to describe the agony of an extensive drawn-out difficulty: long furrows plowed down his back.

Vance Havner writes, "God uses broken things. It takes broken soil to produce a crop, broken clouds to give rain, broken grain to give bread, broken bread to give strength. It is the broken alabaster box that gives forth perfume . . . it is Peter, weeping bitterly, who returns to greater power than ever."

If you have been broken into—as soil penetrated by a plow—take to heart the comfort that a better day lies ahead: "But the Lord is righteous; he has cut me free from the cords of the wicked" (v. 4).

A mother told her son to sit on a stool in his bedroom facing the corner because he had been disobedient. With his face to the wall, he defiantly announced: "I may be sitting down on the outside, but I'm standing on the inside."

We do well to put that boy's attitude to good use when we feel we're being punished for something we haven't done: "I

3Plowmen have plowed my back and made their furrows long. 4But the Lord is righteous; he has cut me free from the cords of the wicked.

may be plowed into, but I'm not plowed under; I may be tied up on the outside, but I'm free on the inside; others may have forgotten me, but the Lord has not."

Thriving

Will things ever be right side up?

When you are hurt, you may not be in too forgiving a mood. The psalmist wasn't. He asked God for three things against the adversaries: bring shame upon them (v. 5), cause them economic ruin (vv. 6,7), and refuse to bless them (v. 8).

Dietrich Bonhoeffer, Christian pastor and theologian martyred by the Nazis in the closing days of World War II, commented that there are some things in the Psalms that can only be prayed purely by Jesus himself. He felt that vengeance requests, like those reflected in these verses, did not belong on the lips of sinful humans who themselves deserve God's punishments. These are the kinds of prayers God grants at the end of the age, when all the mercies of Jesus have been spurned by an ungrateful and rebellious humanity, and finally Christ himself must call for the complete judgment of heaven upon earth. Until then, we are to take up the cry of the Cross, "Father, forgive them" (Luke 23:34).

You're not God, and you will never thrive if you don't take a higher way than spending your time and energy getting even. God will work for the good. Will you?

5May all who hate Zion be turned back in shame. 6May they be like grass on the roof, which withers before it can grow; 7with it the reaper cannot fill his hands, nor the one who gathers fill his arms. 8May those who pass by not say, "The blessing of the Lord be upon you; we bless you in the name of the Lord."

Prayer of response

Lord Jesus, You know best my struggles, pain, and hurt. Thank You that I remain alive, that evil has not gained victory over me. Save me from holding on to wrong attitudes that will bind, hurt, and enslave me far worse than any external enemy. Work Your highest good in my deepest adversity.

My thoughts on Psalm 129 . . .

Relapses

Popular evangelical author A.W. Tozer once described spiritual failure: "Every farmer knows the hunger of the wilderness. . . . No matter how well-prepared the soil, how well-kept the fences . . . let the owner neglect for awhile his prized and valued acres and they will revert again to the wilds and be swallowed by the jungle or the wasteland. The bias of nature is toward the wilderness, never toward the fruitful field."

The fall

You would naturally think that by the time the pilgrim reached the 11th in this series of 15 psalms of ascent, he would be in a jubilant and expectant spiritual and psychological state of mind. Most of the upward climb to Zion lay behind and below. He could see the mountain crest not too far above him.

Have you been climbing a long time, making a lot of progress; but in one fell swoop, you've emotionally tumbled all the way down the trail? You've worked for months to get out of the doldrums, thought you had made progress, and now all the effort seems worthless. You've just gone through what the psalmist speaks of here—a relapse, or Tozer's reversion to wasteland.

With no human help left, you look to God who alone can decipher your need,

¹Out of the depths I cry to you, O Lord; ²O Lord, hear my voice. Let your ears be attentive to my cry for mercy.

219

as a discerning mother understands why her baby cries.

This psalm reminds you that, although you feel you're again at the bottom, in God's reality you're actually more than two-thirds of the way to the top. These are not psalms of descent, but ascent.

Forgiveness

When you deserve God's help, you call for justice. When you don't merit anything, you throw yourself upon the Lord's mercy.

Guilt comes in varying degrees. Sometimes failure appears to be the work entirely of another. You got pushed off the cliff; you didn't jump. Other times you fell prey to temptation. No one forced you. Your own sinful desires took you astray. At all times you must take responsibility for your feelings no matter how you crashed. A relatively innocent person may yet sin by wrongfully reacting to a situation he or she did not create.

The key to getting back on the trail lies in your willingness now to assume personal responsibility for whatever portion of your relapse or failure belongs to you alone.

God will forgive if you will ask. In fact, He's ready to move from forgiveness to forgetfulness by keeping no "record of sins."

Author Lee Davis tells the true story of a much-loved minister in the Philippines who carried the burden of a secret sin he had committed many years before. Even after repenting multiple times, he sensed no peace or forgiveness.

A woman in his parish deeply loved God and claimed to have visions in which she carried on conversations with

[3]If you, O Lord, kept a record of sins, O Lord, who could stand? [4]But with you there is forgiveness; therefore you are feared.

the Lord. To test her, the minister said, "Next time you speak with Christ, I want you to ask Him what sin I committed while I was in seminary."

A few days later he asked, "Well, did Christ visit you in your dreams?"

"Yes, He did," she replied.

"And did you ask Him what sin I committed in seminary?"

"Yes," she answered.

"Well," pressed the minister, "What did He say?"

The godly woman answered, "He said, 'I don't remember.'"

Fellowship

When our relationship with the Lord is restored, we enjoy His presence. The psalm writer anticipates the Lord's appearance with the same intensity as an all-night worker looks forward to the ending of his shift.

Not everyone has such eagerness in waiting. With what disposition do you wait upon the manifestation of His presence: as a child on Christmas Eve waiting to open gifts the next morning, or as a patient waiting for the dentist?

The night watchman spoken of in this psalm has a predictable duration to his night. You have better advantage than the watchman whose expectation was that the Lord would appear to him in the morning. He's with you right now through all the darkness (Matthew 28:20).

Fullness

The Lord does not offer empty words or incomplete solutions to your need. In Him there is "full redemption."

The help you gain from Him enables

5I wait for the Lord, my soul waits, and in his word I put my hope. 6My soul waits for the Lord more than watchmen wait for the morning, more than watchmen wait for the morning.

7O Israel, put your hope in the Lord, for with the Lord is unfailing love and with him is full redemption. 8He himself will redeem Israel from all their sins.

you to testify to others that they likewise "put [their] hope in the Lord."

Yes, Tozer was right. The tendency of the field moves toward relapse. But thank God, there is a higher law and a stronger power at work: the greatness of His might in you.

Prayer of response

Lord Jesus, my emotions are often different from Your reality. My feelings tell me that I fell all the way back down to the bottom, but Your Word tells me I am two-thirds of the way to the top.

My thoughts on Psalm 130 . . .

At Peace Within Yourself

I n their book, *Love Is a Choice,* Christian psychologists Hemfelt, Minirth, and Meier describe the tragic life of Emilia Wesley, sister to her famous brothers, John and Charles, founders of Methodism.

Their mother, Susanna, bore 19 children. Emilia was the oldest. Smart and pretty, she put her own life on hold for years to help her physically weak mother carry the load of housework and caring for the younger children. The family lived at poverty's door.

Emilia developed survival skills, hiding her spinster loneliness in adulthood by successfully developing her own school for girls. At the age of 44 she met Robert Harper who sought her hand in marriage. She didn't really love him, but he was attractive. Perhaps concerned that this might be her last chance for marriage and desperately desiring to be taken care of by another, she married.

What she didn't know was that Robert wanted to marry a successful woman so he could quit working. When their baby arrived, he took Emilia's savings, leaving her with his debts. The sickly baby died.

The tragedy in her life stemmed from parents who did not pay sufficient attention to their own daughter's emotional and developmental needs. Starved for love, she reached out for nurturing from a man she did not know was incapable or unwilling to give her the tender care she sought.

It often happens that way: The undernourished person in childhood repeats in her adult life the calamity of neglect by unwittingly duplicating the dysfunctionalism of the family in which she grew up.

How about you? Is there any hope that things can be different for you, even if your circumstances aren't the same as Emilia's?

I find these 15 psalms of ascent a guide for getting on top. They're designed to move you out of life's valleys and strengthen you on the climb.

At Psalm 131, we're near the end of the long trek upward. What spiritual and emotional muscles has the Holy Spirit been developing as you've fought to recover from the distress (Psalm 120:1) which prompted you to begin the ascent toward recovery? This psalm tells us there are three.

> [1]My heart is not proud, O Lord, my eyes are not haughty; I do not concern myself with great matters or things too wonderful for me.

1. I know my limits and it's okay

Can you accept that you are never going to have some things in life you want?

I have a joyful friend confined to a wheelchair because of an auto accident. She doesn't waste her life by grousing on the what-might-have-beens.

One of the hardest and most necessary things we must do sometimes is let go. What are you fiercely holding on to? You say, "I'm holding on because I have faith." Are you sure it's faith, or is it fear? Fear that if you release your grasp, nothing will be left?

The psalmist, in verse 1, has arrived at the place of inner release. He's no longer holding on to unrealistic expectations about his life. He's replaced the "what if?" with the "what now?" He's not focused on what he can't control, but the things he can.

Almost every day, I repeat this famous prayer: "Lord, grant me the serenity to accept the things I cannot change, the courage to change the things I can, and the wisdom to know the difference."

2. Weaning does not mean starving.

It's hard to be cut off from a familiar and predictable source of nourishment.

The first moments of weaning are frightful. You are used to only one means of ingesting. Now what is familiar has been removed. You're hungry for the way things were. You think you'll die.

But God has other food for you. Just like a baby may resist at first the healthy solid foods fed in mashed spoonfuls, so you may resist the alternative resources God has provided. He sees how upset you are. But in time you will again be calm enough to say, "Like a weaned child is my soul within me" (v. 2).

²But I have stilled and quieted my soul; like a weaned child with its mother, like a weaned child is my soul within me.

3. Help for me means hope for someone else.

This brief psalm ends by giving encouragement to others.

It's hard to shout the victory when you are in the process of recovering from loss, codependency, addiction, or any form of attachment you looked to as a source of support.

But after the weaning, winnowing, weeding, or widowing, you'll have a testimony which will help others. You'll put your arms around a soul just as frightened now as you were then and say with great confidence, "Put your hope in the Lord."

³O Israel, put your hope in the Lord both now and forevermore.

Prayer of response

Lord Jesus, I don't have a problem with the last word of this psalm, "forevermore." I know the long-term future is safe in Your hands. It's the "now" which worries and frightens me. Grant me the strength of Your Spirit to be at peace within myself today.

My thoughts on Psalm 131 . . .

The Finishers

Tanzania's John Stephen Akhwari placed last in the 1968 Olympics marathon. He ran most of the 26-mile course through the streets of Mexico City on a bloody and bandaged leg, wincing pain at every step. Early in the race he had fallen.

Long after all the runners finished, accompanied by a police motorcycle escort illuminating the cold dark evening with flashing green-and-red lights, he entered the stadium for the final lap. The world watched on television as the silent stands broke into a slow, steady rhythmic clapping which grew ever louder as he circled the field and crossed the finish line. They roared as though he had won.

Asked later why he had endured the pain rather than dropping out, Akhwari seemed perplexed by the question and simply answered, "I don't think you understand. My country did not send me to Mexico City to start the race. They sent me to finish the race."

In this psalm, we are only a few steps from the finish line in the 15 psalms of ascent (Psalms 120–134). Will you finish despite setback, hardship, sorrow, or loss?

Hardships

1O Lord, remember David and all the hardships he endured.

The psalm begins with reference to David, injured in a way different from Tanzania's Akhwari, but a model for those who have been spiritually or emotionally bloodied and bandaged.

227

I am fascinated by the opening prayer. "O Lord, remember David and all the hardships he endured" (v. 1). As if the Lord would ever forget.

Hardships. A lifetime of adversity summarized in two syllables. A word encompassing the 10 times Saul tried to kill David, the sin with Bathsheba and consequent sorrows, the rebellion of Absalom, traumas in his own family and staff. They all boil down to one nine-letter word: *hardships.*

How do you make it through such a time? What's the key to finishing?

A worthy goal

David lifted his eyes from his hardships to his objective: to make Jerusalem the dwelling place of God. He outlasted his adversities by having a worthy goal. He clung to it against all odds, and he prevailed.

What sustains you in your journey upward? Do you have an unflagging commitment to make of yourself a dwelling place for God? Perhaps you're very restless because you don't see any progress or hint of resolution in the problems you're dealing with.

You will outlast your trouble if you refuse to give in to it; if you keep your eye instead on what is most important—living in a way that pleases God.

A stated goal

David's companions later remembered the times they heard David verbally express his goal at places like Ephrathah (Bethlehem) and the fields of Jaar. His dream was to capture Jerusalem and turn it into God's capital.

²He swore an oath to the Lord and made a vow to the Mighty One of Jacob: ³"I will not enter my house or go to my bed — ⁴I will allow no sleep to my eyes, no slumber to my eyelids, ⁵till I find a place for the Lord, a dwelling for the Mighty One of Jacob."

⁶We heard it in Ephrathah, we came upon it in the fields of Jaar : ⁷"Let us go to his dwelling place; let us worship at his footstool — ⁸arise, O Lord, and come to your resting place, you and the ark of your might. ⁹May your priests be clothed with righteousness; may your saints sing for joy."

Only those aspirations which are continually repeated ever come true. One-shot emotional impulses have no staying power. Recovery involves getting up again after each setback.

A lasting goal

The psalm writer pleads with God that Jerusalem be kept safe for the sake of David (v. 10). He had worked so hard to gain it—why should God waste such sacrifice and effort?

David's honest heart and heroic struggle elicited a promise from the Lord that the fate of God's people on earth would always be inextricably linked to the success of David's descendants. In David's Son, Jesus our Lord, the words of verses 11 and 12 reach their highest and complete fulfillment. The blessings of life in Jerusalem described in verses 13 through 18, fall to those who are in Christ (Hebrews 12:22,23).

Apply the closing words of this psalm to yourself. "The Lord has chosen you, He has desired you for His dwelling. 'You are where I'm home,' He says, 'and I sit enthroned in you because you desire Me. I will bless you with abundant provisions; I will provide when you are in poverty of any kind. My presence in you will protect and enlighten you as the horn protects the ox and the lamp penetrates the darkness. You will be vindicated and rewarded.'"

Oh, yes. Another runner had won successive marathons at the 1960 Rome Olympics and the 1964 Olympics in Tokyo. He began the race at the 1968 Olympics in Mexico City; but unlike John Stephen Akhwari, he dropped out after

10For the sake of David your servant, do not reject your anointed one. 11The Lord swore an oath to David, a sure oath that he will not revoke: "One of your own descendants I will place on your throne — 12 if your sons keep my covenant and the statutes I teach them, then their sons will sit on your throne for ever and ever."

13For the Lord has chosen Zion, he has desired it for his dwelling: 14"This is my resting place for ever and ever; here I will sit enthroned, for I have desired it — 15I will bless her with abundant provisions; her poor will I satisfy with food. 16I will clothe her priests with salvation, and her saints will ever sing for joy. 17"Here I will make a horn grow for David and set up a lamp for my anointed one. 18I will clothe his enemies with shame, but the crown on his head will be resplendent."

10 miles due to injury. He had a legiti-
mate excuse. So did Akhwari, but
Akhwari finished.

How about you?

Prayer of response

*Lord Jesus, I know what my past
looks like because I have been there.
You're the only One who has seen the
future. Therefore, I have hope because
Your plans for me are good. I am determined to finish, knowing that You will
complete the work You began in me.*

My thoughts on Psalm 132 . . .

At Peace With Others

arl Sandburg, the noted biographer of Abraham Lincoln, tells that a neighbor saw our 16th president lugging his two small sons down the street. Both boys, Willie and Todd, were bawling loudly.

The neighbor asked, "Why, Mr. Lincoln, what's the matter?"

Lincoln answered, "Just what's the matter with the whole world. I've got three walnuts and each boy wants two."

In the actions of his small sons, Lincoln saw mirrored the selfishness and strife that plagues the world.

David, king of Israel and author of Psalm 133, knew something about strife within his family and society. His children fought over power and position. The lack of unity and harmony in his own life lends great poignancy to this psalm, the truth of which he had rarely experienced.

Psalm 133 is positioned as the 14th of 15 psalms of ascent, the prayers of worship used by pilgrims as they climbed from Jericho up to Jerusalem during the three high holy day seasons of the year.

You're not alone

¹How good and pleasant it is when brothers live together in unity!

You are on your own pilgrimage of life. It may seem like forever since you began far below crying for the Lord to hear your distress (Psalm 120). Now the tears are gone. Your stamina has returned. You're breathing easier. You can laugh again. The end lies in view, the steep ascent behind. Just two more

231

small rises, short and quick (Psalms 133 and 134), and your journey of recovery is complete. You will finish after all.

In your darkest night, you may have been unaware of anyone except yourself. You may have even retreated from others for long seasons. You felt you were hurt too many times so you remained oblivious to the companionship of others.

But take a second look. People who love you are alongside. I suspect that the persons who have come closest to you are the ones whom you have given access to your spiritual needs, emotional pain, and relational hunger. They've been on their own climb, and they've made it too. Now is the time for celebrating with them: "How good and pleasant it is when brothers [sisters, family, friends] live together in unity! " (v. 1).

Others: God's special gift

You probably would not select the two examples given by David for being at peace with others: anointing oil for the high priest and the dew of Mount Hermon falling on Mount Zion. He chose these metaphors to make three points.

First, for David unity was rare. He enjoyed precious few tranquil moments with others. Neither his father nor brothers initially had a high opinion of him. His employer Saul hated him without cause. His wife Michal despised him for his devotion to God. His sons fought each other, and one even staged a rebellion against him. It's not surprising, therefore, that he likened harmony to the once-in-a-lifetime anointing of the high priest at his investiture or the rarity of a heavy Mount Hermon—like dew falling on the much-lower-situated Mount Zion.

Paradoxically, God used the very man who lacked harmony in his own life to unify the kingdom of Israel and make its capital the city of peace, Jerusalem. For the followers of the Lord Jesus, unity ought not to be rare. Since we are at peace with God through Christ, we endeavor also to live in peace with others (Romans 12:9–21, especially v. 18).

Second, unity comes in abundance when it occurs. The high priest's head, beard, and clothes got soaked with anointing oil. The dew of Hermon douses the environs of Zion.

The Early Church experienced such copious unity (Acts 2:1,42–47). So may we as we invite the Holy Spirit daily to fill us (Ephesians 5:17–21).

Third, unity comes as a gift from God. Partly lost in the English translation is the threefold repetition of the Hebrew word "descending." The "precious oil poured on the head, *descending* down on the beard, *descending* down on Aaron's beard . . . the dew of Hermon *descending* on Mount Zion" (vv. 2,3). The theme of descending dovetails into the final sentence of this psalm in that both harmony and eternity come down to us as bestowed blessings from the Lord.

The psalms of ascent begin with an emphasis upon "me." They close with an emphasis on "us." The pilgrim's decision to leave behind the old life and call upon the Lord is an intensely personal one (Psalm 120). No one else can make that decision for you. But, as you continue in your upward climb, you will be strengthened by the gifts God gives—loving, caring, and supportive fellow pilgrims.

²It is like precious oil poured on the head, running down on the beard, running down on Aaron's beard, down upon the collar of his robes. ³It is as if the dew of Hermon were falling on Mount Zion. For there the Lord bestows his blessing, even life forevermore.

Prayer of response

Lord, please forgive me for the times I caused disharmony by insisting You or someone else do what I want. Thank You for the precious people who encourage and strengthen me, and thank You for the gift of being at peace with You, myself, and others.

My thoughts on Psalm 133 . . .

Safe at the End of the Day

This intensely personal song of Psalm 134 is for all who struggle through a difficult passage in life. Psalms 120 through 134 track such a pilgrim who makes the arduous climb from a deep valley of need to a mountain peak of full recovery and blessing.

Maybe you've not gone very far or are greatly winded somewhere along the way. This last psalm of ascent provides an uplifting and reassuring vision of your future—of the time when this trial lies behind you and you are again on top. If you're not there yet, let this psalm stand as a photograph for you of what yet will be.

Final fearful thoughts

With this 15th psalm of ascent, the long climb is over.

You wondered if you would ever make it to the top. Evening's shadows cast themselves on the ground ahead.

Is the entrance to the temple already shut, its gates barred for the evening? You hoped you could get there before the doors closed, to that idealized place of peace.

Has this long climb now been for nothing? Have you arrived too late? Made too many mistakes? Was it your last rest on the trail that periously delayed you? Or, the detour down below that you should not have taken?

> ¹Praise the Lord, all you servants of the Lord who minister by night in the house of the Lord.

235

Someone is waiting for you

The light is on inside. The door's ajar. You can get in . . . still. It's not too late. You will enter because those within did not rush off at the appointed closing time. Their tarrying means your entrance.

What can you say of such devoted ones? Those who stayed at their posts of prayer and duty long enough until you too had reached the place of safety and satisfaction? "Praise the Lord, all you servants of the Lord who minister by night in the house of the Lord" (v. 1).

It's the people who kept the night watch of intercession who now make it possible for you to enter: God's special priests who do not punch the clock of duty, but who tarry long hours until every last pilgrim coming up the mountainside has had a chance to make it inside the gates of pearl.

Praise the Lord for all His servants who don't walk off the job of encouragement, prayer, and support when the clock strikes 5. Bless the Lord for their faithfulness as you slip into their evening song of praise. Lift your hands now along with theirs to bless the Lord also . . . in His house.

And remember, our Great High Priest himself never stopped interceding for you (Hebrews 7:25; John 17:13–26).

Others are still behind you

Oh, what it feels like to be in His house. You began your journey from the tents of Kedar (Psalm 120:5). You hated to leave that tent. It was so comfortable, so filled with the illusion of satisfaction. But as a tent it was transitory. It held no permanence for you, no dependable safety. Were you driven out or did you choose to leave? No matter. You headed for the mountain of God.

Now, you are here—the safe place where human hand cannot remove or deny. You are secure in Zion, in its very center, within His holy hill. Pilgrim no more—now you are home. "Lift up your hands in the sanctuary, and praise the Lord" (v. 2).

Your hands once lay heavy at your side. You lift them now: in surrender, palms upward; in adoration, fingers pointed toward the sky.

If you could lift your voice this evening and let your message be wafted by the soft breezes up and over the temple wall, across Zion's field, and downward on the trail . . . it would carry a hopeful word to those camped below tonight who wonder, as you did, if they will ever finish the ascent. "May the Lord, the Maker of heaven and earth, bless you from Zion" (v. 3).

You now have confidence to speak this encouraging word to others not so safely sheltered as you. The blessing of God lies not only *in* Zion with those who minister by night, but *from* Zion for all the pilgrims yet exposed to the dangers on the climb.

²**Lift up your hands in the sanctuary and praise the Lord. ³May the Lord, the Maker of heaven and earth, bless you from Zion.**

Prayer of response

Lord Jesus, this climb toward recovery from loss has stretched me at times seemingly beyond my capacity to endure. Thank You for giving me such a clear vision of a good future. Knowing I'll lift my hands then in praise, I lift them now. The warm light of Your promises is always on for me.

My thoughts on Psalm 134 . . .

Adoration

T ears well up in the eyes of my friend Everett Stenhouse when he talks about his daughter Judy, whose life was taken instantly in an automobile crash several years ago. He tells about the time when Judy was a 3-year-old.

Everett, then pastoring a church, was working in his office when Judy showed up in the doorway. When she had his attention, she asked for a nickel to buy a bag of potato chips. He told her he was busy, and she needed to go back to their house next door.

She returned a second and third time, repeating her request. On the last visit, Everett sternly warned her not to bother him again—that he was very busy.

Time went by, and he heard his office door creak open. He pretended not to notice her standing in the doorway. She remained there silent, looking at him. Finally, he slammed his large hand down on the desk and brusquely demanded, "Well, why are you here again?"

Tearfully, she stretched out her hands and said, "Daddy, I just wanted to love on you."

Everett held out his arms and cradled his darling daughter in his lap. When she slipped away, she had the nickel nestled tightly in her little fist.

In this psalm, the writer is simply inviting us to love on the Lord.

Even when life is tough

Psalm 135 is the first psalm following the 15 psalms of ascent, prayers which reflect the struggle and difficulty of our upward climb in life. It's as though this

¹Praise the Lord. Praise the name of the Lord; praise him, you servants of the Lord, ²you who minister in the house of the Lord, in the courts of the house of our God.

psalm recognizes that when God has delivered us from all our adversities, the appropriate response is for us to worship in His temple.

Thus, this psalm contains not even a hint of trial or sorrow. The battles have all been fought and won. God's work is complete, and His ways have been found perfect.

Perhaps you're not at the finish line in a present difficulty you're passing through. How then can you sing this psalm?

I had to break the news to the wife of one of our church's elders that her husband had died suddenly from a heart attack that day on a ski slope. Church members gathered in shock that next Sunday morning. The announcement time had been planned days before; and in promotion of some kids' event, one of the children's workers popped into the sanctuary dressed as a clown. The clown's appearance was a total disconnection from the somberness of the hour.

Nevertheless

Telling you to love on the Lord when your heart is heavy may seem as emotionally out of place as a clown at a funeral. You honestly don't feel like praising God at all.

That's why a psalm like this can be so helpful. When you don't have words of your own; when you don't feel like saying anything; when your gratitude reservoir is on empty—you can fall back on the written text of Scripture and pray these Spirit-inspired words. Let the Holy Spirit lift you out of your personal world of concern into the broad universe of everlasting truth. In your heart, remain within God's courts.

3Praise the Lord, for the Lord is good; sing praise to his name, for that is pleasant. 4For the Lord has chosen Jacob to be his own, Israel to be his treasured possession.

5I know that the Lord is great, that our Lord is greater than all gods. 6The Lord does whatever pleases him, in the heavens and on the earth, in the seas and all their depths. 7He makes clouds rise from the ends of the earth; he sends lightning with the rain and brings out the wind from his storehouses.

8He struck down the firstborn of Egypt, the firstborn of men and animals. 9He sent his signs and wonders into your midst, O Egypt, against Pharaoh and all his servants. 10He struck down many nations and killed mighty kings — 11Sihon king of the Amorites, Og king of Bashan and all the kings of Canaan — 12and he gave their land as an inheritance, an inheritance to his people Israel.

Praise Him (vv. 1,2). Earthly cares recede during the time we spend in His presence.

The Lord is good (vv. 3,4). His goodness is seen in choosing a people to serve Him. You are also chosen of God. You may not understand all the mystery of that; but for sure you are not some afterthought or a cheap nothing. You are God's treasured possession.

The Lord is great (vv. 5–7). He's got the whole world in His hands. Could He really have lost control over the events in your life?

The Lord redeems (vv. 8–12). He loves His people so dearly that He delivers them from bondage. He didn't just do it for Israel; He delivers His people for all generations (vv. 13,14). Have you thanked Him today for saving you?

Compare (vv. 15–18). You resemble what you worship. If it's an idol (whether metal or mental), you too become unseeing, unhearing, unfeeling, and lifeless. Aren't you grateful you know the living God and that you are growing into His likeness?

Respond (vv. 19–21). The psalm closes as it began—"Praise the Lord." Will you employ these words as the bookends to the morning and evening of this day?

Are you a lot like Everett's little girl? You show up in God's presence most often only wanting a nickel so you can have His resources to satisfy your own appetites. This psalm tells us we should take occasions to come into God's presence with nothing on our mind except to love Him.

13Your name, O Lord, endures forever, your renown, O Lord, through all generations. 14For the Lord will vindicate his people and have compassion on his servants.

15The idols of the nations are silver and gold, made by the hands of men. 16They have mouths, but cannot speak, eyes, but they cannot see; 17they have ears, but cannot hear, nor is there breath in their mouths. 18Those who make them will be like them, and so will all who trust in them.

19O house of Israel, praise the Lord; O house of Aaron, praise the Lord; 20O house of Levi, praise the Lord; you who fear him, praise the Lord. 21Praise be to the Lord from Zion, to him who dwells in Jerusalem. Praise the Lord.

Prayer of response

Lord Jesus, I remember how You welcomed children into Your arms and blessed them. They just wanted to be close to You. Forgive me for too often coming as a demanding adult, insisting You put something I want into my grasping hand. I come to you today as Your child, just to say, "I love You."

My thoughts on Psalm 135 . . .

True Love Lasts

A marriage counselor asked a husband whose marriage had gone bad after 18 years, "How did you know it was over?"

"When she stopped putting toothpaste on my brush in the morning," he replied. "When we were first married, whoever got up first would roll toothpaste on the other's brush and leave it lying on the sink. Somewhere along the line we stopped doing that for each other, and the marriage went downhill after that."

Perhaps the husband's explanation of the deterioration of his marriage may be off base or overly simplistic; but true love is expressed, as the poet Elizabeth Barrett Browning put it, in "the nameless unremembered acts of kindness and of love." When someone within a relationship stops doing the small things—whether putting toothpaste on the brush, taking the garbage out in the morning, or giving the predictable hug and kiss of goodbye or welcome—it's often a signal that the underlying emotional attachment has waned.

Here before us is a psalm which celebrates the truths later encapsulated by the apostle Paul in these three words, "Love never fails" (1 Corinthians 13:8).

Take a moment and review the immediate context of this psalm. Preceding it are the psalms of ascent (120–134), prayers for the pilgrim on the upward journey of emotional and spiritual wellness. The object of the climb is to reach God's holy temple on Zion, the place of shalom where your life is integrated instead of broken, healed instead of hurt, and at ease rather than "disease." No wonder Psalm 135 fills up with language of heartfelt praise to God for arriving at last within a secure haven.

Psalm 136 continues the service of worship in the temple. You recite it standing in a vast assembly of other pilgrims who give uniform witness of God's watchful love and care. The leader of the worship service recites a phrase describing some aspect of God's character and nature. Your part is to recite in unison with other pilgrims, "His love endures forever." Twenty-six times within this psalm you will repeat the refrain, "His love endures forever." Such repetition steadily drives home the truth about God into the deepest recesses of your mind, heart, and soul.

The themes of this psalm may be grouped into four major reasons for expressing thanks to the Lord for His true and lasting love.

1. God loves you because it is His nature to do so

Simply put, "God is good." Not a shadow of evil or wrongful intent toward you resides in Him. As God of gods and Lord of lords, His supreme greatness over all other authority guarantees that His love for you can never be overthrown. J.B. Phillips said, "God's love can outlast anything. It is, in fact, the one thing that still stands when all else is fallen."

2. God's love is seen through His acts of creation

Join the psalmist in viewing creation as an opportunity not only to stand in awe, but as a testimony of God's love for the human race. His everlasting love is seen within His wonders: the making of heaven, earth, water, lights, sun, moon, and stars.

[1]Give thanks to the Lord, for he is good. His love endures forever. [2]Give thanks to the God of gods. His love endures forever. [3]Give thanks to the Lord of lords . . . [4]to him who alone does great wonders . . . [5]who by his understanding made the heavens . . . [6]who spread out the earth upon the waters . . . [7]who made the great lights . . . [8]the sun to govern the day . . . [9]the moon and stars to govern the night . . . [10]to him who struck down the firstborn of Egypt . . . [11]and brought Israel out from among them . . . [12]with a mighty hand and outstretched arm . . . [13]to him who divided the Red Sea asunder . . . [14]and brought Israel through the midst of it . . . [15]but swept Pharaoh and his army into the Red Sea . . . [16]to him who led his people through the desert . . . [17]who struck down great kings . . . [18]and killed mighty kings . . . [19]Sihon king of the Amorites . . . [20]and Og king of Bashan . . .

3. God's love is seen through His acts within Israel's history

He employs His power over the enemies of His people: human potentates such as Pharaoh and mighty kings like Sihon and Og, or the natural elements such as Red Sea and desert. He brings His people to their promised land.

Likewise in your life, He thrusts aside whatever would prevent His purposes from being attained. In His time, He removes them all.

4. God's love is seen through His care for His people

God never forgets you when you are in the deepest valleys (v. 23). He frees you from your enemies (v. 24)—sometimes instantly (the Red Sea) and other times through a process (wilderness walking and gradual conquest of Canaan). He meets your needs (v. 25).

Every day He puts toothpaste on your brush, for "His love endures forever."

21and gave their land as an inheritance . . . 22an inheritance to his servant Israel . . . 23to the One who remembered us in our low estate . . . 24and freed us from our enemies . . . 25and who gives food to every creature . . .

26Give thanks to the God of heaven. His love endures forever.

Prayer of response

Lord Jesus, You will not forsake me nor give up on me. You will not cast me aside nor love me today but leave me tomorrow. You will not betray me, hang up on me, or slam the door against me. Thank You that Your love for me never comes to an end.

My Thoughts on Psalm 136 . . .

Away Games

Psalm 137

At the close of each major league baseball season, I evaluate the standings of all the teams in each league. Almost without exception, the top teams have the best record for away games. All but a handful of the worst teams have a winning record at home, but only the great team consistently wins on the road.

Psalm 137, written at the time of the Babylonian captivity of Israel in the sixth century B.C., illustrates how difficult it is to retain a winning spiritual edge when you do not have home court advantage. Look at the three ways the psalmist employs the word "remember" to describe the beginning, duration, and conclusion of all "away" games.

The memory that brings discouragement: *"When we remembered Zion"*

¹By the rivers of Babylon we sat and wept when we remembered Zion. ²There on the poplars we hung our harps, ³for there our captors asked us for songs, our tormentors demanded songs of joy; they said, "Sing us one of the songs of Zion!"

When something happens to hurt you deeply, you'll probably first experience the feelings of the psalmist: memories of better days, sorrow, and an inability to sing for joy.

How can you make merry when you're so far from where you really want to be, in the company of persons who don't care for you at all and demand impossible things from you?

247

The memory that brings hope: *"If I do not remember you"*

The question, "How can we sing the songs of the Lord while in a foreign land?" (v. 4), is answered by the truth that we must sing or die. You can't win the away games if you adopt an attitude of defeat. The psalmist knows he can't let his mouth go dry; he must not let the negative memories of captivity overwhelm his memories of joy.

V. Gilbert Beers, former editor of *Christianity Today*, tells about his great-great-grandmother to the eighth great, Catharine duBois. One day in 1663, Minnisink Indians swept down from the Catskill Mountains, killed several inhabitants of the little settlement now known as Paltz, New York, and took a number of women and children captive. Among them were Catharine duBois and her infant daughter Sara. For 10 weeks they were held in the mountains, while search parties looked for them in vain.

Feeling confident they would escape reprisal, the Indians decided to celebrate their success by burning Catharine and Sara. A cubicle pile of logs was arranged, upon which the bound mother and daughter were placed. When the Indians lit the torch to ignite the logs, all of Catharine's descendants were about to be annihilated with her.

Beers notes that a most human response at that moment would have been for Catharine to scream at her tormentors and curse them for her suffering. But instead, she burst into song, turning the foreboding Catskill forest into a cathedral of praise with a Huguenot hymn she had learned in France. The words were from Psalm 137.

[4]How can we sing the songs of the Lord while in a foreign land? [5]If I forget you, O Jerusalem, may my right hand forget its skill. [6]May my tongue cling to the roof of my mouth if I do not remember you, if I do not consider Jerusalem my highest joy.

The Minnisink, of course, had not asked for a song (v. 3); but they were so captivated with Catharine's singing that they demanded another song, then another, and then another. And while she sang "the songs of Zion," her husband, Louis and his search party burst upon the scene and rescued her (and all her descendants).

Saints of all ages—whether the psalmist of 137 or Catharine before the Minnisinks or Paul in the Philippi jail—have learned the absolutely essential ingredient to winning on the road: You must sing the songs of Zion—whether you feel like it or not.

The memory that guarantees victory: *"Remember, O Lord"*

The Lord will remember. That's the psalmist's comfort and hope. Is it yours?

Unlike the exiles to Babylon, we do not pray revenge upon those who cheered at our misfortune or a gruesome death for their babies. But we do take solace in the truth that the Lord will prevail ultimately, and that His judgments are true and righteous.

We unite with the end of this psalm when we share in the certainty of final outcome. The Lord has the last word over all our adversities. Even in "away" games we know victory is ours through Christ our Lord.

7Remember, O Lord, what the Edomites did on the day Jerusalem fell. "Tear it down," they cried, "Tear it down to its foundations!" 8O Daughter of Babylon, doomed to destruction, happy is he who repays you for what you have done to us — 9he who seizes your infants and dashes them against the rocks.

Prayer of response

Lord Jesus, I'm having a hard time right now because I too feel like the psalmist— I'm in a strange land. The negative voices are so much louder than the helping voices. Give me eyes and ears today to see the heavenly cloud of witnesses who cheer me on. Grant me voice today to sing the songs of Zion in this most difficult place.

My thoughts on Psalm 137 . . .

Upperside or Underside?

Psalm 138

I n the last years of her life, Corrie Ten Boom, author of *The Hiding Place* and honored for her work in sparing the lives of Jewish people from the Nazis, often began her testimony by holding up before the audience a piece of embroidered cloth.

First, she showed the beauty of the embroidered side with all the threads forming a beautiful picture, which she described as God's plan for our lives. Then she would flip over the cloth to show the tangled and confused underside, illustrating how we so often view our own lives from a human standpoint.

She then quoted the poem of the weaver:

**My life is but a weaving,
between my God and me,**

*I do not choose the colors, He worketh steadily.
Oftimes He weaveth sorrow, and I in foolish pride,
Forget He sees the upper, and I the underside.
No 'til the loom is silent and the shuttles cease to fly
Will God unroll the canvass and explain the reason why.
The dark threads are as needful in the weaver's skillful hand
As the threads of gold and silver in the pattern He has planned.*

The challenge of the Christian life is to trust God with the upperside when all you see in your own life are the threads of tangled confusion.

With Psalm 138, we begin a series of eight psalms hearing for the last time the prayers of the man David who continued to worship the Lord amid all the underside sorrows and setbacks. How did he survive "walk[ing] in the midst of trouble" (v. 7)? This psalm tells us.

Never stop worshipping

In Psalms 135 and 136, the focus was on community worship. But this psalm reflects the intimate tones of "I" and "me."

What is your response to the Lord on this particular day of your life? What prayer, if any, do you choose to lift upward to Him? You can begin any day without praise, or choose every day to worship. David's choice was always clear because it was rooted, not in his feelings, but in his will and from all his heart (v. 1).

But what does he mean when he says, "before the 'gods' I will sing your praise?" The gods with a small "g" represent your decision to praise the Lord in the face of whatever in your life remains as a strong power against you. You minimize their threats by magnifying His name.

You make a conscious decision to point your life in the direction of His temple (v. 2), to look toward the Lord rather than away from Him. When you turn your face toward Him you find the reality of His love and faithfulness. You walk in the confidence that the Lord's exaltation of His name and Word above all things means that all His everlasting promises to you personally will come true.

You gain strength in His presence (v. 3), and great desire for all—even chiefs of state—to know and worship the Lord you serve (vv. 4,5).

Never stop trusting

There is a fascinating connection between the thought in verses 4 and 5 as

¹I will praise you, O Lord, with all my heart; before the "gods" I will sing your praise. ²I will bow down toward your holy temple and will praise your name for your love and your faithfulness, for you have exalted above all things your name and your word. ³When I called, you answered me; you made me bold and stouthearted. ⁴May all the kings of the earth praise you, O Lord, when they hear the words of your mouth. ⁵May they sing of the ways of the Lord, for the glory of the Lord is great.

compared to the beginning of verse 6. David invites kings of the earth to praise the Lord, and then immediately notes that it's the prayers of the lowly that God "knows," while the proud He only "knows from afar." In other words, God lovingly watches over the poor-in-their-own-eyes rather than the powerful-in-their-own-eyes.

Perhaps, like David, you have "walk[ed] in the midst of trouble" (v. 6), much deeper and longer than you thought you could endure. But your fear and despair ultimately proved weaker than the Lord's protective care. He shelters you even in the harshest winter of your life.

The psalm closes with one of the most comforting and reassuring words a child of God could ever hear: "The Lord will perfect that which concerneth me" (v. 8, KJV). Why? Because His love endures forever and He does "not abandon the works of [His] hands."

The apostle Paul picks up the same theme in his letter from prison to the Philippians: "Being confident of this, that he who began a good work in you will carry it on to completion until the day of Christ Jesus" (1:6).

Are you on the underside today? Then, as the gospel song puts it in truth parallel with this psalm, "When you can't see His plan, when you don't understand, trust His heart." He will fulfill His purpose for you.

⁶Though the Lord is on high, he looks upon the lowly, but the proud he knows from afar.

⁷Though I walk in the midst of trouble, you preserve my life; you stretch out your hand against the anger of my foes, with your right hand you save me.

⁸The Lord will fulfill his purpose for me; your love, O Lord, endures forever — do not abandon the works of your hands.

Prayer of response

Lord Jesus, I so often wonder if I'm making any progress at all. So many things have turned out differently than I wished or thought best. But today I renew again my trust in You. My life is not my own, but Yours. Weave in me the tapestry that most pleases You.

My thoughts on Psalm 138 . . .

A Psalm of Intimacy

For the first 12 ¹/₂ years of marriage, our pet dog was a white poodle named Boomer. A few months after his death, Sunshine came into our lives for the next 15 years—a beautiful apricot poodle.

We put Boomer's name tag on Sunshine's collar, and Sunshine never knew the difference. The dog does not have a capacity to know his own identity, to engage in introspection, or to look into a mirror and ask: "Who am I?"

Not so with us!

"Know thyself," Socrates said. Psalm 139, and the whole of Scripture, goes a giant step beyond Socrates by saying, "God knows you far better than you know yourself."

How well does God know you?

¹O Lord, you have searched me and you know me.

God's knowledge of you is based upon His own investigative searching (v. 1). The underlying Hebrew word for "search" means "to dig." The Lord "digs" into you—not with a careless thrust of a shovel, but with the painstaking sifting of an archaeologist probing the layers of your soul. When His digging into you is done, there's nothing about you He doesn't know.

²You know when I sit and when I rise; you perceive my thoughts from afar. ³You discern my going out and my lying down; you are familiar with all my ways. ⁴Before a word is on my tongue you know it completely, O Lord.

He knows your routines (vv. 2,3). At any given time, He knows whether you're sitting or standing, going in or coming out.

He knows your thoughts (v. 4). Persons close to me tell me that often they know

255

what I'm thinking by looking at the expression on my face. God doesn't have to get that close to read me since He "perceives my thoughts from afar" (v. 2). He even knows what I'm going to say next.

He knows everything (v. 5). You can't escape His inventory. He's got you hemmed in "behind and before." Were David alive today, he would probably say that God has x-rayed your every intention and act. He's got His hand on you: not a light touch, but a solid clamp.

How do you respond to such knowledge (v. 6)? Two reactions are possible: (1) Awful! When a favorite Bible teacher of mine was a little boy, his mother would send him out to play by saying, "Now remember, Willard, the eye of God is watching you." His adolescent view of God was as a disembodied giant eye, and the thought frightened him. Perhaps you're unnerved by how well God knows you. But David had a different reaction: (2) Wonderful! Just think how important you are to God that He would make himself intimately aware of you!

How near is God to you?

Simply and summarily put: "You can't get away from Him" (v. 7). He's with you in the highs and lows (v. 8), in the far-off places (vv. 8–10), and the darkest nights—even the ones of your own making (vv. 11,12).

How involved is God with you?

He made you. From the time you were a single cell, He watched over you microscopically and embryonically (vv. 13–15). He laid down the genetic code and DNA that determined your peculiar and individual characteristics. But more than

5You hem me in — behind and before; you have laid your hand upon me. 6Such knowledge is too wonderful for me, too lofty for me to attain.

7Where can I go from your Spirit? Where can I flee from your presence?

8If I go up to the heavens, you are there; if I make my bed in the depths, you are there. 9If I rise on the wings of the dawn, if I settle on the far side of the sea, 10even there your hand will guide me, your right hand will hold me fast.

11If I say, "Surely the darkness will hide me and the light become night around me," 12even the darkness will not be dark to you; the night will shine like the day, for darkness is as light to you.

13For you created my inmost being; you knit me together in my mother's womb. 14I praise you because I am fearfully and wonderfully made; your works are wonderful, I know that full well. 15My frame

that, He foresaw the development of your own personal history (v. 16). Nothing you have done has taken Him by surprise.

Although the Lord has access to all your hidden faults and sins, David takes such all-compassing knowledge as a comfort rather than a fright (vv. 17,18). God can count the hairs on your head (Matthew 10:30), but you can't count the sum of God's thoughts toward you. He remains focused on you, attentive to you. You are very much on His mind.

Reactions

David offers two prayers as a response to the Lord's all-inclusive knowledge of his life.

First, he does the normal and the natural. He asks God to look at the persons who wronged him (vv. 19–22). "Do something about them," he cries. If the Lord would just make your external circumstances more friendly and less hostile!

On second thought, David takes the high road to spiritual maturity. He asks the Lord to change him (vv. 23,24).

This psalm began with an admission that God had already searched, yet at the end of the psalm David invites a new search. (Compare verse 1 with verse 23.) Why?

When you realize God knows everything about you, but still loves you—you respond lovingly to Him. You want Him to know you completely. In the intimacy of your relationship with Him you find: (1) rest in the present because He knows your anxious thoughts, (2) redemption over the past because He forgives your offensive ways, and (3) reassurance about the future because He leads you in the way everlasting.

was not hidden from you when I was made in the secret place. When I was woven together in the depths of the earth,

¹⁶your eyes saw my unformed body. All the days ordained for me were written in your book before one of them came to be.

¹⁷How precious to me are your thoughts, O God! How vast is the sum of them! ¹⁸Were I to count them, they would outnumber the grains of sand. When I awake, I am still with you.

¹⁹If only you would slay the wicked, O God! Away from me, you bloodthirsty men! ²⁰They speak of you with evil intent; your adversaries misuse your name. ²¹Do I not hate those who hate you, O Lord, and abhor those who rise up against you? ²²I have nothing but hatred for them; I count them my enemies.

²³Search me, O God, and know my heart; test me and know my anxious thoughts. ²⁴See if there is any offensive way in me, and lead me in the way everlasting.

Prayer of response

Lord Jesus, please dig into me. As You search, I ask You to carry away the thoughts, habits, and actions that offend You; and to repair the wounds that only You can heal. Thank You that although You know everything about me, You still accept and love me.

My thoughts on Psalm 139 . . .

Destructive Relationships

T he late John Macbeath in his commentary *The Wayfarer's Psalter* summarized this psalm as "a painful protest against the cruelties that man can practice against his fellow man." He noted the comparison of man to the animals, made in an earlier century by Jacob Behman: Human beings "can be like a wolf, cruel and merciless; like a dog, snappish, malicious, envious; like a serpent, stinging, subtle, treacherous; like a hare, timorous, frightened; like a fox, sly, thievish, artful."

In this psalm, David exemplifies all the qualities in a hare (rabbit), while his enemies combine all the ferocious elements of wolf, wild dog, serpent, and fox. He knew the trauma of a daily threat against his very existence as a human being.

Perhaps the danger facing you is not parallel. Your enemies may not be seeking to kill you in a literal sense. They may not even regard themselves as enemies. But whoever threatens or causes spiritual, emotional, or physical harm to you is most certainly no friend.

¹Rescue me, O Lord, from evil men; protect me from men of violence, ²who devise evil plans in their hearts and stir up war every day.

Five pressure points

Before David paints a picture of his problems for God to see, he starts by expressing his complete dependence upon the Almighty, "Rescue me, O

Lord." He possessed the good spiritual sense to know that you should never try to handle your pressures on your own.

Further, he avoided a tendency common among those who suffer abuse from others. He put the blame squarely where it belonged: not on himself, but on "evil men." Here are the weapons (or patterns) used by such individuals.

1. *Force (v. 1)*. The synonym for "evil men" is "men of violence," people who take what they want whether they are entitled to it or not. Violence need not always be physical: Something can be taken from you by heartless acts within a relationship.

2. *Intentional (v. 2)*. Things do not just "happen." Rather, the "evil" devise "evil plans." The act simply manifests the character.

If you are a victim of abuse, it's absolutely vital that you not accept responsibility or guilt for how the other person has behaved. You are not the source of the evil—they are! Don't let someone manipulate you by making you feel responsible for his or her bad behavior.

3. *Habitual (v. 2)*. You cannot be at peace with an individual who "stirs up war every day." A proverb applies this same principle to the home: "A quarrelsome wife [or husband] is like a constant dripping" (Proverbs 19:13).

4. *Hurtful speech (v. 3)*. Sharp tongues and poisoned lips describe a person who uses words to slice and dice. Not only do such words cut, they kill love, respect, and self-worth.

5. *Hidden agendas (vv. 4,5)*. David's danger lay in stealth opponents. He could not be sure when or where the next attack would come from because it was

³They make their tongues as sharp as a serpent's; the poison of vipers is on their lips. Selah

⁴Keep me, O Lord, from the hands of the wicked; protect me

"hidden," "a snare," "a net," and "a trap." No wonder David says, "Selah" or, "Just think of it!" Is there someone who always seems to be looking for the next way to get you? You are not at fault for their choices.

Praying for deliverance

David could see no human way out. Either God would help him or his enemies would triumph. So, he turns to the Lord (vv. 6,7). Note he turns to the Lord *with confidence:* affirming their close personal relationship ("You are my God") and expectation of help. Calling the Lord "Sovereign" and "my strong deliverer, who shields" conveys that you know He's in control even if you're not. David asks the Lord to step in not simply to save his own skin, but because the evil persons will only get worse if God doesn't help (v. 8). Selah. Just think about that.

Then, David does what we often do in prayer—give the Lord some help by telling Him what we think He ought to do:

- Give the wrongdoers a good taste of their own medicine (v. 9).
- Send them to hell (v. 10).
- Clean out all the bad people from society (v. 11).

The psalm ends, however, on the high ground of New Testament faith by leaving final results with God (vv. 12,13). If there's nothing more you can humanly do, reach for that place of trust where you "know that the Lord secures justice for the poor and upholds the cause of the needy."

from men of violence who plan to trip my feet. ⁵Proud men have hidden a snare for me; they have spread out the cords of their net and have set traps for me along my path. Selah

⁶O Lord, I say to you, "You are my God." Hear, O Lord, my cry for mercy. ⁷O Sovereign Lord, my strong deliverer, who shields my head in the day of battle — ⁸do not grant the wicked their desires, O Lord; do not let their plans succeed, or they will become proud. Selah

⁹Let the heads of those who surround me be covered with the trouble their lips have caused. ¹⁰Let burning coals fall upon them; may they be thrown into the fire, into miry pits, never to rise. ¹¹Let slanderers not be established in the land; may disaster hunt down men of violence. ¹²I know that the Lord secures justice for the poor and upholds the cause of the needy. ¹³Surely the righteous will praise your name and the upright will live before you.

Prayer of response

Lord Jesus, let it become a settled assurance in my life that You do all things well. You will prevail. Deliver me from pessimism and despair. May I say with absolute confidence in You that I know that You will either deliver me from, or shield me in, every destructive relationship or circumstance.

My thoughts on Psalm 140 . . .

Protection

What protection do you have in the face of adversity, particularly an adversity generated by another person?

David wrestles with that question in this psalm—the trauma caused by an "enemy." It's a familiar theme in David's prayers.

Take comfort from David's endless struggles. God permitted him to write his psalms so we would not fail in faith when our own sufferings do not come to an end all at once. Yes, time and struggle are needed if you are to overcome. David asked God to act quickly (v. 1), but emergencies on earth are not always emergencies in heaven.

What are the protections you need in your dificult times?

Worship

Prayerlessness and withdrawal from God during adversity only intensify your problems. David practiced the truth in the gospel song: "Take your burdens to the Lord and leave them there."

¹O Lord, I call to you; come quickly to me. Hear my voice when I call to you.

In temple sacrifices, incense served the practical purpose of perfuming the stench of burning animal parts. Your problems, by themselves, can make you nauseous. Prayer deodorizes the foulness of your circumstances by perfuming them with praise and trust in the Lord.

263

264 / A Psalm in Your Heart

In lifting your hands, you take the posture of a supplicant yielding yourself to God and His perfect will. Your upraised hands surrender your need to the Lord and bring the peace of His presence in what otherwise would be a completely unmanageable situation.

Self-control

Your tendency when deeply injured is to mouth off. You need others to feel your pain. That's why David placed a filter on his words by asking the Lord to put a guard over his mouth. Don't surrender your tongue to revenge, rage, self-pity, and blame. Ask the Lord to give you discretion over what you say and who you say it to. Leave more unsaid than spoken.

Avoidance

The short New Testament letter of Jude tells us that when the archangel Michael disputed with the devil about the body of Moses, he did not dare bring a slanderous accusation against him, but said, "The Lord rebuke you." In other words, when you fight the devil, be careful you do not become like him. Michael acted like the good angel he was. Too many have shipwrecked their faith by acting like the devil when fighting the devil.

David recognized the same danger, and asked the Lord to help him avoid acting like the evil persons who had caused him grief. If another person has misused or abused you, set a different standard for your own conduct—even in dealing with them.

²May my prayer be set before you like incense; may the lifting up of my hands be like the evening sacrifice.

³Set a guard over my mouth, O Lord; keep watch over the door of my lips.

⁴Let not my heart be drawn to what is evil, to take part in wicked deeds with men who are evildoers; let me not eat of their delicacies.

⁵Let a righteous man strike me —it is a kindness; let him rebuke me —it is oil on my head. My head will not refuse it. Yet my prayer is ever against the deeds of evildoers; ⁶their rulers will be thrown down from the cliffs, and the wicked will learn

Correction

Take good advice. Consider it fortunate when a good and godly person warns you about your attitudes or behavior.

Anger

No emotion is more misunderstood by believers than anger. Anger is a gift from God to help you create distance between yourself and the wrongdoer. If, for example, you see an adult mistreating a child and you don't become angry, then something is wrong with you. In the same way, you need to let anger create distance between you and someone who violated your trust.

David is so angry he asks the Lord to push his enemies off cliffs and desecrate their graves. Notice, however, David didn't volunteer for the job. He found a way to release anger without destroying himself or others.

Perspective

"My eyes are fixed on you, O Sovereign Lord," David affirms.

It's no easy task bringing your focus back upon the Lord rather than on your external circumstances or internal feelings. The aspect of "eyes fixed" connotes a steady, and unbroken gaze.

You must avoid the mistake of glancing only occasionally at God during the time you are wounded. You can't afford to go a single day without integrating His Word into your life, or conversing with Him in prayer.

that my words were well spoken. 7They will say, "As one plows and breaks up the earth, so our bones have been scattered at the mouth of the grave."

8But my eyes are fixed on you, O Sovereign Lord; in you I take refuge —do not give me over to death. 9Keep me from the snares they have laid for me, from the traps set by evildoers. 10Let the wicked fall into their own nets, while I pass by in safety.

Prayer of response

Loving Heavenly Father, keep me secure from all harm. Save me from the harm I would do myself by thinking and acting in ways that are not wholesome. Save me from the harm launched against me by others or by circumstances over which I had no control. Help me to discern true from false friends, and grant me the wisdom and power to obey sound advice.

My thoughts on Psalm 141 . . .

Alone, But Not Alone

Psalm 142

Can the Lord hear you from deep within a cave, a darkened place where you are physically or emotionally cut off from others—a place so lonely and difficult you ask: "Does anyone even know I'm here?"

Here's a psalm from such a cave.

The historical record of David's life relates the two times he hid in a cave: at En Gedi when he sneaked up on the unsuspecting Saul and cut off a part of his clothes (1 Samuel 24:3) and in the cave of Adullam (1 Samuel 22:1). Psalm 57 was written from the En Gedi cave, and it carries a buoyant mood in comparison to the doleful tone of Psalm 142. At En Gedi, David's men were with him, but at Adullam initially he was alone and in hiding for his life.

The kind of cave you're in often determines the tone of the prayer you pray. This psalm fits best the cave of Adullam: an extended period of frightful depression, deep anxiety, desperation, and feelings of utter abandonment.

Cry for help

Note the strong words. They express emotions borne out of intense personal crushing and affliction.

It's a cry, not a prayer of routine words.

It's a loud cry, testifying to the deep hurt involved.

The voice is lifted up. From within the recesses of the cave, the sound

¹I cry aloud to the Lord; I lift up my voice to the Lord for mercy. ²I pour out my complaint before him; before him I tell my trouble.

bounces off the walls, gathering intensity until it funnels out the open mouth of the cave on its journey heavenward. Although David is in the cave because of threatened danger, his cry indicates that his pain is greater than his instinct to remain hidden.

The complaint is poured out to God. It is not the one-time cry of momentary discomfort, but the prolonged anguish of a person who sees no resolution and who has been greatly wronged.

Confidence in the Lord

Notice the yin and yang of the soul in trial: from pain to peace, and back to pain again. Momentarily, David's anguish is broken by the calming truth: "When my spirit grows faint within me, it is you who know my way" (v. 3); but a breath later he despairs anew: "I have no refuge; no one cares for my life" (v. 4). Peace and pain play against each other on the tennis court of the soul. Which one wins is determined by God's mercy and a person's trust in Him.

David never accepted defeat as God's last word. Having confessed that he had no refuge, he immediately corrects himself: "O Lord . . . You are my refuge, my portion in the land of the living" (v. 5).

Like David, you may have no human solution to your desperate need.

You cannot handle some things by yourself. So never boast about how strong you are. Never say within yourself, *I can handle anything.* You may later find yourself in a cave where God teaches you that you are not as strong as you think.

From the cave, David contemplates

³When my spirit grows faint within me, it is you who know my way. In the path where I walk men have hidden a snare for me. ⁴Look to my right and see; no one is concerned for me. I have no refuge; no one cares for my life. ⁵I cry to you, O Lord; I say, "You are my refuge, my portion in the land of the living."

and contrasts his weakness with God's strength (v. 6).

Comfort for the future

The psalm closes on an up note. David anticipates a future day of release from the cave when he'll look back and praise the Lord. No longer will he be alone, but he will be surrounded by others who similarly recognize God's great goodness.

An old spiritual says, "Nobody knows the trouble I've seen." In a very real sense, pain is always individual. Others may empathize with you—even share their own similar experiences—but only you can fully know your pain.

The good news is, the Lord knows your weakness and that you need His strength. Some things are too strong for you. Unless the Lord frees you from your cave of need, despair, depression, illness—you will be forced to remain there.

Don't lose hope! These days in the cave will pass.

⁶**Listen to my cry, for I am in desperate need; rescue me from those who pursue me, for they are too strong for me.**

⁷**Set me free from my prison, that I may praise your name. Then the righteous will gather about me because of your goodness to me.**

Prayer of response

Lord Jesus, I remember You once told
the disciples that they would leave you
all alone, yet you were not alone for
your Father was with you (John 16:32).
In this cave, there are so many things I
do not have; but the one thing most
valuable I do possess: Your presence.
You don't leave me. You don't forsake
me.

My thoughts on Psalm 142 . . .

My Spirit Grows Faint Within Me

Psalm 143

Again we find David crushed in spirit, deep in despair, and hurting terribly.

It's so encouraging to know the Holy Spirit wanted the journal of David's psalms in the Bible. The inclusion of his psalms of heartache lets us know that often inner sorrow takes a long time to fight, that healing processes do not necessarily happen overnight. When your own recovery drags out over an extended time, you are tempted to think that God has forsaken you, that you are a spiritual abnormality.

Be encouraged. You're as normal as one of God's great (and very flawed) saints: David. Quit being so hard on yourself. God is not down on you because your progress is slow.

My plea

¹O Lord, hear my prayer, listen to my cry for mercy; in your faithfulness and righteousness come to my relief. ²Do not bring your servant into judgment, for no one living is righteous before you.

David never stands on his own accomplishments or personal merit as a basis for seeking or deserving God's help. If God helps at all, it's mercy undeserved. It's not your faithfulness or righteousness which clasps you to the Lord; it is His.

Who can ever pass God's inspection (v. 2)? David knows better than to offer himself as a "yes" to that question. It's, therefore, a comfort to know you are not alone in this matter of unrighteousness. If all are unrighteous before Him, then you have as good a chance as anyone else for His mercy.

David banks on his cry for mercy being heard because God is faithful and righteous (v. 1). His righteousness insures He will be faithful; and His faithfulness insures He will be righteous.

My plight

Enemies pressured David. Notice the effect of such external hounding:

You are reduced as a person. To be crushed (v. 3) means to be compacted. Your self-worth is minimized. You don't feel like a whole person. The crushing David speaks of is "to the ground." You've never felt so little.

You do not understand. How could this have ever happened to you? You "dwell in darkness" (v. 3). Darkness serves as a metaphor for lack of illumination. The night-time of the soul brings the despair of unanswered questions.

Your "spark" is gone. David describes it as "my spirit grows faint within me and my heart . . . dismayed" (v. 4). You feel an overall numbness, weariness, and brokenness.

The turning point comes as you consciously begin to reflect on who God is and what His works are (v. 5). Remember how God has helped you in the past, and how He acts to save His people.

David reaches only to the Lord for satisfying his deepest needs, describing his soul as thirsting "for you like a parched land" (v. 6). When your inner life is cracked and dry, it's time to lift your hands in supplication and surrender. "Lord, please send Your rain upon my parched spirit."

³**The enemy pursues me, he crushes me to the ground; he makes me dwell in darkness like those long dead.**

⁴**So my spirit grows faint within me; my heart within me is dismayed. ⁵I remember the days of long ago; I meditate on all your works and consider what your hands have done.**

⁶**I spread out my hands to you; my soul thirsts for you like a parched land. Selah**

My petitions

David's desire for a speedy answer stems from his concern that he cannot hold out much longer (v. 7). Unless God acts, he's headed for the pit (v. 8).

Your prayers will shape your behavior. If you ask for God's unfailing love in the morning (v. 8), will you become a loving person the rest of the day? If you ask the Lord to show you the way you should go (v. 8), will you then go in that direction? If you ask Him to rescue you (v. 9), will you then hide yourself in Him? If you ask the Lord to teach you His will (v. 10), will you then do it? If you ask the Good Shepherd to lead you (v. 10), will you then walk on "level ground" rather than the roller coaster where your feelings dominate over your faith?

What great petitions!

Show me . . . Rescue me . . . Teach me . . .Lead me . . .These are the prayers of a person who wants to live!

How about you? Have you felt like giving up? Perhaps you have even entertained thoughts of self-destruction. You need the closing words of this psalm: a desire for the Lord to preserve your life (v. 11), and to destroy what's destroying you (v. 12).

⁷**Answer me quickly, O Lord; my spirit fails. Do not hide your face from me or I will be like those who go down to the pit. ⁸Let the morning bring me word of your unfailing love, for I have put my trust in you. Show me the way I should go, for to you I lift up my soul. ⁹Rescue me from my enemies, O Lord, for I hide myself in you. ¹⁰Teach me to do your will, for you are my God; may your good Spirit lead me on level ground. ¹¹For your name's sake, O Lord, preserve my life; in your righteousness, bring me out of trouble. ¹²In your unfailing love, silence my enemies; destroy all my foes, for I am your servant.**

Prayer of response

Lord Jesus, unless You act for me, I will be destroyed, my enemies will prosper and justice will be trampled on. I want to live: Lord, preserve my life. I want peace: Lord, bring me out of trouble. I want power over my adversaries: Lord, help me to forgive and to trust You that You will make the same grace available to them that You have made to me.

My thoughts on Psalm 143 . . .

On the Mend

I n this psalm, we meet an optimistic David. He's out from the cave of desperate circumstances (Psalm 142) and no longer faint in spirit (Psalm 143). He's ready instead to engage his adversaries and is supremely confident of success.

In his storybook for children of all ages, *Oh, the Places You'll Go!* the venerable Dr. Seuss counsels:

> And when you're in a Slump,
> you're not in for much fun.
> Un-slumping yourself
> is not easily done.

Here's a psalm to help you "un-slump."

Revitalized confidence

¹Praise be to the Lord my Rock, who trains my hands for war, my fingers for battle.

The will to survive, to overcome, must get into your spirit if you are going to heal up from any adversity. Thus, David begins this prayer asking God to shape him up: "Train my hands for war, my fingers for battle" (v. 1). You know you're on the mend when you're ready to fight again. In the place of being a passive victim to whoever or whatever rolled on top of you, you're ready to get off the mat and slug it out.

You will never overcome your problems by living with a defeatist mentality or an irresponsible attitude which says, "Well, you know there's nothing I can do."

Oh, yes there is! You can ask the Lord to get you in fighting condition.

But that's not enough. You can be in the best shape but still lose. David knows that, and in the next 10 verses throws himself upon God for help. Thus, these first 11 verses represent a fairly good ratio of what you need to prevail. For every one part you contribute (v. 1), recognize your loving God weighs in with 10 parts (vv. 2–11).

He protects you in a multitude of venues: sometimes putting you within the walls of an impenetrable fortress and other times protecting you with only a thin shield on the battlefield (v. 2).

You'll be amazed how much attention and concern God gives you (vv. 3, 4).

Sometimes He'll use His mighty arsenal to scatter and shoot down your enemies (vv. 5,6); at other times, He simply plucks you out of raging waters (vv. 7,8). You can't predict how God will help you because He chooses to fight differently on your behalf today than He did yesterday. That's why your praise won't grow stale—each deliverance merits "a new song" to "the One who gives victory" (vv. 9,10).

However, David is not out of trouble yet (v. 11). When you're in a long-term struggle with an adversity, you understand readily the mood switch between verses 10 and 11. In one moment, you feel absolutely confident of success; the very next minute you realize how utterly dependent you are on the Lord's help.

Security about the future

On-the-mend people feel secure about the future. Do your top three confidences about tomorrow parallel those of David?

Family (v. 12).

A distraught mother came to her pas-

²He is my loving God and my fortress, my stronghold and my deliverer, my shield, in whom I take refuge, who subdues peoples under me. ³O Lord, what is man that you care for him, the son of man that you think of him? ⁴Man is like a breath; his days are like a fleeting shadow. ⁵Part your heavens, O Lord, and come down; touch the mountains, so that they smoke. ⁶Send forth lightning and scatter the enemies; shoot your arrows and rout them. ⁷Reach down your hand from on high; deliver me and rescue me from the mighty waters, from the hands of foreigners ⁸whose mouths are full of lies, whose right hands are deceitful. ⁹I will sing a new song to you, O God; on the ten-stringed lyre I will make music to you, ¹⁰to the One who gives victory to

tor and requested prayer for her daughter who was a prostitute. The pastor looked straight into the mother's eyes and admonished her, "Don't call your daughter a prostitute any more. Call her, 'Beautiful daughter.'" The mother began praying for her girl through this new lens of faith. She caught an entirely different picture of what God could make her daughter, and the Lord worked through her faith to make it happen.

David employs the same principle here: anticipating the day when his sons will be "well-nurtured plants," and his daughters, "decorative pillars."

Finances (v. 13).

In David's day, there were no bank savings accounts, stock portfolios, retirement plans, or social security. Wealth was measured by produce ("barns full") and livestock. Jesus tells us that since our Heavenly Father provides for our needs (Matthew 6:25–34), our focus shouldn't be on finances but on His kingdom. The apostle Paul discovered there's so much blessing in following Jesus that even when you have nothing, you have everything (2 Corinthians 6:10).

Security (v. 14).

How terrible not to feel safe! This psalm closes by reminding us of God's protection for His people, a promise never fully realized until we abide within the four walls of the heavenly city (see Revelation 21:1 to 22:5).

kings, who delivers his servant David from the deadly sword. 11Deliver me and rescue me from the hands of foreigners whose mouths are full of lies, whose right hands are deceitful.

12Then our sons in their youth will be like well-nurtured plants, and our daughters will be like pillars carved to adorn a palace.

13Our barns will be filled with every kind of provision. Our sheep will increase by thousands, by tens of thousands in our fields;

14our oxen will draw heavy loads. There will be no breaching of walls, no going into captivity, no cry of distress in our streets.

15Blessed are the people of whom this is true; blessed are the people whose God is the Lord.

Prayer of response

Lord Jesus, I'm so much like David. One moment, I think I'm on the mend, successfully dealing with my disappointments and conflicts; and, the very next second I panic and throw myself completely upon You for help. I'm so blessed to be one of Your people (v. 15). Because You are my Lord, I have a future and a hope.

My thoughts on Psalm 144 . . .

Our Great God

C onsider the immensity of the universe.

Imagine that the thickness in a single piece of paper represents the 93-million-mile distance from the earth to the sun, light traveling 8 seconds at the speed of 186,282 miles per second. Next, using the same ratio in paper thickness, lay page after page on top of one another until the stack is 71 feet high. You now have the distance to the nearest star beyond our own sun: 26 trillion miles or 4 $1/3$ light-years.

The diameter of our galaxy at 100,000 light-years takes a 310-mile-high stack of paper. When you get to the edge of the universe, or as far as the telescopes can see, it would require a stack of paper 31 million miles high, the thickness of each page representing the distance between earth and sun.

Our earth is to the universe what a lady bug is to the forest. You and I are the size of invisible specks on the lady bug.

1I will exalt you, my God the King; I will praise your name for ever and ever. 2Every day I will praise you and extol your name for ever and ever. 3Great is the Lord and most worthy of praise; his greatness no one can fathom.

From A to Z

In Psalm 145, this last of 73 psalms attributed to him, David empties his pen telling the glory of God, a "greatness no one can fathom" (v. 3). So many of his psalms focus on his acute pain in life; here, his eyes look upward rather than inward. It's a hopeful example for any child of God who has endured adversity. In the end, praise swallows up all our griefs and complaints.

This psalm does not lend itself to an outline inasmuch as it is written as an acrostic, each verse beginning with a subsequent letter of the Hebrew alphabet. There are eight such psalms, five of which bear David's name. It's David's way of saying: "God is great from A to Z."

At the beginning, David says, "I will exalt you" and "extol your name for ever and ever" (vv. 1,2). How do you make God any bigger than He already is! What does it mean to exalt, extol, or magnify Him? Isn't He far greater than you can even imagine?

Let's face it. Objectively, you will never change God. You cannot make Him bigger or smaller. The problem is in the subjective realm. Have you permitted God to become small in you? When you praise and extol the Lord, you are changing the size of God in you.

That's what David does throughout this psalm. He's saying, "Lord, you are absolutely wonderful. No one has you figured out" (v. 3).

From generation to generation

His deeds, however, reach beyond creation into human history. He acts on behalf of His people, one generation telling His mighty acts to the next (vv. 4–7). We're still telling the stories of His deliverance of Israel from Egypt and the greatness of His love and power in Christ Jesus, our Lord.

But His actions are not confined to the past. "The Lord *is* gracious and compassionate . . . *is* good to all" (vv. 8,9). The faith never dies out because His mighty acts never cease; rather His "dominion endures through all generations" (vv. 10–13).

You may be the invisible speck on the

[4] One generation will commend your works to another; they will tell of your mighty acts. [5] They will speak of the glorious splendor of your majesty, and I will meditate on your wonderful works. [6] They will tell of the power of your awesome works, and I will proclaim your great deeds. [7] They will celebrate your abundant goodness and joyfully sing of your righteousness.

[8] The Lord is gracious and compassionate, slow to anger and rich in love. [9] The Lord is good to all; he has compassion on all he has made. [10] All you have made will praise you, O Lord; your saints will extol you. [11] They will tell of the glory of your kingdom and speak of your might, [12] so that all men may know of your mighty

lady bug in the forest of the created universe, but your needs are not lost to Him. Ponder His loving care for you: The Lord upholds you when you fall down, lifts you when you're bowed down, gives you food at the proper time, and opens His hand to satisfy your desires (vv. 14–16).

Your hymn of praise affirms the Lord's work in your own life. He's righteous and loving (v. 17), near when you call (v. 18). He meets your deepest needs (v. 19) and protects you (v. 20).

For ever and ever

That's how David sees God in this last psalm. It would be dishonest not to note that in earlier psalms David didn't always exude such confidence. At times, God's help seemed delayed or distant. Often, David felt vulnerable and unprotected. God didn't make snap rescues or function on David's timetable. This psalm shows that it takes time to see that the Lord truly was with us in the wilderness, the darkness, and the difficult place. Go on trusting in the Lord; and when it's all done, you'll see the whole and not the half.

The bottom line, when you review all God has done for you, is a heart full of praise (v. 21).

acts and the glorious splendor of your kingdom. [13]Your kingdom is an everlasting kingdom, and your dominion endures through all generations. The Lord is faithful to all his promises and loving toward all he has made.

[14]The Lord upholds all those who fall and lifts up all who are bowed down. [15]The eyes of all look to you, and you give them their food at the proper time. [16]You open your hand and satisfy the desires of every living thing.

[17]The Lord is righteous in all his ways and loving toward all he has made. [18]The Lord is near to all who call on him, to all who call on him in truth. [19]He fulfills the desires of those who fear him; he hears their cry and saves them. [20]The Lord watches over all who love him, but all the wicked he will destroy.

[21]My mouth will speak in praise of the Lord. Let every creature praise his holy name for ever and ever.

Prayer of response

Lord, I can neither fathom Your creative power nor Calvary love. But You never asked me to understand You. Instead You invite me to praise and love You. I do that gladly. I am so little. You are so great. I humbly ask You to magnify Your presence in my life this day.

My thoughts on Psalm 145 . . .

Hold Secure

King Duncan tells about an elderly man out walking his grandson. "How far are we from home?" he asked the boy.

"Grandpa, I don't know," came the answer. The old man good-naturedly tossed back, "Sounds to me as if you're lost."

"Nope," the grandson replied as he looked up at his granddad, "I can't be lost. I'm with you."

Do you feel the same way as you walk with God? Don't be surprised then if a frequent "Praise the Lord" falls out of your lips.

The last five psalms all begin and end with that phrase, "Praise the Lord"—one word in the underlying Hebrew text: "Hallelujah" (*hallel* meaning praise and *ujah* for Yahweh or Jehovah).

Grateful for His presence

Perhaps your heart is so burdened with problems and questions that you rarely, if ever, praise Him. Maybe You hold Him responsible that things aren't better for you. Such condemnation only shrivels your faith. Look at all the needy people mentioned in this psalm: oppressed, hungry, imprisoned, blind, bent down, alienated, orphan, and widowed. Every one of them has reason to blame God. But they don't. Why? You never get better if you bite the hand that helps you. God is committed to healing you, not hurting you.

1Praise the Lord. Praise the Lord, O my soul. 2I will praise the Lord all my life; I will sing praise to my God as long as I live.

283

Who else have you looked to for help? You wanted affirmation, approval, understanding, intimacy, communion, relationship, joy, laughter, camaraderie, friendship, and love. You depended on another person, a "prince" (or princess) to meet those needs (v. 3). But, that person didn't stay with you—either by choice or death (v. 4).

Who then will you rely upon? The psalmist answers: "Blessed is he whose help is the God of Jacob . . . " (vv. 5,6). Your solution lies in turning to the God of the struggler.

Grateful for His help

Jacob knew well the see-saw between the thrill of victory and the agony of defeat. He enjoyed short years of fulfillment and endured long years of loneliness and intense burden. He was not his father's favorite son. His brother hated him. His father-in-law demeaned and cheated him. The woman he loved died in childbirth. Most of his children became a grief. But Jacob endured. How? He kept true to the identity of his name Jacob, "he who grasps the heel" (Genesis 25:26). Life could strip everything away from him, but he refused to release his grip on God (Genesis 32:22–32). And God did for him what his father, brother, wife, kids, and father-in-law could not or would not do—God helped him.

It's embedded in the character of God: He helps the struggler.

He upholds the cause of the oppressed (v. 7). God knows when you're caught in the squeeze, when you come under unrelenting pressure. He's committed to helping you.

³Do not put your trust in princes, in mortal men, who cannot save. ⁴When their spirit departs, they return to the ground; on that very day their plans come to nothing.

⁵Blessed is he whose help is the God of Jacob, whose hope is in the Lord his God, ⁶the Maker of heaven and earth, the sea, and everything in them — the Lord, who remains faithful forever.

And gives food to the hungry (v. 7). He knows when your resources are exhausted. You may not get the food you want; but when you're hungry, you'll gladly eat what He provides.

The Lord sets prisoners free (v. 7). Sometimes He brings freedom instantly; other times He permits you to emerge after great exertion like a butterfly from the cocoon.

The Lord gives sight to the blind (v. 8). Sin or passion or depression blind you. It's the Lord's good pleasure to give you insight, to see things as they really are.

The Lord lifts up those who are bowed down (v. 8). Burdens bend the back. The Lord comes to help lift, not push down.

The Lord loves the righteous (v. 8). Therefore, He loves Jesus and whoever Jesus holds close.

The Lord watches over the alien and sustains the fatherless and the widow (v. 9). Here are life's three most frightening prospects: alienated, orphaned, or widowed. God watches not simply to observe, but, to help and defend.

But he frustrates the ways of the wicked (v. 9). Here's the only negative in the list. God has determined that wrong will not win.

When you grab hold of what God is like, then you'll start to put the same qualities in your own life. If you're not a struggler, then you must be a helper of the struggler.

What else can be said? God reigns forever (v. 10). You're held secure because God is with you.

7He upholds the cause of the oppressed and gives food to the hungry. The Lord sets prisoners free, 8the Lord gives sight to the blind, the Lord lifts up those who are bowed down, the Lord loves the righteous.

9The Lord watches over the alien and sustains the fatherless and the widow, but he frustrates the ways of the wicked.

10The Lord reigns forever, your God, O Zion, for all generations. Praise the Lord.

Prayer of response

Lord, a century from now You will reign. When the earth has melted and dissolved, You will reign. My health may go, my financial resources may dry up, my friends may leave, the dearest to me may die; but You'll never leave me nor forsake me. Since I eternally rely on You, I trust You also with the present moment.

My thoughts on Psalm 146 . . .

Well-treated

Emile Gaugin's death in the early 1980s passed practically unnoticed. His famous father, the painter Paul Gaugin, at the age of 51 consorted with a 17-year-old Tahitian mistress. Emile was the result.

But Paul Gaugin died when Emile was 3. Emile spent his life in poverty, mocked by his fellow Tahitians for the years he spent in the streets of Papeete, sleeping and begging. He fathered 11 children, and in their youth they often helped him try to earn money by passing off his sketches to tourists as original Gaugins. But Emile never came close to his father's talent. By the time of his death at the age of 80, only one of Emile's children had anything to do with him.

When Emile was born, Paul Gaugin celebrated the event by doing two paintings: one now in the Hermitage Museum in St. Petersburg and the other owned by the Rockefeller family. Emile was often heard to say, "If I owned but one of my father's paintings, I would have been a rich man."

> **¹Praise the Lord. How good it is to sing praises to our God, how pleasant and fitting to praise him!**

This psalm paints a far different picture. God does not orphan nor neglect you. Rather, if you spend time in His presence, you'll find ample reasons to sing "Hallelujah" or "Praise the Lord" (v. 1). Look at how well He treats you.

If He repairs Jerusalem, He also rebuilds you

Jerusalem has been conquered and torn down more than any living city in history. God's rebuilding, regathering,

287

and repairing are all the more special because He did not limit His help to one or two occasions.

Did the enemy break into your life, demolishing what you held close and dear? Did you fail God, experience His help, and then fail again? Do you now wonder if He's washed you from His hands? Consider His great patience and grace. He's not desirous of your remaining in ruins. He's committed to helping you get back up on your feet, wounds healed, and heart no longer broken.

If He names the stars, He's not lost track of you

It's no harder for Him to start up a sun than for you to light up a match. Even scientists can't figure out the immensity of space, but God tracks all His stars by name.

From pondering God's power over the heavens, the psalmist turns to personal application. If deep space doesn't manage itself, what mortal could conceive of existing independent from God? That wicked one will God bring down, but the individual who recognizes he or she is nothing without God—that humble person God sustains. Aren't you grateful? Don't you feel like singing thanks (v. 7)?

If He sustains the earth, He'll meet your need as well

He made and manages the ecosystem: the interrelationship and interdependency of clouds to rain to vegetation to cattle and birds (vv. 8,9). The speed, stamina, and endurance represented in the legs of a horse or human might be impressive

²The Lord builds up Jerusalem; he gathers the exiles of Israel. ³He heals the broken-hearted and binds up their wounds. ⁴He determines the number of the stars and calls them each by name. ⁵Great is our Lord and mighty in power; his understanding has no limit. ⁶The Lord sustains the humble but casts the wicked to the ground.

⁷Sing to the Lord with thanksgiving; make music to our God on the harp.

⁸He covers the sky with clouds; he supplies the earth with rain and makes grass grow on the hills. ⁹He provides food for the cattle and for the young ravens when they call. ¹⁰His pleasure is not in the

qualities to admire (v. 10). You certainly wish you had legs strong enough to out-run any danger or support any burden. Don't worry. God's not impressed with what you have. Rather, He delights when you tell Him you can't make it on your own—that you need His help (v. 11).

Take a moment to extol Him (v. 12) for guarding (v. 13) and satisfying you (v. 14).

Even as He makes winter (vv. 15–17) and summer (v. 18), He's with you in both the cold/difficult and warm/pleasurable seasons of life.

If He speaks, He desires you to listen

We are not left on our own to try and figure out who God is. The psalmist notes the special privilege the people of Israel were given when God revealed himself to them as to no other. You have even greater advantage for you have more knowledge of God than that given by Moses and the prophets, for God has finally and completely spoken to us by His Son (see Hebrews 1:1–3). What a tragedy if I do not listen when God speaks.

How much better, instead, to respond with a final "Praise the Lord" to the great truth that God has not given us the silent treatment. He has told us everything we need to know about Him and ourselves. Isn't that wonderful?

strength of the horse, nor his delight in the legs of a man; ¹¹the Lord delights in those who fear him, who put their hope in his unfailing love.

¹²Extol the Lord, O Jerusalem; praise your God, O Zion, ¹³for he strengthens the bars of your gates and blesses your people within you. ¹⁴He grants peace to your borders and satisfies you with the finest of wheat.

¹⁵He sends his command to the earth; his word runs swiftly. ¹⁶He spreads the snow like wool and scatters the frost like ashes. ¹⁷He hurls down his hail like pebbles. Who can withstand his icy blast? ¹⁸He sends his word and melts them; he stirs up his breezes, and the waters flow. ¹⁹He has revealed his word to Jacob, his laws and decrees to Israel. ²⁰He has done this for no other nation; they do not know his laws. Praise the Lord.

Prayer of response

Lord, I delight in Your unfailing love (v. 11). You do not neglect me, mistreat me, or fail to provide for my every need. You are not a Paul Gaugin who leaves his son to fend for himself, bereft of a father's love and resources. I am so privileged to be Your child.

My thoughts on Psalm 147 . . .

Maestro to Heaven and Earth

Psalm 148

A s the youngest child of itinerant preacher-parents, I spent a good deal of time alone—entertaining myself with make-believe.

One of my favorite activities involved turning on the radio or record player. I stood in the middle of the room with my boyish arms flailing away as I "directed" my orchestra and singers. I loved the crescendos, urging my musicians with furious motion to extend their fullest energies. Unfortunately, to this day, I still can't even read a note of music. But every once in a while when I hear great music, I look around to see if anyone else is in the room. If not, I raise my arms and revert to childhood—maestro again for a moment.

I see Psalm 148, this third "Praise the Lord" or "Hallelujah" psalm (Psalms 146–150), much the same way. The psalm writer, as conductor, takes his position in the wide-open spaces, lifts his orchestra baton and bids the heavens (vv. 1–6) and earth (vv. 7–14) to join in a symphony of praise to God.

The heavens above

Why don't you take the baton yourself and become the maestro bidding the universe to break out in song to the Lord?

¹Praise the Lord. Praise the Lord from the heavens, praise him in the heights above.

One thing I don't recall doing as a child: I don't remember ever acting as a conductor when I was sad. I hammed it up only when I was happy. Some psalms uniquely fit moments of great sadness (Psalm 88) or painful emotional need

291

(Psalm 23), but this psalm is for glad hearts.

You're so in love with God. Life is blessed and full. You cannot contain the joy within yourself. When your "cup runneth over," the grass looks greener, the stars brighter, the sky more blue. Like the psalmist, you want the whole world to celebrate with you.

You lift your baton and bid the heavens above to strike up music in praise to God (v. 1). And you then turn to those who dwell in the heights—angels and heavenly hosts—to immediately join in (v. 2).

Could it be that God is doing something within you that merits praise from heavenly beings? Did they hang on the edge of their seats as they witnessed how God kept you in the nick of time from going over the precipice? Could it be they heard Jesus call your name while He was dying at Calvary? Or did they listen to Him lift up your need during His intercession at the right hand of the Father (Romans 8:34)? Are they now ecstatic that you have responded to Him—that His death, resurrection and intercession for you have not been in vain? Is it possible they see the future yet ahead for you—and are quite ready to praise God for all the good yet to issue forth?

Oh angels! Praise Him for His goodness to me. Let the whole universe join in (vv. 3–6).

The earth below

You lifted your baton for heaven to exalt God in song; now you look across open fields and bid earth to join in harmony with the music from above.

2Praise him, all his angels, praise him, all his heavenly hosts.

3Praise him, sun and moon, praise him, all you shining stars. 4Praise him, you highest heavens and you waters above the skies. 5Let them praise the name of the Lord, for he commanded and they were created. 6He set them in place for ever and ever; he gave a decree that will never pass away.

Everything in nature should praise Him (vv. 7–10)—on sea, in air, on land. But did you notice the small phrase tucked into verse 8 which provides another reason for praise: "stormy winds that do his bidding"? Perhaps you feel that storms only destroy. But the aftermath of storm is rebuilding. Will you trust the Lord that your own storm "will do His bidding"—that what devastated you will become the means by which the Lord repairs or rebuilds you into an even more beautiful habitation of His Spirit?

You've now got all heaven and earth praising Him—it's time to point the baton to the choir of humanity. It's their turn to join the song. Every human person should praise Him—from big shots (v. 11) to little kids (v. 12).

This psalm closes by letting us know the why behind the song: There's no one else worthy of such praise (v. 13), and God has acted to redeem His people (v. 14). Notice the closing crescendo: "He has raised up for his people a horn." In biblical language, "horn"—as in a bull's horn—projects the symbol of help, strength, and power. In the words of Zechariah, the father of John the Baptist, we see this promise fulfilled in Jesus: "Praise be to the Lord, the God of Israel, because he has come and has redeemed his people. He has raised up a horn of salvation for us" (Luke 1:68,69).

It's time to point the baton toward your own heart. Will you too enter into the worship of heaven and earth with a "Praise the Lord!" from your own lips?

7Praise the Lord from the earth, you great sea creatures and all ocean depths, 8lightning and hail, snow and clouds, stormy winds that do his bidding, 9you mountains and all hills, fruit trees and all cedars, 10wild animals and all cattle, small creatures and flying birds, 11kings of the earth and all nations, you princes and all rulers on earth,

12young men and maidens, old men and children.

13Let them praise the name of the Lord, for his name alone is exalted; his splendor is above the earth and the heavens.

14He has raised up for his people a horn, the praise of all his saints, of Israel, the people close to his heart. Praise the Lord.

Prayer of response

Lord Jesus, in You today I have a horn. I am saved and protected by Your power. I add my voice to "the music of the spheres" and sing a heartfelt "How great Thou art!" Your splendor covers all my stains. I love You, my Creator and Redeemer.

My thoughts on Psalm 148 . . .

A Grateful Heart

L egend has it that a man found the barn where satan (I never capitalize his name) kept his seeds ready to be sown in the human heart. The seeds of discouragement far outnumbered all others because they could be made to grow most anywhere.

When satan was questioned, he reluctantly admitted that there was one place where he could never get discouragement seeds to thrive. "And where is that?" asked the man

"In the heart of a grateful person," came the answer.

The final five psalms all begin and end with one word in the Hebrew tongue: "Hallelujah," meaning "Praise to the Lord." Unlike many of the other psalms, you won't find any discouragement in these. I look at these psalms of closure in the same way as the songs contained in the Book of Revelation. At the end of the day, when all of life is reviewed and eternity peeks over the eastern horizon like the rising sun, nothing is left but praise and gratitude.

Psalm 149 "fast forwards" us to the end, showing us final results for both God's people (vv. 1–5) and God's enemies (vv. 6–9).

> ¹Praise the Lord. Sing to the Lord a new song, his praise in the assembly of the saints. ²Let Israel rejoice in their Maker; let the people of Zion be glad in their King. ³Let them praise his name with dancing and make music to him with tambourine and harp.

Delightful praise

"Sing to the Lord a new song!" Why is your song new? Only you can describe the Lord in reference to His care for you personally. No one else has your identical testimony. Other saints may sing in praise of God's attributes of majesty, love, and power—but you alone know specifically and personally how God has ministered to you.

But your solo is quickly surrounded by the voices of the mighty choir to which you belong (vv. 2–5). Sorrow banished. No tears. Just joy—undiminished infectious joy. Laughter unrestrained. Heaven come down. Depression all gone. In its place, gladness, dancing, tambourine, and harp. But, that's not all.

Remember when "all night long [you] flooded [your] bed with weeping and drenched [your] couch with tears" (Psalm 6:6) or lay upon a "sickbed" (Psalm 41:3)? The bed—where you thrashed the night, relived hurtful memories, dwelled endlessly on the what-might-have-beens—has become now the very place where you sing songs of joy (v. 5).

Delicious vindication

This psalm closes by asking God to help you triumph over adversaries (vv. 6–9). The psalmist relishes the moment when the tables are turned on the ungodly. Jesus' heart was broken at the prospect that any would perish (John 3:16), but His deep love for the human race did not abolish the awful consequences for any who spurn His grace. How can there be salvation if there is no damnation? What is there to be saved from?

We live in an era when even many professing Christians are tempted not to take God's judgments seriously. This psalm—and indeed the whole Bible—tells us there are only two ends for any human being: salvation (vv. 1–5) or damnation (vv. 6–9).

⁴For the Lord takes delight in his people; he crowns the humble with salvation.

⁵Let the saints rejoice in this honor and sing for joy on their beds.

⁶May the praise of God be in their mouths and a double-edged sword in their hands, ⁷to inflict vengeance on the nations and punishment on the peoples, ⁸to bind their kings with fetters, their nobles with shackles of iron, ⁹to carry out the sentence written against them. This is the glory of all his saints. Praise the Lord.

C. S. Lewis explains the two ends this way: "I would pay any price to say truthfully 'All will be saved.' But my reason retorts, 'Without their will, or with it?' If I say, 'Without their will,' I at once perceive a contradiction; how can the supreme act of self-surrender be involuntary? If I say 'With their will,' my reason replies, 'How, if they will not give in?'"

Heaven would be hell for those who still want to break the commandments, tell God to mind His own business, use the Lord's name in vain rather than in worship, and repudiate the life and love of Jesus Christ.

The gratitude in this psalm flows directly out of understanding that God can be taken at His word. It's in His character to save the humble and punish the haughty.

A young Scottish pastor, somewhat doubtful in his own faith, called on an elderly lady in his congregation who was dying. Bothered somewhat by her calm assurance, he asked her how she could be so confident. "Oh," she replied. "If I should awake in eternity to find myself among the lost, the Lord would lose more than I would; for all that I would lose would be my immortal soul, but He would have lost His good name."

That's the reason for our gratitude—not in who we are, but in who He is. We can take Him at His word.

Prayer of response

Lord Jesus, as I near the end of the Psalms, I step momentarily into the future. I envision the victory. I seize to my heart the day when all will be well. Let my life add yet another new song to the anthem of all the saints in heaven and on earth.

My thoughts on Psalm 149 . . .

From all the Saints

My friend Elizabeth Mittelstaedt, founder and publisher of *Lydia* magazine (the largest evangelical periodical in Europe), told me the story about a fidgety little boy in church who pulled on his tight shirt collar and stared at the hat of the lady in front of him. He was bored by the sermon that should have been over already.

His big brown eyes wandered around the sanctuary and became glued on the stained-glass windows. In those windows were men and women in a sea of colors, and they radiated as uniquely formed gems—in contrast to the stern faces of the people in the pews around him.

"Mommy," he whispered not too quietly, "who are those people in the windows up there?"

"Saints," she snapped back. "Now, be quiet."

The next day in religion class the teacher asked, "Can someone describe a saint to me?"

The little boy, excited, squiggly and impatient, waved his hand and said, "I can. I can."

"Yes, good Tobias," the teacher said. "Explain it to us."

"They are colorful, transparent, and the sun shines through them," he said.

"And how would you know that?" the teacher asked.

"I saw them yesterday in the church stained-glass windows," he said.

> ¹Praise the Lord.
> Praise God in his sanctuary; praise him in his mighty heavens.

Perspective on the past

As we look at the very last psalm, we find those colorful, transparent, and sun-shining-through-them saints clos-

299

ing the Bible's hymnbook, the Psalter, with one final great hallelujah. Throughout the psalms we have witnessed the continual example of godly persons praying during the great personal problems, deeply staining sins, tragic personal misfortune, physical illness, advancing age, overwhelming adversaries and obstacles, lonely valleys of depression, feelings of abandonment by others and even God, hurt and anger, and unrelenting sorrow. They struggled with unanswered prayers, delayed answers, denied answers.

But they also celebrated victories of God's intervention and kept returning to express their trust in the Lord even when they did not understand what He was up to, or why He seemed so long in coming to their aid.

In short, the prayers of the saints in the psalms are just like our own. A true saint hides nothing. He or she doesn't wear a slick gloss of cosmetic perfection, as though neither a worry nor a dark thought has ever crossed the mind. No, saints are those colorful and transparent people who, in the many-hued circumstances of life, keep letting the Son shine through them.

Praise now and evermore

Then comes the time for the last hallelujah, the final amen.

All ends well in God. Life has a successful resolution. God kept His word and worked for the good in your life. There were days when you did not see where He was taking you or what good He was doing for you—but now eternity makes it all so plain. Nothing but joy awaits. No more recitation of sorrow or need; just pure, unrelenting satisfaction and fullness. The final psalm shows not even a ripple of discontent.

At the end, you are a singing fountain. As with all the praise psalms, you are encouraged to take the song you sing then and jam it into the present. Move the future joy into the present hour. If Psalm 150 marks the exit song for all saints, then why not sing it today?

Verse 1 gives the where of praise—the sanctuary and the heavens. The sanctuary on earth may be multiple: the temple in Jerusalem for the psalmist, the church for the body of Christ, the heart for each individual believer. But praise ascends beyond earthly containment into the very sanctuary of heaven itself.

Verse 2 gives the why of praise. Exalt Him for His deeds and His character. Praise Him for His acts of power in your own life—even those you disagreed with and fought against. Sometimes He hurt you to protect you from a greater harm. Everything He did or did not do for you arose out of His love. No one could be more faithful, kind, just, loving, and full of mercy.

Verses 3–5 give us the how of praise. Eight instruments are named, plus dance. Dancing represents the body overcome with joy—the profound surge of emotion attached to this high moment of release and boundless happiness.

Verse 6 gives us the who of praise—everything that has breath. Do you have breath today? Then praise Him.

²Praise him for his acts of power; praise him for his surpassing greatness.

³Praise him with the sounding of the trumpet, praise him with the harp and lyre, ⁴praise him with tambourine and dancing, praise him with the strings and flute, ⁵praise him with the clash of cymbals, praise him with resounding cymbals.

⁶Let everything that has breath praise the Lord. Praise the Lord.

Prayer of response

Lord Jesus, as I close the Psalms I lift my voice in one final act of praise. Thank You for Your presence in the canyon valleys, for being with me on the long upward trail. Thank You for sustaining me. You never left me nor forsook me. I praise You today, Lord. My life comes from You and will one day return to You. Help me daily to be Your colorful, transparent, and Son-shining-through saint.

My thoughts on Psalm 150 . . .